Java™ Performance and Scalability
Volume 1

Java™ Performance and Scalability
Volume 1

Server-Side Programming Techniques

Dov Bulka

Addison-Wesley

**Boston • San Francisco • New York • Toronto • Montreal
London • Munich • Paris • Madrid
Capetown • Sydney • Tokyo • Singapore • Mexico City**

Many of the designations used by manufacturers and sellers to distinguish their products are claimed as trademarks. Where those designations appear in this book and we were aware of a trademark claim, the designations have been printed in initial capital letters or all capitals.

The authors and publisher have taken care in the preparation of this book, but make no expressed or implied warranty of any kind and assume no responsibility for errors or omissions. No liability is assumed for incidental or consequential damages in connection with or arising out of the use of the information or programs contained herein.

The publisher offers discounts on this book when ordered in quantity for special sales. For more information, please contact:

Pearson Education Corporate Sales Division
One Lake Street
Upper Saddle River, NJ 07458
(800) 382-3419
corpsales@pearsontechgroup.com

Visit us on the Web at *www.awl.com/cseng/*

Library of Congress Cataloging-in-Publication Data
Bulka, Dov.
    Java performance and scalability / Dov Bulka.
      p.   cm.
    Includes bibliographical references and index.
    Contents: v. 1. Server-side techniques
    ISBN 0-201-70429-3
    1. Java (Computer program language) I. Title.

QA76.73.J38 B84 2000
005.13'3—dc21   00-025661

ISBN 0-201-70429-3

Text printed on recycled paper.
1 2 3 4 5 6 7 8 9 10-ML-04 03 02 01 00
First printing, May 2000

To my sisters, Miri Amir and Dvora Sarig,
my brother, Zeev Bulka,
and last but not least,
my wife, Cynthia Powers Bulka.

Contents

List of Figures

Chapter 5

Chapter 6

Chapter 7

Chapter 8

Chapter 9

Chapter 10

Chapter 11

Preface

Performance has been one of the dominant concerns hovering around Java from its infancy. Regardless of an order of magnitude speedup resulting from just-in-time (JIT) compilers, HotSpot, and other advances in JVM technology, the performance issue is still a legitimate concern. The reality facing Java programmers is that it is very easy to write slow Java programs. Java is a performance mine field and expert guidance is a must.

Given the importance of performance to Java developers, it is somewhat surprising that no book has been dedicated to this important topic. Almost any other Java-related issue has had multiple books dedicated to it—RMI, JNI, JDBC, threads, networking, and the list goes on. Conspicuously absent has been Java performance. It has been mentioned in passing by many authors but, to my knowledge, rarely has there been more than a chapter discussing it. This book is aiming to fill that gaping hole. It is entirely focused on Java performance issues from start to finish.

This book is written for Java programmers by a Java programmer. This is an important fact. It is very likely that the Java performance issues that I have dealt with in my code will surface in your code as well. The Java optimization techniques that you will find here will significantly elevate the performance and scalability of your Java programs.

There's plenty of material to cover. Let's get started.

Introduction

Java performance has been a hot issue ever since the arrival of Java in the mid 1990s. In the early days, performance was a serious concern as first-generation Java virtual machines (JVMs) executed Java programs by interpreting byte-codes. The addition of just-in-time (JIT) compilers to the JVM has allowed it to compile Java bytecodes to machine-specific instructions on the fly and to skip bytecode interpretation on subsequent invocations of compiled methods. Depending on the specific workload, JIT compilers have roughly increased Java speed by an order of magnitude. The Java HotSpot technology has added the ability to selectively compile the performance-critical methods, apply massive inlining to that code, and use the latest and greatest in garbage-collection algorithms. Those impressive advances in JVM speed have given significant momentum to the claim that the performance of Java programs is now entirely determined by the program's architecture, otherwise known as high-level design. If you believe that, then the next logical conclusion is that it really does not matter whether you program in Java, C++, C, or assembly language. As long as your overall program design is rock-solid, the implementation language should not matter. Most programmers will perceive the previous statement as clearly false. It is much faster to convert an ASCII string to uppercase in assembly language than to try to do the same in Java. The logical conclusion was false because the underlying premise was false. Java performance is not entirely determined by the program's high-level design. A solid high-level design is a necessary condition for high-performance software, but it is not sufficient.

If program architecture is not the whole story, then what else is there? What factors determine the speed of our Java programs? The following issues immediately come to mind.

- *The physical machine*. The speed of any program, Java or not, is influenced to a large extent by a variety of hardware issues such as the speed of the processor, number of processors, size of cache and memory, as well as speed of peripheral devices [HP96, PH97, PFI98]. If upgrading any one of these hardware elements can bring performance to the required level, then that would be the easiest solution. This solution is not always available, however. After all, processor speed is finite and so is the size of the cache, memory, and number of processors that can be added to a machine. In addition, you may be working under a cost constraint that will make the hardware upgrade route less attractive. It may also be the case that your Java solution is evaluated in a competitive bid against other Java solutions on the same exact hardware. In that scenario, the hardware dimension is a nonfactor, as everybody runs on the same platform. Usually, the fastest, most scalable solution wins the business.

- *The Java virtual machine* (JVM) *implementation*. The JVM is a software program that executes your Java class files in accordance with the Java language specifications [GJS96, LY97]. There are many JVM implementations [JE99] and, just like any other software solution, some are faster than others.

- *System and JVM tuning parameters*. Every platform allows the system administrator to tinker with its resource allocation. For instance, if you throttle the number of threads or sockets available to a server, you may inhibit the server's throughput. Similarly, tweaking the Java runtime initialization parameters could sometimes influence performance to some extent, particularly the size of the memory heap.

- *Application architecture*. The overall architecture plays an important role in determining application performance. No amount of micro-tuning will compensate for a fundamentally flawed design. A bubble-sort will not catch up to a quicksort even if you inlined the whole thing. In procedural programming, application architecture (or high-level design) would be the functional decomposition of a large task into smaller subtasks. In an object-oriented world, it would be described in terms of the class hierarchy and object message-passing. The important subtopic of data structures and algorithms falls in this category of application architecture. Technically speaking, an algorithm is any finite computation that could be carried out by a Turing machine. We will use the term algorithms in the more popular and restricted sense, referring to those computations that access, insert, delete, update, sort, compress, and otherwise manipulate collections of data. This topic is independent of any specific programming language and a detailed discussion of it is outside the scope of a Java-specific performance book. The interested reader should pursue the classic Knuth volumes [KNU97a, b, c] as well as Aho, Hoperoft, and Ullman [AHU74] and Binstock and Rex [BR95]. This topic has been studied extensively and received intense coverage in the literature. Duplicating that knowledge here would be redundant; and in my experience, most programmers have a firm grasp on the efficiency of algorithms and data structures.

- *Java Developer's Kit (JDK).* The JDK is a large collection of reusable Java classes that form the building blocks for complex Java applications. The JDK provides such a rich foundation that synthesizing complex software solutions in Java is remarkably easier than doing the same in other languages. This is the strength of the JDK. It is also its performance weakness. The only way you can provide a widely applicable set of building blocks is by making them generic. Unfortunately, dramatic performance optimizations often demand the narrowing of the problem domain into a specific, very small subset. In addition, some JDK constructs are much faster than others, and often you can achieve significant speedup by selecting faster constructs within the JDK.

- *Memory management.* There are many reasons why Java is so popular, and portability is not the only one. By taking over garbage collection, the JVM has freed the programmer from the delicate and error-prone task of managing memory. Although we don't see it in our source code, there's substantial computational effort under the covers to make it happen. Failure to pay proper attention to the underlying garbage-collection issues could sink Java performance.

- *Efficient coding.* When you fail to factor out constant computations such as

```
for (int i=0; i < vector.size(); i++) {
  // do something that does not modify vector size...
}
```

you have committed a (minor) performance coding mistake. The repeated calls to `vector.size()` should be factored out. Small-scale issues of that nature do not belong under the application architecture umbrella. If architecture is reserved for high-level design issues, coding issues will be home for the rest of the implementation issues of smaller scale.

The goal of this book is to provide you, the Java programmer, with the required expertise to build highly efficient Java applications or to optimize existing ones. We will direct the spotlight on the typical and dominant performance pitfalls and demonstrate solutions to those performance challenges. We will work our way towards highly efficient Java by studying most of the performance elements enumerated above. Each of the optimizations we discuss will fall into the quadruple category of application architecture, JDK efficiency, garbage collection, or efficient coding.

In a book dedicated to Java performance, how can we possibly leave out a serious discussion of various JVM implementations and their internals? Well, you have to keep in mind what our goal is. If this as a Ph.D. dissertation on Java performance, covering JVM internals and various implementation approaches would be mandatory. Every topic with performance relevance would have to be included. This, however, is not a dissertation. The only topics that will be covered are those that can potentially help Java programmers to achieve the goal: efficient, scalable Java code. Peripheral issues that do not get us closer to that goal did not make the cut. A study of JVM implementations is intellectually stimulating but rarely does it provide any insight towards modifying your Java coding and design for higher performance. If a certain JVM implementation uses direct object pointers as opposed to handles, it makes no difference to your code. Does it matter what algorithms are used for garbage collection? It may make a difference for the speed of the JVM but will not affect the design of your Java source code. One way or another, you are encouraged to keep object proliferation to a minimum and alleviate the demand on garbage collection. That is a good idea across all JVM implementations. If you follow the guidelines provided in this book, you may not have to depend on the quality of the garbage-collection implementation. You will keep object creation to a minimum and recycle objects as much as you can.

On a related note, we will also not attempt to crown the JVM performance king by benchmarking JVMs. Chasing this issue would be a fruitless exercise.

JVM implementations change too fast to keep track of in a book. JVM benchmark numbers change constantly and become quickly obsolete. The JDK, in comparison, changes very slowly, so it makes more sense to focus on the JDK rather than the various JVMs.

Java Speed

Before we delve into the issue of programming language performance, we should state clearly that talking about the performance of a language is a popular misuse of the terminology. A programming language does not have any speed. It is not slow nor fast. We can only discuss the speed of software programs written in a particular programming language. It is a convenient phrase, however, so I will continue to misuse the terminology and make frequent mention of Java performance where I actually mean the performance of programs written in Java.

Why is Java performance an issue in the first place? Have you ever heard anybody complain about the performance of assembly-language code? Probably not. Similarly, the issue of C performance traps and pitfalls has been equally void of content. All performance discussions of C code centered around topics such as the program's high-level design, the use of algorithms and data structures, and small-scale implementation issues. It has never been about the intrinsic cost of the language constructs themselves. *Writing Efficient Programs* by Jon Bentley [BEN82] is an excellent book covering those issues in a language-neutral manner. As a matter of fact, the coding examples were in Pascal. Why is it difficult to find text covering the performance pitfalls of the C language? Because there are very few of them. Again, inefficient C code is rarely linked to language constructs. Why is Java any different?

The speed of a code snippet is determined by the number of CPU cycles it takes to execute. On a modern processor, with sufficient cache space, CPU cycles will directly correlate to machine instructions; the compiler translates your source to these instructions. Even a Java program eventually executes on a physical machine as a stream of machine-specific instructions. If you wrote an assembly-language program, it would be fairly easy for you to estimate its speed. There is a one-to-one mapping from assembly-level statements to machine instructions. You could estimate the CPU cycle cost by counting the number of statements in your assembler code. There are no hidden surprises in assembly-language code. You pretty much have to construct everything from scratch. If you needed to convert a timestamp to GMT date format, you'd know how costly it is because your implementation would consist of hundreds of assembler statements that would consume thousands of CPU cycles (statements in a loop execute more than once). Java presents the other extreme. You want a GMT string representation of the current time? It is as easy as

```
String s = (new Date()).toString();
```

This simple statement leaves us absolutely clueless with respect to the enormous computational complexity hidden behind it. Since programmer time has become substantially more expensive than the cost of CPU cycles, the evolution of programming languages moves from fast, do-it-yourself low-level languages to higher-level languages that mask the complexity, substantially increase programmer productivity, and as a trade-off, produce slower code.

Most performance comparisons contrast Java to C/C++, not assembly language, but the point made above still holds. C and C++ allow the programmer finer control over programming constructs. Fine, low-level control, normally translates into faster execution. Take memory management for example. In C/C++, this is a delicate and error-prone task. But you can do it faster in C/C++ than in Java, where you have absolutely no say about memory management and garbage-collection implementation.

The portability and ease of use that helped Java take the programming world by a storm have a price tag. They inevitably mean that complexity is hidden away in the JDK library and the JVM implementation. Hidden complexity leads to performance surprises that can be staggering in magnitude. Where hidden surprises abound, you need knowledge to navigate around. Providing this knowledge is the goal of this book. This is an ambitious goal and undoubtedly some important optimizations may be missing. I'm sure you'll set me straight at dov_bulka@hotmail.com.

The Test Environment

In the course of our discussion we will often contrast several ways to achieve a given computational task. In order to pick the performance winner in each scenario, we will usually measure the speed of each programmatic alternative. Our typical test environment consisted of a single-processor PC powered by a

333 MHz Pentium-Pro processor. The operating system was NT 4.0, running the Sun 1.2.2 JDK.[1] This is the default environment, unless stated otherwise. In some scenarios we have used a 12-way AIX server with the 1.1.6 JDK from IBM. In other measurements we also used a 4-way Netfinity server (4×200 MHz, Pentium-II, NT 4.0) using the IBM 1.1.7 Win32 JDK. In all test scenarios that involve networking, the communication link was a 100 Mbps Fast Ethernet. Any time we stray from the default environment stated above (333 MHz Pentium-Pro, NT 4.0, Sun 1.2.2) it will be clearly stated. Each test environment exhibits a single JVM(JDK). If you are looking for JVM(JDK) comparisons, you will not find them in this text. The performance observations found here are JVM-invariant, which means that they hold true across all JVMs. If some optimization gives you some boost on JVM X, it may get you a little less on JVM Y, but we will not sweat such minor differences. If, on the other hand, JVM X outperforms JVM Y by a wide margin, we really should not worry about JVM Y for very long. The competitive forces of the capitalist economy will relegate JVM Y to the sidelines very quickly. Typically, a significant optimization on JVM X will be significant on JVM Y as well.

One crucial aspect of our test environment is that we always run with the JIT enabled. The JIT is worth, on average, an order of magnitude boost in speed. If you disable the JIT, you have essentially given away performance.

You will also notice that we measure the performance of code segments by repeatedly executing it inside a loop. The number of loop iterations will vary as we try to bring the loop execution time to the one- to ten-second range. We need the measurement to run long enough to eliminate irrelevant and transient factors such as JIT compilation. If we only ran a small number of iterations, all measurements would look alike. They would just about measure the speed of JIT compilation. In real-life applications, the JIT will compile a method once and subsequent invocations will execute the compiled method. For that reason, the speed of the JIT is not interesting to us, only the speed of the compiled code.

Before You Optimize: A Word of Caution

Code optimization is a transformation performed on a given source code that produces a new code entity. That transformation has various characteristics:

---

[1] JIT enabled. HotSpot was not used.

- It must preserve program correctness. You don't have the liberty of speeding up a fragment of code at the expense of sacrificing correctness.

- The resulting code is more efficient than the original one.

- The resulting code is often less generic and consequently less reusable. Many optimizations are the result of narrowing the problem domain and taking advantage of domain-specific assumptions.

- The resulting code is often not as simple as the original one. It is often more complex, less readable, less maintainable, and harder to modify and extend. It may also be less reliable.

As you can tell, software optimization is filled with potential negatives. An overdose of optimizations could wreak havoc on many important characteristics of your software design and implementation. Optimization is like a medication. A small, recommended dose is designed to help. An overdose could be very harmful; so optimizations, like medicine, should be applied carefully.

To protect your software from the potentially negative consequences, two habits are recommended. First, you should profile your program prior to taking any optimization action. Profiling will help you detect the 20 percent of your code that executes 80 percent of the time. This 20 percent is the performance-critical code. There's no point is optimizing anything outside that critical path. That also means that if you apply optimizations randomly to your source code, you will be wasting energy 80 percent of the time without reaping any benefits.

The second recommendation is to insist on getting a substantial return on your investment. The effort in modifying code and reducing readability and other metrics is your investment. What you hope to get in return is higher performance. My favorite optimizations are those that net a huge performance gain for little effort and minute impact on the existing design and implementation. The 80–20 principle works its magic here as well: 20 percent of the available optimization ideas will deliver 80 percent of the potential speed boost. The rest of the optimizations are not worth bothering with because the return on investment will have diminishing returns.

Organization of This Book

We start with a discussion of `String`, `StringBuffer`, and the `StringTokenizer` classes. Those are some of the most frequently used classes in Java programs. When you profile typical Java programs, particularly if they have anything to do with the Web, you are very likely to find string manipulation methods at, or very near, the top of the list of your performance hot spots. Understanding the performance implications of string manipulation is crucial and a very good place to start a discussion of Java performance. This is the topic of Chapter 1.

Typical performance optimizations have to strike a delicate balance between program speed and other important software metrics such as flexibility, simplicity, reliability, reuse, and more. It is not often that we can gain significant performance without sacrificing anything at all. These are the best kind of optimizations. They remove pure overhead without paying for it. Optimizations of this kind are discussed in Chapter 2.

Chapter 3 explores the performance of the Java collections. We will focus on the dominant collection types such as `Vector`, `Hashtable`, and `ArrayList`.

One of the most valuable techniques in the arsenal of the performance engineer is caching. Chapter 4 will explore various manifestations of caching and how they can help circumvent costly Java computations.

If you are looking for a Java networking chapter, the closest thing to it is Chapter 5, which discusses the more general issue of Java I/O streams. Chapter 5 drives home some important general I/O streams performance issues. Socket I/O is just a special case of I/O streams.

Memory management and garbage collection is another crucial issue to Java performance. Relying on improvements in JVM garbage-collection algorithms is one way to help the performance cause. A better way would be to reduce the number of objects your Java program creates. Chapter 6 will provide several options for object recycling.

As we said earlier, programmers are costly, CPU power is not. In some scenarios, customers are willing to absorb the fact that Java applications are somewhat short on speed, given that throwing more CPU power at it can compensate for the lack of efficiency. In other words, I can live with a slower Java program if the addition of CPUs can elevate it back to the required performance level. However, the move from a single-processor machine to a symmetric multiprocessor (SMP) does not guarantee higher performance. In fact, a poorly designed program could see performance degrade on an SMP box. Chapter 7 will discuss the design and implementation of programs designed to maximize scalability on the SMP architecture.

True to form, Java has gone a long way to simplify the task of distributed computing via remote method invocation (RMI.) Naturally, if a complex task is made to look very easy, there must be a performance trade-off somewhere. We will quantify it in Chapter 9. This will be followed by a discussion of servlets and Java Server Pages (JSP) performance in Chapter 10.

The various optimizations discussed throughout this book could provide dramatic improvements to the performance and scalability of typical Java code. To substantiate that claim, we download a Java Web server code from the Web and quadruple its performance by applying some of the optimizations explained in earlier chapters. That interesting exercise is performed in Chapter 11. This chapter puts an exclamation point on the usefulness of the performance observations made earlier in the book. These optimizations are for real.

Acknowledgments

Bringing a book to market is the culmination of the work of many people. I'd like to thank Julie DeBaggis, my editor at Addison-Wesley, for skillfully leading this project. Writing a book is often described as a grueling experience. Not this one. Working with Julie on this book was enjoyable from beginning to end.

I have been fortunate enough to hang around some very talented friends and colleagues who have helped to shape and contribute optimization ideas, review them, or all of the above. I must confess that if I managed to make some observations far into the Java performance sky, it is only because I was standing on their shoulders. They are, in no particular order:

Chet Murthy

Josh Engel

Yomtov Meged

Scott Snyder

Andy Citron

Chris Seekamp

Last, but not least, I am grateful to the reviewers provided by Addison-Wesley. Their feedback, positive and negative, was extremly valuable. In particular, I'd like to thank

Mary Dageforde

Malcolm Sparks

J. D. Baker

Paul Barford

Elisabeth Freeman

Howard Harkness

Elliott Hughes

Tim Lindholm

Peter Sparago

Finally, I take sole responsibility for the views expressed in this book. It should not be assumed that my friends, colleagues, or reviewers necessarily endorse my views on Java performance and scalability.

1

Java Strings

Java `String` and `StringBuffer` objects are two of the most frequently used class instances in Java programs. It is definitely so in Web-enabled applications. In the same way that scientific applications crunch numbers, Web applications are primarily string-crunching machines. Understanding the issues underlying Java string performance is therefore important for developers attempting to write high-performance Web applications in Java. A solid application design is necessary for application performance but is definitely not sufficient. There are many important performance issues lurking in the JDK details, many of which are unintuitive. This chapter presents a detailed study of those issues with regard to Java `String`, `StringBuffer`, and `StringTokenizer` objects.

Optimization 1: `String` Concatenation

One operation that is frequently found in Java code is string concatenation. As it turns out, there is substantial effort under the Java covers to make this happen. If you read the comments in `StringBuffer.java` (Sun's JDK 1.2.2) you will find out that the simple statement

```
String p = a + b;   // a, b are String objects
```

is compiled by the Java compiler into

```
String p = (new StringBuffer()).append(a).append(b).toString();
```

We can already spot two objects created by the above statement:

- `StringBuffer`
- The `String` return value created by `toString()`

This is not all. Each `String` and `StringBuffer` has a private `char` array to hold the individual characters of the string. That lifts the object count even higher. They happen to share this array for efficiency, so our object count only goes up to three. New objects inflict a performance penalty twice: once upon creation and later by creating more work for the garbage collector. The reason that `String` addition is so inefficient is that `String` objects are immutable. You cannot take a `String` whose value is "a" and extend it into "ab". You have to create a brand new `String` object for "ab". Fortunately, the `String` class has a close relative in Java that can do the job more efficiently. The `StringBuffer` object is a string that is allowed to change. The ability to modify `String-Buffer` objects makes them a more efficient alternative when it comes to string concatenation. For the sake of comparison, we measured the performance of code using either class to perform string concatenation. The first measures the speed of `String` concatenation:

```
String s = new String();
long start = System.currentTimeMillis();   // <+++ Start timing

for (int i = 0; i < 10000; i++) {
   s += "a";
}

long stop = System.currentTimeMillis();   // <+++ Stop timing
```

The second test does the same for `StringBuffer`:

```
StringBuffer s = new StringBuffer();
long start = System.currentTimeMillis();   // <+++ Start timing

for (int i = 0; i < 10000; i++) {
   s.append("a");
}

long stop = System.currentTimeMillis();   // <+++ Stop timing
```

The difference is pretty dramatic, as shown in Figure 1.1. The `StringBuffer` class is by far more efficient than `String` for this particular usage.

The reason the `StringBuffer` append is so dramatically more efficient is that new objects are not generated by

```
s.append("a"); // s is a StringBuffer
```

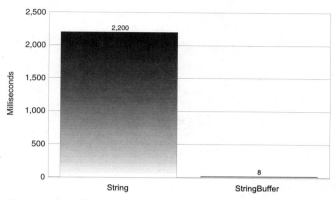

Figure 1.1.   Comparing `String` and `StringBuffer` appends

A single character is added to the internal buffer maintained by the `String-Buffer` implementation. The only time a new object is created in this scenario is when the buffer is full and must be expanded, but this occurs infrequently. In the case of `String` append, on the other hand, the statement

```
s += "a"; // s is a String
```

is converted into

```
s = (new StringBuffer()).append(s).append("a").toString();
```

which is guaranteed to create a few objects every time. The generous creation of superfluous objects is one of the most serious problems in practical Java programs. With that said, `String` concatenation does not always generate new objects. In the following text we will dissect a large misconception. Take a look at the loop

```
for (int i = 0; i < 100000; i++) {
    String s = "Hello " + "John " + "Parker";
}
```

It may look as if a whole lot of `String` concatenation is going on in this loop. In fact, there is none. The compiler has enough information to figure out that the resulting `String` would be "Hello John Parker". The compiler creates a `String` object

```
__temp = "Hello John Parker";
```

and the loop is converted into

```
for (int i = 0; i < 100000; i++) {
    String s = _temp;
}
```

The execution speed of this loop is phenomenal since it is just a bunch of inexpensive assignments. In fact, the performance of

```
String s = "Hello " + "John " + "Parker";
```

is equivalent to that of

```
String s = "Hello John Parker";
```

and also just as fast as

```
String s = hello + john + parker;
```

where `hello`, `john`, and `parker` are class members defined as

```
private static final String hello = "Hello ";
private static final String john = "John ";
private static final String parker = "Parker";
```

If, however, you have chosen to build the `String` in distinct steps, you may get into trouble. The compiler is not likely to apply the above optimization to code such as

```
String s = "Hello ";
s += "John ";
s += "Parker";
```

As a matter of fact, while the loop

```
for (int i = 0; i < 100000; i++) {
    String s = "Hello " + "John " + "Parker";
}
```

executed in less than 1 millisecond, the loop

```
for (int i = 0; i < 100000; i++) {
    String s = "Hello ";
```

```
    s += "John ";
    s += "Parker";
}
```

took 1,370 milliseconds, a huge difference. A gap of three orders of magnitude is visually difficult to appreciate, so I'll spare you the graphical chart representation.

In many situations, the building blocks of a String are not all available during compile time. Some of the ingredients are dynamic and computed on the fly. To mimic this situation, let's modify our loop a little:

```
for (int i = 0; i < 100000; i++) {
    String s = "Hello " + i + " John Parker";
}
```

Now we have the index i stuck in the middle of the String so the compiler cannot construct the String. We really have to concatenate the fragments during run time. I've seen lots of people trying to outsmart the compiler by rolling their own append, as in

```
StringBuffer sb = new StringBuffer();
sb.append("Hello ");
sb.append(i);
sb.append(" John Parker");
String s = sb.toString();
```

Now this is exactly what the compiler does when it is faced with the statement

```
String s = "Hello " + i + " John Parker";
```

So what's the point of rolling your own StringBuffer? When we compared the performance of 100,000 iterations of those two forms, their execution time was almost identical, at roughly 3,225 milliseconds. There was no advantage there. The only time you can really outsmart the compiler is when you have an intelligent guess with respect to the size of the resulting String. By default, the StringBuffer is initialized with a capacity of 16. We had more than 16 characters, so we took a performance hit. The following optimization actually makes sense as we allocate the StringBuffer to have an initial capacity of 32 and we prevent it from ever needing an expansion in capacity:

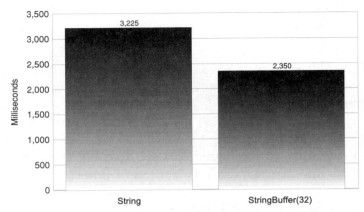

Figure 1.2.   Compare `String` to `StringBuffer` performance

```
StringBuffer sb = new StringBuffer(32); // Only change
sb.append("Hello ");
sb.append(i);
sb.append(" John Parker");
String s = sb.toString();
```

One-hundred thousand iterations of this code have executed in 2,350 milliseconds, which is better than the execution time of

```
String s = "Hello " + i + " John Parker";
```

Figure 1.2 compares the speed of the naive `String` concatenation to an explicit `StringBuffer` construction when sufficient buffer space has been allocated ahead of time.

Naturally, if the size of the resulting `String` is less than 16, there is no point in rolling your own `StringBuffer`. Stick to the notational convenience of the `String` + operator.

Optimization 2: Fight Object Overpopulation

The previous optimizations focused on the specific issue of `String` concatenation. The real issue is actually bigger than that. It is the issue of object proliferation in Java programs that is at the core of many Java performance issues. The `String` class just happens to be an excellent example of what could happen to Java performance if you don't watch your object count. The fact that

String objects are immutable forces the creation of a new String object anytime you want to change it in any way. If you want to add a single character to a string, you have to create a brand new String object. In C++ you could do the same by simply adding this character to the existing object. To say that Java could be just as fast as C++ because of JIT, HotSpot, or static compilation, is to miss the point that some decisions that are inherent in the Java language design, are taking away some optimization opportunities like the one just mentioned, as well as the big decision to prevent programmers from managing their own memory. This is not a criticism of those design decisions, as they provide immense benefit to other important software metrics (not to mention that the popularity of Java ratifies those decisions). However, we should not be blind to the fact that they take a toll on performance in a way that compilation and massive inlining (HotSpot) may not be able to fix.

Let's look at a concrete example involving object creation. If you need to print some String objects to a file, should you execute

```
printWriter.print(x+y);
```

or would it be better to use

```
printWriter.print(x);
printWriter.print(y);
```

The latter consists of two print() calls and may intuitively feel as the less efficient choice. The measurement results will surprise you. Let pw be a buffered PrintWriter object:

```
PrintWriter pw =
    new PrintWriter(
        new BufferedWriter(
            new FileWriter("junk.out")));
```

We compared 1,000,000 iterations of

```
pw.print("one " + i);
```

to the same number of iterations of

```
pw.print("one ");
pw.print(i);
```

where i is an `int` ranging from 0 to 999,999. The first test clocked in at 22,900 milliseconds. It consisted of a single `print()` statement but was forced to create `String`, `StringBuffer`, and `char[]` objects to accommodate the `String` concatenation. The second test was faster. It executed in 15,700 milliseconds. Although we had doubled the number of `print()` calls, we have skipped the many objects flowing out of the `String` concatenation. This should serve as a warning that overzealous creation of objects could hurt the performance of your Java code. See Figure 1.3.

As Java programmers, we should keep a watchful eye on the number of objects our code generates on the performance-critical path. We make coding decisions that could greatly affect the object population for better or worse. Let's look at another example.

We have spent considerable effort up to this point giving `String` concatenation a bad name. Actually, you could do worse. If you wanted to concatenate the strings a, b, and c, you could perform a multistep construction such as

```
s = a;    // s, a, b, and c are all pre-existing String objects
s += b;
s += c;
```

This construction is very wasteful in terms of object creation. A statement such as

```
s += b;
```

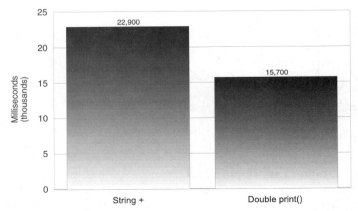

Figure 1.3.   Overabundance of objects takes a toll on performance

is equivalent to

```
s = s + b;
```

which is converted to

```
s = (new StringBuffer()).append(s).append(b).toString();
```

This, as we already know, creates a `StringBuffer` object, a `String` object, and a `char[]` object that is shared by both `String` and `StringBuffer` objects. Taken together, code such as

```
s = a;
s += b;
s += c;
```

creates six additional objects that must be disposed of later by the garbage collector.

The alternative is to use

```
s = a + b + c;
```

which is converted to

```
s = (new StringBuffer()).append(a).append(b).append(c).toString();
```

which only creates three additional objects. We compared 100,000 iterations of the above constructions, and the single-step construction

```
s = a + b + c;
```

was twice as fast as the multistep one. See Figure 1.4.

The issue of the object population explosion is so important to Java performance that we will drive it further with one more example before we (temporarily) let it go. If you have recently migrated to Java from C or C++ you may be tempted to do the following when a case-insensitive string compare is required:

```
ucA = a.toUpperCase();     // a, b , ucA and ucB are all strings
ucB = b.toUpperCase();
boolean bool = ucA.equals(ucB);
```

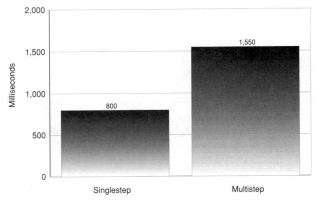

Figure 1.4. You could do worse than `String +`

This would be fairly natural in C or C++. Uppercase both strings and then compare them. It would not work very well in Java. Unlike C and C++, you cannot modify the `String` object in place. In Java we must create new `String` objects to hold the uppercase versions. To avoid the creation of ucA and ucB objects, you could do the following

```
boolean bool = a.equalsIgnoreCase(b);
```

Comparing 1,000,000 iterations of both versions, we find that the latter is more than an order of magnitude faster than the former. See Figure 1.5.

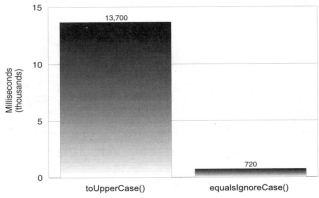

Figure 1.5. `toUpperCase()` creates a new `String` object

Optimization 3: `String` Equality

The next step in our coverage of popular `String` operations is the testing of `String` objects for equality. `String` comparison is right up there in popularity with the `String` concatenation and append. These operations frequently pop up in Java code. When it comes to `String` comparison, we have two flavors depending on case sensitivity. The `equals()` method checks for an exact match that is case-sensitive. The `equalsIgnoreCase()`, as you can imagine, will accept two strings as equal even if their individual characters differ in case. The following three classes test various aspects of the `String` `equals()` comparison. The first class compares two identical strings. The second compares two strings of the same length that differ in case. The third compares two strings of unequal length:

```
public class Equals_1 {              // Compare two identical strings
    public static void main(String args[]) {
        String s = "H"+"elloWorld";  // These two Strings...
        String p = "HelloWorl"+"d";  // ...have identical characters

        long start = System.currentTimeMillis();  // <+++ Start timing
        for (int i = 0; i < 10000000; i++) {
            s.equals(p);
        }
        long stop = System.currentTimeMillis();  // <+++ Stop timing

        System.out.println( " time = " + (stop - start) );
    }
}


public class Equals_2 {              // Compare two strings of same
                                     // length but different case
    public static void main(String args[]) {
        String s = "HelloWorld";
        String p = "HelloWorlD";

        long start = System.currentTimeMillis();  // <+++ Start timing
        for (int i = 0; i < 10000000; i++) {
            s.equals(p);
        }
        long stop = System.currentTimeMillis();  // <+++ Stop timing
        ...
    }
}
```

```
public class Equals_3 {      // Compare two strings of different length
   public static void main(String args[]) {
      String s = "HelloWorld";
      String p = "HelloWorld1";

      long start = System.currentTimeMillis();  // <+++ Start timing
      for (int i = 0; i < 10000000; i++) {
         s.equals(p);
      }
      long stop = System.currentTimeMillis();   // <+++ Stop timing
      ...
   }
}
```

The execution times of the above tests are given by Figure 1.6.

The absolute fastest of the bunch was the Equals_1 class comparing two identical String constants. Since Java String objects are immutable, there is no
need to generate two separate instances of an identical string constant. The
JVM exploits this feature to create two separate references to a single String
object. The equality of the references is the very first check performed by the
equals() method. For that reason, Equals_1 is our fastest test case. The
Equals_2 test case compared two strings that were almost identical except that
they differed in the case of one character. Consequently, those two String references could not share a single representation and that is reflected in the
speed of this test. The speed of Equals_2 was crippled even further by the fact
that the two strings under comparison differed in the last character only. We
had to march all the way down the string to discover the character mismatch.

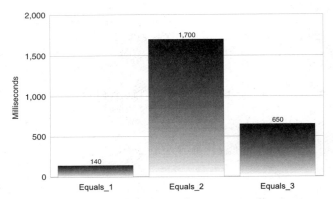

Figure 1.6. Performance of String equality tests

The last test case, `Equals_3`, was significantly faster than the previous one. The reason is that the two strings were of unequal length. A popular implementation of the `String equal()` method has a shortcut that checks for string length early in the computation. If the strings are not equal in length, they are definitely not equal, which tends to speed things up by avoiding the tedious task of comparing one character at a time.

Now what about string comparison when case sensitivity is ignored? Generally, this comparison should be slower because it introduces another dimension of complexity into the character comparisons. We have two versions of this test. The first compares strings of equal length that differ in the case of the last character. The second compares strings of unequal length.

```
public class IgnoreCase_1 {            // equalsIgnoreCase on strings
                                       // of equal length
    public static void main(String args[]) {
        String s = "HelloWorld";
        String p = "HelloWorlD";

        long start = System.currentTimeMillis();  // <+++ Start timing
        for (int i = 0; i < 1000000; i++) {
            s.equalsIgnoreCase(p);
        }
        long stop = System.currentTimeMillis();  // <+++ Stop timing
        ...
    }
}

public class IgnoreCase_2 {            // equalsIgnoreCase on strings
                                       // of unequal length
    public static void main(String args[]) {
        String s = "HelloWorld";
        String p = "HelloWorld1";

        long start = System.currentTimeMillis();  // <+++ Start timing
        for (int i = 0; i < 1000000; i++) {
            s.equalsIgnoreCase(p);
        }
        long stop = System.currentTimeMillis();  // <+++ Stop timing
        ...
    }
}
```

Figure 1.7 adds the last two test cases into the mix.

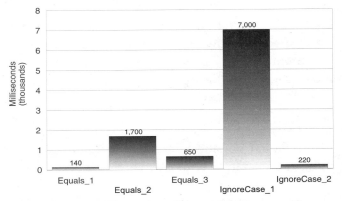

Figure 1.7.   The various flavors of `String` equality

The `IgnoreCase_1` test case had the worst results. It compared two strings of equal length while being case-insensitive. There were no shortcuts for this scenario. The code had to compare one character at a time and take uppercase and lowercase considerations into account. The second test case was much faster. Even though it ignored case, the strings were of unequal length, providing this implementation with a shortcut. One interesting and unintuitive result is that the `equalsIgnoreCase()` method was faster than `equals()` for strings of unequal length (`IgnoreCase_2` and `Equals_3`). The `equalsIgnoreCase()` method performs its length check earlier in the computation than `equals()` does. That's why it is faster in the case of unequal strings. The surprising outcome here is that if the strings you are comparing are unlikely to have identical length, the `equalsIgnoreCase()` will be a faster comparison. This observation, however, may be highly dependent on the particular JDK being used. You may want to test this claim with regard to your JDK before taking any action on it.

Optimization 4: Characters to Bytes and Back

An article appearing in *Java Report* [WB99] has correctly pointed out that broad, generic software solutions tend to compromise performance. The essence of performance optimizations is to take advantage of narrow assumptions. This is in direct opposition to the force driving reusable software design—to be applicable in a wide variety of situations. The authors did not provide an example, but we will fill that gap and make the point painfully concrete.

The getBytes() method of the String class is the most compute-intensive method of the class. Even a single call to getBytes() can manifest itself as a performance hot spot in your code. This method copies characters from the String object into a byte array. Each Unicode character may be converted into one, two, or even three bytes. The correct decision is made by the getBytes() implementation and is costly. It is simpler in the case of ASCII characters (because ASCII is a small subset of the Unicode set.) Each ASCII character is converted into a single byte by truncating one byte of the two-byte Unicode representation. The need to support char-to-byte conversion in various character encodings takes a tremendous toll on the complexity and efficiency of this method. The StringGetBytes class measures a baseline for the performance cost of calling getBytes():

```
public class StringGetBytes {
    public static void main(String args[]) {
        String s = "HelloWorld";

        long start = System.currentTimeMillis();   // <+++ Start timing
        for (int i = 0; i < 1000000; i++) {
            byte[] b = s.getBytes();
        }
        long stop = System.currentTimeMillis();   // <+++ Stop timing
        ...
    }
}
```

As you will see shortly, there's a substantial performance penalty to using getBytes(). However, you can often bail out fairly easily. It may be the case that your application manipulates ASCII strings that do not necessitate character-encoding conversion. We encountered such a scenario on the WebSphere application server where we manipulated HTTP strings that were guaranteed to be ASCII by the HTTP protocol. Since performance is a high priority for an application server, we [SS98] have created a homegrown version of get-Bytes() that works on ASCII strings only:

```
public class MyGetBytes {

    public static byte[] asciiGetBytes(String buf) {
        int size = buf.length();
        int i;
        byte[] bytebuf = new byte[size];
```

```
    for (i = 0; i < size; i++) {
        bytebuf[i] = (byte) buf.charAt(i);
    }

    return bytebuf;
}

public static void main(String args[]) {
    String s = "HelloWorld";

    long start = System.currentTimeMillis();   // <+++ Start timing
    for (int i = 0; i < 1000000; i++) {
        byte[] b = asciiGetBytes(s);
    }
    long stop = System.currentTimeMillis();   // <+++ Stop timing

    System.out.println( " time = " + (stop - start) );
}
}
```

The test case using our homegrown asciiGetBytes() has outperformed the original by a wide margin, as shown in Figure 1.8.

Our asciiGetBytes() solution is a huge performance winner precisely because we have diluted the power and generality of the original String.getBytes(). The original can handle any character encoding whatsoever, but ours can only do ASCII; but that's okay. If the strings that we are manipulating are ASCII, then the awesome power of getBytes() is wasted on us. What we really want is a narrowly focused and fast solution to address our very particular need.

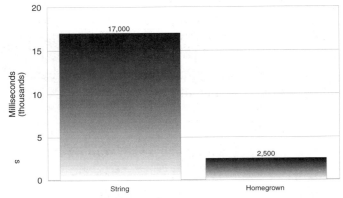

Figure 1.8.   Comparing String.getBytes() to a homegrown one

Naturally, an analogous case exists in the opposite direction when you want to convert bytes to a String object of Unicode characters. You encounter this scenario anytime you read from a byte stream and want to convert what you read into a String. The String class provides a method to construct a Unicode String from a byte array. If b is a byte array, as in

```
byte[] b = "HelloWorld".getBytes();
```

you could invoke the following method to create a String out of it:

```
String s = new String(b);
```

We measured the performance of this constructor, and it is very poor. We used the following test:

```
byte[] b = "HelloWorld".getBytes();

long start = System.currentTimeMillis();   // <+++ Start timing

for (int i = 0; i < 100000; i++) {
    String s = new String(b);
}

long stop = System.currentTimeMillis();   // <+++ Stop timing
```

This is the same problem that we had with getBytes(). The mapping between the sets of bytes and Unicode characters is compute-intensive. This is what you have to live with if you must convert from one character-encoding to another, but what if your data source and sink are both ASCII and the conversion is trivial? We need an ASCII shortcut. This time, instead of rolling our own solution, we will use a method already available in the String implementation. This method is deprecated, so we may have to revisit it in the future. For now, it is still supported and a significant performance winner. (I doubt that support for it will be dropped unless an equally efficient alternative is made available.) The method we are talking about is the constructor

```
public String(byte ascii[], int hibyte) { ... }
```

In our test loop above we simply replaced

```
String s = new String(b);
```

with

```
String s = new String(b,0);   // This works only on ASCII
```

The performance of the deprecated byte-to-char converter has outperformed the officially recommended one by a wide margin. Figure 1.9 compares the execution time of 100,000 iterations of the loop shown earlier in this section.

Some people may suggest that in a world dominated by the Internet, internationalization of data is a must and opportunities to optimize ASCII-only data may be rare. This idea is wrong. Such optimization opportunities are abundant even in the HTTP protocol that powers the Web. The HTTP protocol enforces the use of ASCII-only format for all protocol headers as well as other portions of the HTTP message (request line, response status, and more.) When a Web server manipulates the request line of an HTTP request ("GET /myURL HTTP/1.1"), it is guaranteed to be working with an ASCII string. Treating this string as a generic Unicode string will be less efficient.

Optimization 5: `StringTokenizer`

The `StringTokenizer` class is a perfect example illustrating why Java makes programmers so productive. The `StringTokenizer` is a powerful and flexible class that encapsulates the tedious nitty-gritty details of parsing a string behind a simple, easy-to-use interface. Power and flexibility, however, do not

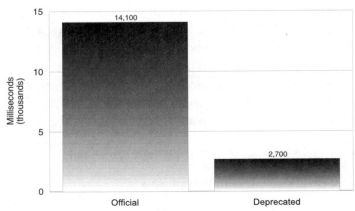

Figure 1.9.   The fast byte-to-char converter has been deprecated

often go hand in hand with high performance. More often than not, they push in opposite directions. High-performance code is typically dependent on narrowly focused simplifying assumptions. This idea—which we repeat many times over—is fundamental for software performance engineering.

When you design general-purpose code such as the JDK, you cannot make too many simplifying assumptions because your target audience is diverse. The JDK must satisfy the needs of a large set of Java applications. Your application, on the other hand, is a very special one. It has a specific task in a specific domain. As such, you probably don't need the full power of any JDK class. You need only the subset that you depend on.

Say that you profiled your application, identified the performance-critical path (that 20 percent of the code that executed 80 percent of the time), and found out that the StringTokenizer is gobbling up your CPU. In that case (and in that case only), you may consider replacing the StringTokenizer with a StringBuffer and use the indexOf() and substring() to parse out the tokens [SF99]. Let's do that.

Our first implementation will use the default StringTokenizer:

```
private static void jdkTokenizer(String s) {
      String sub = null;
      StringTokenizer st = new StringTokenizer(s,",");

      try {
          while ( (sub = (String) st.nextToken()) != null) {
          // Normally, you would compute something useful here...
          // ...but not now as we are trying to isolate the ...
          // ...performance cost of a StringTokenizer
          }
    }
    catch (NoSuchElementException e ) {}
}
```

Our next version is a homegrown replacement for the StringTokenizer:

```
private static void mySimpleTokenizer(String s) {
      String sub = null;
      int i = 0;
      int j = s.indexOf(",");
```

```
while ( j >= 0) {
    sub = s.substring(i,j);
    // Normally, you would compute something here
    i = j+1;                    // skip over comma we already found
    j = s.indexOf(",",i);       // find next comma
}

sub = s.substring(i);          // Don't forget the last substring
}
```

The first version, using the JDK's StringTokenizer, works fine but it is not very fast. One-hundred thousand invocations of it using the string "a,b,c,def,g" has executed in 3,100 milliseconds. Our alternative tokenizer implementation (mySimpleTokenizer()) improved execution speed to 900 milliseconds, as shown in Figure 1.10.

You may wonder what are we doing that makes our homegrown tokenizer so much faster than StringTokenizer. In a very simplistic answer, we are faster because we are less powerful. Our code makes a specific assumption that the set of delimiters is made of a single character. The StringTokenizer does not make such a strong assumption. It is powerful enough to handle a larger set of delimiters at once. We also make a very subtle assumption that we don't have consecutive delimiters such as "a,b,,,c,,d." To put this on a more concrete footing, notice that in order to find the end of the next token, all we have to do is a single call to indexOf(). The StringTokenizer, on the other hand, without the benefit of our assumptions, must call indexOf() for every character in the string in order to decide if it belongs in the set of delimiters or not. There's a

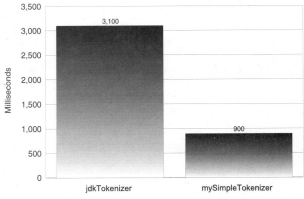

Figure 1.10.   A StringTokenizer compared to a homegrown one

very important performance principle that we are glossing over here—that generic code, flexible enough to cope with a wide variety of inputs, naturally cannot make very strong assumptions about the nature of its input and, as a consequence, has limited opportunities for optimizations. The StringTokenizer implementation is not bad at all. It is actually very fast for what it set out to accomplish. It's just that it is too powerful for its own good (performance-speaking).

This brings up an interesting twist. Take an HTTP request, for example. The first line looks something like

```
GET /servlet/HelloWorldServlet HTTP/1.0
```

or in general

```
<method> <URL> <protocol version>
```

This request arrives on a socket as a byte stream. We have two choices from here on.

- We can convert the byte stream to a String and then parse the String into its constituent parts (method, URL, and version).

- Alternatively, we could parse the byte stream directly and then convert the tokens into String objects.

It all boils down to the following decision: Do we prefer to parse a String or a byte array? So we have a third tokenizer version that parses a byte array representing "a,b,c,def,g" and then converts the individual tokens into String objects.

```
private static void byteTokenizer(byte[] b) {
    String sub = null;
    int i = 0;
    int j = 0;

    while ( j < b.length) {
        if (b[j] == ',') {
        // Typically, you would use the String here...
        i = j+1;  // skip over comma we already found
        }
```

```
        j++;
    }

    // Don't forget the last substring
    sub = new String(b,0,i,b.length-i);
}
```

First, notice that when we convert a byte sequence into a `String`, we opted to use the deprecated method:

```
sub = new String(b,0,i,b.length-i); // hibyte is 0. ASCII conversion
```

instead of

```
sub = new String(b,i,b.length-i);  // Proper Unicode conversion
```

Optimization 4 explains why we like those deprecated conversion methods. They are much faster if your input stream is ASCII.

This last attempt was faster than the default `StringTokenizer` but fell short of the performance of our alternative `mySimpleTokenizer()`. Executing 100,000 invocations of `byteTokenizer()` has taken 2,800 milliseconds. The repeated creation of a `String` object from a byte array has taken a toll on performance. Figure 1.11 exhibits our three attempts at tokenizing a character string.

Another interesting point to draw from Figure 1.11 is that it is faster to create a `String` object using the `substring()` method than to construct a new `String`

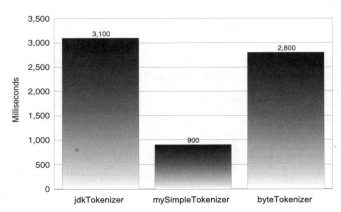

Figure 1.11.   Homegrown tokenizing is faster

object from a byte array. The JDK implementation is leveraging the fact that the underlying String object is immutable and allows the new String object (created by substring()) to refer to the original character array of the containing string. As a result, no copying of data is required. On the other hand, when a new String object is created from a byte array, each byte in the array corresponds to a newly allocated two-byte Unicode character. Both memory allocation and data copy are required in this case.

The 80–20 principle (Optimization 15) states that only 20 percent of your code is performance-critical. In other words, in 80 percent of your code, performance issues are secondary and are overwhelmed by other important issues of software engineering such as readability, maintainability, programmer-productivity, and more. You should definitely use the JDK's StringTokenizer in the vast majority of your code in which performance is irrelevant. In the performance-critical path, you may consider replacing the StringTokenizer with a simpler, faster variation along the lines of a homegrown parser.

Optimization 6: `charAt()` ∎

I normally don't like overly defensive programming that starts every method with multiple sanity checks on the input arguments. I'm not opposed to checking the validity of the arguments, but I only want to do it once. What happens in practice is that we check the validity of the same conditions over and over. For example, if I determined the length of a String, I can guarantee the validity of the character access:

```
int len = s.length()
for (i = 0; i < len; i++) {
    char c = s.charAt(i);
    ...
}
```

If the length of the String is 50, then the charAt() implementation will perform 50 validity range checks on the input index, all of them redundant and not really necessary in this case. We have performed an implicit range check already when we computed the length of the String. The typical charAt() method checks that the character index is positive and that it does not fall outside the String length. The problem with excessive sanity checks is that they get between you and the CPU cycles. A modern processor can do many things simultaneously. It can execute an instruction, decode another, and fetch the next instruction after that. That's how we keep the pipeline humming. It is very difficult though, to fetch the next instruction if you don't have a clue what the next instruction is. It is a conditional branch instruction that introduces uncertainty with regard to the location of the next instruction. Introducing such bubbles into the processor pipeline causes delays.

To make matters worse, we take a simple one-line method such as charAt(), and we triple its pathlength by introducing range checks. Take the asciiGet-Bytes() method from Optimization 4. It is dominated by the cost of the many invocations of charAt(). I found this by profiling, a strategy that is highly recommended prior to hacking your elegant design.

```
public static byte[] asciiGetBytes(String buf) {
    int size = buf.length();
    int i;
    byte[] bytebuf = new byte[size];

    for (i = 0; i < size; i++) {
        bytebuf[i] = (byte)buf.charAt(i);
    }

    return bytebuf;
}
```

Unfortunately, modifying the JDK is illegal, so we cannot modify the String.java implementation. However, I am still curious about the performance implications of range checking in often-called methods such as charAt(). Just for the fun of it, let's rewrite this method so we can quantify the performance impact. The new and improved charAt() is named fastCharAt():

```
public char fastCharAt(int index) {
    return value[index + offset];   // Offset is the point in the
                                    // buffer where this
                                    // String begins.
                                    // It could be substring of a
                                    // larger String...
}
```

We can use fastCharAt() in asciiGetBytes() to replace the calls to charAt(). A million invocations of asciiGetBytes() has taken 2,500 milliseconds using the old charAt(). It executed in 1,900 milliseconds when using fastCharAt(). See Figure 1.12.

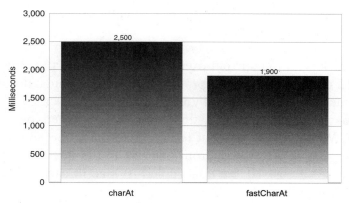

Figure 1.12. A faster charAt()

There's a similar issue with the charAt() method of the StringBuffer class. It is even worse there because the method is synchronized; so even in the presence of no contention, we suffer the cost of grabbing and releasing a lock. I don't know about you, but in my code the vast majority of String and String-Buffer objects are confined to a single thread and all synchronization issues are nonexistent. If I code a fastCharAt() for StringBuffer that does no synchronization and no sanity checking, I get an even bigger bang for the buck.

Modifying String.java was just an exercise. We cannot do it in practice, so let's back off. It turns out, however, that we have yet another surprising alternative when it comes to replacing frequent calls to charAt(). Instead, you could copy the String characters into a char[] object and iterate over the individual characters by indexing directly into the array. That is a potential performance win on three fronts:

- It skips the range checking of the charAt() method.

- It avoids the method call overhead.

- It eliminates the integer addition inside charAt() that adds the requested index to the offset at which the String begins (return (offset+index);)

There's a potential downside as well. We must copy the character array from the String object to another character array. The cost of that copy operation should be weighed against the expected savings of avoiding repeated calls to charAt(). Surely, there's a crossover point at which copying the character array will be faster than making repeated calls to charAt(). Next we design a test to look for that cutoff point.

We will stick with the current exercise of converting a String object to a byte array. You don't really need a profiler to convince yourself that the asciiGet-Bytes() method is dominated by the loop iterating over the String characters. It is also rather obvious that this loop is dominated by repeated calls to charAt(). We ran a sequence of tests converting a String to a byte array. We varied the size of the String from one test to the next. Starting with a string "HelloWorld" of size 10, we quadrupled its size in each subsequent test via a command-line argument:

```
String s = "HelloWorld";
int n = Integer.parseInt(args[0]);

for (int i = 1; i < n; i++) {
    s += s;
    s += s;
}
```

The String s is the one we convert into a byte array via

```
for (int i = 0; i < 100000; i++) {
    byte[] b = asciiGetBytes_arrayCopy(s);
}
```

The converter method using array copy is given by

```
public class MyGetBytes {
    ...
    static char[] recycleCharBuff = new char[8192];

    public static byte[] asciiGetBytes_arrayCopy(String buf) {
        int size = buf.length();
        byte[] bytebuf = new byte[size];
        char[] charBuff = null;            // The char array destination

        if (size < 8192) {                 // Trying to reuse
            charBuff = recycleCharBuff;    // an existing buffer
        }                                  // so that we won't
        else {                             // have to create a
            charBuff = new char[size];     // new object
        }                                  // every time
```

```
    buf.getChars(0, size, charBuff, 0);  // Copy the char[]

    for (int i = 0; i < size; i++) {
        bytebuf[i] = (byte) charBuff[i]; // Direct indexing
    }

    return bytebuf;
  }
}
```

Other than replacing charAt() with direct addressing, notice also that we are trying hard to avoid the creation of a new char[] object. We are trying to recycle a static class variable to serve as a scratch buffer. To our big surprise, the crossover point has occurred very early. The array copy has outperformed the version using charAt() almost from the start. It was roughly the same for a String of size 10, but then the array copy took the lead for good and was 2.5× faster for a String of size 640. See Figure 1.13. Each pair in the chart consists of the charAt() version on the left and the array copy on the right. This chart exhibits the relationship between the String length and execution speed.

This surprising lesson could be applied in diverse scenarios, any time the charAt() method is proved by the profiler to be a performance hot spot. In our case, even as few as 20 consecutive calls to charAt() have already justified the switch to an array copy. This is counterintuitive because performance engineers tend to recoil when faced with data copy operations. This is another reminder that gut feelings should not be relied upon in software optimization.

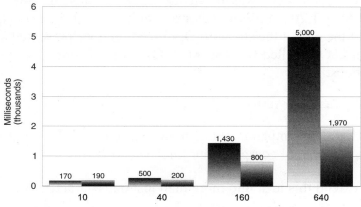

Figure 1.13. Array copy plus direct indexing outperformed charAt()

Optimization 7: Prefer `charAt()` to `startsWith()`

The `String` class provides a method called `startsWith()` to decide if the string starts with a given substring. In practice, I've seen many programs using this method to check if the string starts with a particular character, as in

```
if (s.startsWith("a")) {...}
```

This works fine, but from a performance perspective this method is a misuse of the `String` API. The `startsWith()` method was meant for bigger tasks than just checking the first character. The code implementing `startsWith()` makes quite a few computations preparing itself to compare its prefix with another string. All these computations are a waste of time if all we are really after is the first character. In this case, it makes more sense to use the `charAt()` method, as in

```
if ('a' == s.charAt(0)) {...}
```

To prove the point, we measured the performance of both constructs. We timed the execution speed of ten million invocations of

```
bool = s.startsWith("a");
```

and compared it to

```
bool = (s.charAt(0) == 'a');
```

As expected, `charAt()` was much faster. It executed in 740 milliseconds as opposed to a 1,200 milliseconds execution time of `startsWith()`. However, this is not the end of the story. In Optimization 6 we presented a faster form of `charAt()` that we called `fastCharAt()`. Our third version gives performance yet another boost:

```
bool = (s.fastCharAt(0) == 'a');
```

This last version is much faster than the previous two. It executed in 180 milliseconds. Figure 1.14 compares our three versions.

You can extend this idea into more than just one character. For example,

```
bool = (s.fastCharAt(0) == 'a' && s.fastCharAt(1) == 'b');
```

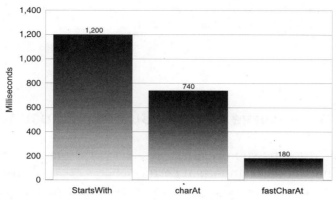

Figure 1.14. Faster alternatives for `startsWith()`

is faster than

```
bool = s.startsWith("ab");
```

although the performance returns start to diminish as the length of the substring grows.

In Figure 1.14, `fastCharAt()` is 4× faster than `charAt()`, whereas in Figure 1.12 the difference is nowhere near that dramatic. This perceived inconsistency is due to the nature of the distinct test cases used in those two experiments. The test case for Figure 1.14 was entirely dominated by character indexing operations, as in

```
bool = (s.fastCharAt(0) == 'a');
```

The test case generating Figure 1.12 was different. Character indexing played an important role in the overall performance but it did not dominate to the same extent as in Figure 1.14. There were other costly operations such as object creation:

```
public static byte[] asciiGetBytes(String buf) {
    int size = buf.length();          // This counts for for some CPU
                                      // cycles...
    int i;
    byte[] bytebuf = new byte[size];  // ...and this is costly as
                                      // well...
```

```
for (i = 0; i < size; i++) {
    bytebuf[i] = (byte)buf.charAt(i);
}

return bytebuf;
}
```

Optimization 8: Reserve `StringBuffer` Capacity

One of the criticisms you often hear against performance tuning is that it can negatively impact other important performance metrics such as readability and reliability, to name just two. This observation is true in many cases; that is why you often have to insist on a large performance return for your coding and design investment. Sometimes, however, you can get "free" optimizations that help performance without exacting a toll anywhere else. This is the kind we prefer. The `StringBuffer` capacity issue is one such example.

When you define a `StringBuffer` object

```
StringBuffer sb = new StringBuffer();
```

the `StringBuffer` constructor will create a character array of a default size, typically 16. This is the initial capacity. As you append characters to the `StringBuffer`, you may exceed its capacity. At that point, a nontrivial step takes place. The `StringBuffer` has to allocate a new character array with larger capacity, copy the old contents into the new array, and eventually discard the old array (during GC). Typically, the new capacity will be twice as large as the old one, so this expansion step will not take place very often. However, there is a very simple optimization that does not compromise quality. In many situations you can tell in advance how big your `StringBuffer` is likely to be. In that case, you can reserve enough capacity during construction and prevent the `StringBuffer` from ever needing expansion:

```
StringBuffer sb = new StringBuffer(1024);
```

We created a `StringBuffer` object above whose initial capacity is 1,024. Of course, you only want to allocate 1,024 bytes if you think that the `String-Buffer` has a reasonable chance to approach this size. Otherwise, you should choose a smaller size to conserve memory as well as avoid wasting cycles on instance zeroing.

This optimization in itself is not likely to be detectable. However, a collection of such small optimizations can add up to something measurable. The key is that this optimization is both very easy and does not compromise quality.

Key Points

- Most Java compilers are intelligent enough to collapse

```
String s = "a" + "b";
```

into

```
String s = "ab";
```

at compile time. No concatenation will take place at run time.

- Replacing

```
String s = x + y;
```

with

```
String s = (new StringBuffer()).append(x).append(y).toString();
```

is no optimization at all. This is exactly what the compiler generates. It will speed things up only if you know (or have a good guess) the expected length of the resulting character string, as in

```
String s =
    (new StringBuffer(32)).append(x).append(y).toString();
```

- The following

```
String s = "a" + "b" + "c";
```

is faster than

```
String s = "a";
s += "b";
s += "c";
```

- Comparison of two `String` objects is faster if they differ in length.

- If two `String` objects are of equal length, `equalsIgnoreCase()` is far more expensive than `equals()`. This is in line with expectation.

- When we compare two `String` objects, more often than not, they will differ in size. In this case, we were surprised to find out that `equalsIgnoreCase()` performed better than `equals()`. This, however, is an artifact of the JDK implementation and could be easily fixed. Don't count on it, but keep it in mind.

- The `getBytes()` method of the `String` class is extremely expensive. We have provided a faster alternative for ASCII strings.

- Generic, powerful classes are often forced to trade away performance in exchange for function. On a performance-critical path, you could roll your own string parser that will probably outperform the `StringTokenizer` by a significant margin.

- The same holds for byte-to-char conversion. The recommended `String` constructor to build a `String` object from a byte array is very slow. The deprecated one is much faster. Don't hesitate to use it if you are only handling ASCII characters.

- The comparison

```
('a' == s.charAt(0))
```

  is faster than

```
s.startsWith("a");
```

- The `StringBuffer` default capacity is 16. If your character string is likely to be larger than that, you might as well reserve larger capacity by using the appropriate `StringBuffer` constructor.

2

Pure Overhead

Performance optimization often has to strike a delicate balance between competing forces. This is perhaps why it is referred to as optimization as opposed to performance maximization. Performance optimization often requires the sacrifice of some other software goal. Important goals such as flexibility, maintainability, cost, and reuse must often give way to the demand for performance. It is unusual when a performance fix, in an otherwise high-quality piece of code, does not compromise any other software development goals. Sometimes we are fortunate when the elimination of simple coding mistakes results in higher performance without any sacrifice. The optimizations we discuss in this chapter fall into this category. They improve performance while sacrificing very little or nothing at all. These are the kinds of optimizations we all like.

Optimization 9: Useless Computations

Ideally we don't want to compute anything unless we are going to use the results. Software perfection means we compute what we need, all of what we need, and nothing but what is absolutely necessary. The degree to which we deviate from that ideal directly corresponds to our program's inefficiency. If I had a dime for every time I detected useless computations in commercial code, I'd be very rich by now. The easiest example that comes to mind is tracing. Let's take the world's simplest implementation of a trace facility:

```
public class Trace {

    private static boolean loggingIsOn = false;

    public static void log (String msg) {
        if (loggingIsOn == true) System.out.println(msg);
    }
```

```
public static void setLoggingIsOn(boolean newState) {
    loggingIsOn = newState;
}

public static boolean logging() {
    return loggingIsOn;
}

}
```

The `Trace` class contains a private static member, `loggingIsOn`, indicating the state of the application. It can be in one of two states: It is either logging trace messages to `System.out` or, if logging is disabled, it does nothing. A typical usage would be something along the lines of

```
public void doIntTrace(int i) {
    Trace.log("Enter doIntTrace(). Input arg is " + i);
    myInt = i+1;
    Trace.log("Exit doIntTrace()");
}
```

(`doIntTrace` is my naming convention meant to remind me that I'm doing an integer manipulation and that I'm tracing it.) `doIntTrace()` is a very simple method. It assigns a value to an integer member called `myInt`. This method logs trace messages upon method entry and exit. When tracing is on, we really don't care about performance. We don't anticipate people turning on trace during production. Our performance concern has to do with the impact of the tracing machinery when tracing is off. It must not have a noticeable effect on application performance. Now, every programmer knows that I/O is expensive. The author of the following `Trace` class has taken care of that. No I/O is performed if tracing is off.

```
public class Trace {
    ...
    public static void log (String msg) {
        if (loggingIsOn == true) System.out.println(msg);
    }
    ...
}
```

Is this sufficient to make tracing overhead negligible? Let's measure. We'll take a simple method and measure it with and without trace messages. We have already shown the code for `doIntTrace()`. The corresponding method stripped out the trace:

```
public void doInt(int i) {
    myInt = i+1;
}
```

We then proceed to measure the execution time of the loop that follows,

```
for (int i = 0; i < 1000000; i++) {
    doInt(i);
}
```

and compare it to

```
for (int i = 0; i < 1000000; i++) {
    doIntTrace(i);
}
```

The plain `doInt()` loop executed in 250 milliseconds, whereas the addition of tracing to the second loop (`doIntTrace()`) has slowed down execution to 10.4 seconds (10,400 milliseconds.) This is a huge degradation by two orders of magnitude. To see where our cycles went I profiled it with

```
java -Xrunhprof:cpu=times TraceTester 10000
```

For profiling purposes, we only ran the loop 10,000 times. The profiling output follows.

Rank	Self	Accum	Count	Trace	Method
1	13.11%	13.11%	10000	19	TraceTester.doIntTrace
2	7.38%	20.49%	10000	50	java/lang/String.<init>
3	7.38%	27.87%	10000	25	java/lang/StringBuffer.<init>
4	5.74%	33.61%	10000	41	java/lang/StringBuffer.append
5	4.92%	38.52%	10000	5	java/lang/StringBuffer.append
6	4.92%	43.44%	10000	39	java/lang/StringBuffer.append
7	4.10%	47.54%	10000	14	java/lang/String.length
8	4.10%	51.64%	10000	40	java/lang/StringBuffer.<init>

(continued on next page)

Rank	Self	Accum	Count	Trace	Method
9	4.10%	55.74%	10000	52	java/lang/String.length
10	3.28%	59.02%	10000	16	java/lang/String.getChars
11	2.46%	61.48%	5808	51	java/lang/String.charAt
12	2.46%	63.93%	10000	30	java/lang/String.length
13	2.46%	66.39%	20000	31	Trace.log
14	1.64%	68.03%	1	17	TraceTester.intTraceRun
15	1.64%	69.67%	10000	38	java/lang/StringBuffer.length
16	1.64%	71.31%	10000	45	java/lang/Object.<init>
17	1.64%	72.95%	10000	49	java/lang/StringBuffer.getValue
18	1.64%	74.59%	10000	48	java/lang/StringBuffer.toString

As you can tell, the overhead of creating the parameter `String` in

```
Trace.log("Enter doIntTrace(). Input arg is " + i);
```

has absolutely destroyed performance. What went wrong? Looking at the profile, the overhead of the two additional calls to `Trace.log()` was negligible in this test (only 2 percent.) The bigger issue with this `Trace` implementation is the creation of `String` objects that end up being dropped on the floor.

In the typical case where the `String` cannot be constructed at compile time, we are forced to unconditionally create a `String` object to be passed as an argument to the `Trace.log()` method. As the code stands, this `String` is going to be created whether tracing is on or off; that does not matter. When the `log()` method checks the state of the trace, it is too late. The `String` object as already been computed. This exacts a performance toll twice: once upon the creation of the object and again during garbage collection. The more objects you have around, the harder garbage collection has to work to clean them up. This is a perfect example of a useless computation. We go through a nontrivial computation to produce results that are ignored in the typical execution scenario.

This tracing stuff is not a figment of my imagination. I've actually seen it in practice more than once. I've seen this sin committed in Java as well as

C++. The performance of an application server I was working on has plummeted by a factor of 10 after the Java code has been contaminated by a tracing facility similar to the one presented here. It was much worse than the simple example given earlier. A typical trace message looked something like the following:

```
Trace.log("Enter method X with two integer arguments: " +
        " a = " +
        a +
        " b = " +
        b);
```

There's a substantial amount of work involved in creating this argument String: two integer-to-string conversions, one StringBuffer creation, and a bunch of StringBuffer.append() calls. All these painful computations are for nothing. Tracing is off and the resulting String is thrown away.

The solution is pretty simple. Don't perform premature computations. The Trace class provides the caller a way to determine the tracing state. Don't create the argument String unless tracing is on, as in the following:

```
public void doIntTrace2(int i) {
    if (Trace.logging()) Trace.log("Enter doIntTrace2(). Input arg is " + i);
    myInt = i+1;
    if (Trace.logging()) Trace.log("Exit doIntTrace2()");
}
```

We check for the trace state first and if it is off, we don't bother calling the log() method at all. Consequently, the String argument to log() will not be constructed in that case.

If we repeat the test we performed earlier using the new and improved doIntTrace2(), this version of conditional trace executes in 350 milliseconds. See Figure 2.1.

Now this is much better than unconditional calls to the log() method but still bad in comparison to no tracing at all. The remaining difference is due to the call overhead of Trace.logging(). We are not done yet. The rest will be taken care of by Optimization 10.

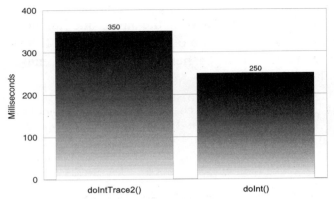

Figure 2.1.   Tracing impact on performance

Optimization 10: Don't Trace Trivial Methods

In Optimization 9 we have seen the dramatic effect that trace messages can have on performance. The problem is that we cheated to some extent. We looked at a specific example that exaggerated our point. The impact of trace logging on performance was skewed because the method we chose to trace was trivial. It did very little computation and was a leaf node method—it did not invoke any other method. When you add code to such trivial methods, it is going to skew the performance measurement. To set the record straight, let's trace a more substantial method:

```
public void doDate() {
    myDate = (new Date()).toString();
}
```

This method computes the current date and converts it to a String. The following method adds tracing:

```
public void doDateTrace() {
    if (Trace.logging()) Trace.log("Enter doDateTrace()");
    myDate = (new Date()).toString();
    if (Trace.logging()) Trace.log("Exit doDateTrace()");
}
```

When we executed 100,000 invocations of these two methods, they both clocked in at around 28 seconds. The performance impact of tracing was not detectable.

The example using Date may be going too far in the other extreme. The Date class is my favorite when I need to exhibit a CPU hog. So in Optimization 9 we gave the impression that tracing was harmful, and here we are saying that it is not such a big deal. The truth is that those two conflicting assertions could actually co-exist in peace. Their validity is context-dependent.

The impact of tracing depends heavily on the methods being traced. The moral of this story is that you should avoid tracing methods that are trivial because the addition of trace would double their cost. You should definitely avoid tracing trivial methods that are frequently invoked on the performance critical path. In my days as a C programmer, it was common to have large complicated functions. This is no longer the case. I haven't run any scientific study of this fact but it wouldn't be far-fetched to assert that object-oriented code tends to break down the code into many frequent invocations of small methods (which we call trivials). If we blindly trace every method on the critical path, we will almost definitely hurt performance.

Optimization 11: Making Overhead Vanish

Our trace implementation was such that you could turn tracing on and off during program execution. There is a variation that turns the trace into a debug facility to be used only during application development. This strategy is actually pretty common in large-scale development. The code is littered with debug statements during development and test, and then you just turn debug off when you ship the finished product. If we used our Trace class as a debug machinery, we would still have some residual overhead in the form of the if statements, such as

```
if (Trace.loggingIsOn) {...}
```

At the very least the condition will be evaluated. There's a fairly easy way to correct this and eliminate the Trace entirely by exposing the Trace state variable as

```
class Trace {
    public static final boolean loggingIsOn = false;
    ...
}
```

The member `loggingIsOn` is assigned the value `true` when we debug and `false` when we ship the product. In this case a statement such as

```
if (Trace.loggingIsOn) {...}
```

is essentially equivalent to

```
if (false) {...}
```

because `Trace.loggingIsOn` is a static final member whose value is false and is never going to change (without a recompilation). This is dead code; a decent compiler should recognize and remove it. What we give up with this design is the ability to turn tracing on and off dynamically without having to recompile.

Optimization 12: Premature Object Creation ▪

In C you can declare new variables at the beginning of a scope:

```
void f() {
   int i;
   ...
   if (...) {
      struct Date x;       // Object x is defined inside the scope ...
                           // ... where it is used
                           // Date is a user-defined struct

      init(&x);            // Initialize object x
      ...                  // Object x only used here
   }
   ...
}
```

Since the `struct` definition did not exact any performance penalty, most of us got into the habit of defining all the local variables up front, as in

```
void f() {
   int i;
   struct Date x;         // Object x is defined outside the scope ...
                          // ... where it is used
                          // Date is a user-defined struct
   ...
   if (...) {
      init(&x);           // Initialize object x
```

```
      ...                          // Object x only used here
   }
   ...
}
```

While this was okay in C, it would be a costly idea to bring this habit forward to your Java programs. The cost of using object x, in C, is in having to initialize it. That would happen only inside the scope where it is being used. What we did in C was separate the definition step from the initialization step. In Java, however, what you may find is something like

```
void f() {
   int i;
   Date x = new Date();     // Date x is constructed outside the ...
                            // ... scope where it is used
   ...
   if (...) {
      ...                   // Date object x only used here
   }
   ...
}
```

If we don't execute the scope in which x is used, then the effort that goes into the definition of x is pure overhead. It consists of

- Allocating a new object

- Executing the constructor logic

- Garbage collecting the object sometime in the future

This problem has a very easy solution: Define your objects in the scope that uses them, as in

```
void f() {
   int i;
   ...
   if (...) {
      Date x = new Date();          // Date x is constructed inside the ...
                                    // ... scope where it is used
      ...                           // Date object x only used here
   }
   ...
}
```

You don't want to pay for services that you don't consume. If you define your objects in the appropriate scope, you will not pay for needless overhead.

Optimization 13: Don't Initialize Twice ▮

In Java, you can initialize a data member on the same line at which you define it. For example

```
public class X {
    private Vector v = new Vector();

    public X() {
    }
    ...
}
```

You may wonder at what point the member v gets initialized. The answer is simple—it gets initialized in the constructor. The statement

```
v = new Vector();
```

is silently added to the X constructor even if you did not put it there. The generated constructor code is equivalent to

```
public X() {
    super(); // Call superclass constructor
    v = new Vector();
}
```

What happens if the programmer chooses to initialize a member to a default value in the definition as well as the constructor?

```
public class X {
    private Vector v = new Vector();      // First initialization

    public X() {
        v = new Vector();                 // Second one
    }
    ...
}
```

What happens is that the member is redundantly initialized twice. The resultant constructor becomes

```
public X() {
    super ();
    v = new Vector();        // First initialization
    v = new Vector();        // Second one
}
```

We compared the performance of class X

```
public class X {                // Member v is initialized twice
    private Vector v = new Vector();

    public X() {
        v = new Vector();
    }
}
```

to the performance of Y where the member is correctly initialized only once:

```
public class Y {
    private Vector v = new Vector();

    public Y() { }
}
```

We measured the time to construct 100,000 objects of either type and, as expected, constructing Y objects was almost twice as fast as X objects since the Y constructor was doing only half the work for the same net result. See Figure 2.2.

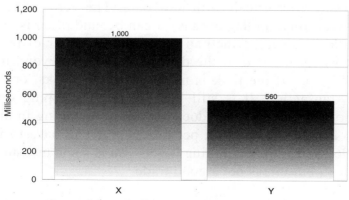

Figure 2.2. The impact of double initialization

This is one of those optimizations that never occurred to me until I saw it in commercial code. Subsequently, I have observed this type of mistake in code quite often.

Optimization 14: Do You Really Need to Zero-Out a Buffer? ∎

Quite often when I scan code for potential optimizations, I find data structures that get initialized with zeros or blanks, for no good reason. When you dig further into the code, you find that the zero (or blank) values are never really used or relied upon in any way. It's almost like a programming knee-jerk reaction to zero-out a data structure just in case. Buffers used for socket communication provide a perfect example:

```
BufferedInputStream is = new BufferedInputStream(s.getInputStream());
byte[] buf = new byte[4096];
...

for (int i = 0; i < buf.length; i++) { // Zero-out the stale buffer
                                       // contents
    buf[i] = 0;
}

int numBytesRead = is.read(buf, 0, buf.length);
```

The buffer buf is repeatedly used to read data from the socket. The contents of the buffer (from a previous transaction) are considered junk at this point, so we eradicate it by overwriting the buffer with zeros. But we really don't have to do that. The presence of old data does not bother me because I'm going to overwrite it with new data. The zero value itself does not serve as a termination flag because it can be, and often is, a legitimate part of the data. The read() method returns the number of bytes read, which indicates where the end of the data is. Anything beyond it is junk, and I really don't care if the junk is made of zeros, blanks, or old data from a previous transaction. It is still junk. Explicitly wiping out the previous contents of this buffer really does not buy us anything in the way of functionality. It is also a drag on performance if you have to iterate over the loop 4,096 times. The only thing it gets you is some measure of psychological comfort, but this is not a good trade.

Optimization 15: The 80–20 Principle   ■

The 80–20 rule has many applications: 80 percent of the execution scenarios will traverse only 20 percent of your source code; 80 percent of the elapsed time will be spent in 20 percent of the functions encountered on the execution path. The 80–20 rule is the dominating force driving the argument that premature optimization is a sin. If you randomly optimize everything you can think of, not only do you waste 80 percent of the effort, you will also hack the design beyond repair. Optimization is like medicine—very helpful in small doses, but an overdose could be harmful.

The HTTP specification is a 100-page document that describes all possible HTTP requests that a Web server must handle. Most of the HTTP requests that traverse the Web these days are very simple. They contain only a small subset of the possible HTTP headers that a request could potentially contain. Finding out what these typical request headers look like is fairly simple. Since Microsoft and Netscape have a dominating share of the browser market, all you need to do is peek at the request headers sent by these two browsers. This is yet another manifestation of the 80–20 rule—20 percent of your possible inputs will occur 80 percent of the time. I'm not advocating breaking away from standards. Far from it. Your code must comply with the standards. It is simply that we can give typical inputs preferential treatment to speed them up.

HTTP request headers determine the request type and will often traverse separate execution paths. An efficient use of programmer resources is to tune those 20 percent of the request types that appear 80 percent of the time.

There's another point to the 80–20 idea. Not only do you need to focus on the typical execution path, you should take advantage of the fact that most of your input data is going to come from a narrow range of the whole input space. Some examples follow.

The HTTP Accept header is part of an HTTP request. It specifies what document formats are acceptable to the browser. The HTTP specification allows for the Accept header to have any combination of uppercase and lowercase. When you read a string token and want to determine if it is the Accept header, it is not enough to perform a

```
headerName.equals("Accept:");
```

We need to perform a case-sensitive string compare. To be HTTP compliant, the correct action should be

```
if (headerName.equalsIgnoreCase("Accept:"))  {
    // This is the Accept header
}
```

However, `equalsIgnoreCase()` is not cheap. This is where our domain expertise must come into play. Because Microsoft and Netscape have a commanding share of the browser market, we can focus on the header they send. The Accept header happens to be "`Accept:`". Now this is only one of the many upper- and lowercase combinations that HTTP allows, but it is the one we are going to receive 95 percent of the time, so it is the one we care about. The following test tries to take advantage of that:

```
if (headerName.equals("Accept:") ||      // An intelligent gamble...
    headerName.equalsIgnoreCase("Accept:"))  {

    ... // This is the Accept header. Do something with it.
}
```

In 95 percent of the inputs, the `equals()` test is going to succeed, and we will never call the more expensive `equalsIgnoreCase()`.

The last code sample leads us right into another 80–20 issue of evaluation order. It is often the case that conditional expressions are built as a logical combination of subexpressions. When we examine expressions of the form

```
if (e1 || e2) {...}
```

or

```
if (e1 && e2) {...}
```

the order of evaluation has performance implications. Take the former `if` statement as an example:

```
if (e1 || e2) {...}
```

If (e1 || e2) evaluates to false, we lost. Both subexpressions, e1 and e2, must be evaluated. However, in the case in which (e1 || e2) is true, if e1 is true, e2 will not be evaluated and the overall cost of the expression is reduced. In the following discussion, we narrow our attention to the case in which (e1 || e2) is true.

If e1 and e2 are equally likely to evaluate to true, then the subexpression whose computational cost is smaller should be placed first in the evaluation order. If, on the other hand, e1 and e2 are of equal computational cost, then the one most likely to evaluate to true should appear first. In a more general situation, let

> p1 = the conditional probability that e1 is true, given that (e1 || e2) is true
>
> c1 = computational cost of evaluating e1

Define the weight of an expression to be the product

w1 = p1 * c1

The evaluation order of a logical OR expression should be in ascending order of weight. The subexpression whose weight is smallest should go first. Our example above only dealt with two subexpressions, but this easily extends to any number of subexpressions in a logical OR expression.

Previously, we encountered a conditional statement checking for an HTTP Accept header:

```
if (headerName.equals("Accept:") ||      // An intelligent gamble...
    headerName.equalsIgnoreCase("Accept:"))  {

    ... // This is the Accept header. Do something with it
}
```

In this case,

- e1 is headerName.equals("Accept:")

- e2 is headerName.equalsIgnoreCase("Accept:")

In the case in which the `if` statement is `true`, `e2` will evaluate to `true` 100 percent of the time since it is a case-sensitive string compare. So $p2 = 1.0$. The subexpression `e1` will evaluate to `true` only 90 percent of the time. So $p1 = 0.9$. The computational cost is roughly given by:

$c1 = 100$ instructions

$c2 = 1,000$ instructions

The overall weights are:

```
w1 = c1 * p1 = 90
w2 = c2 * p2 = 1000
```

Therefore,

```
if (e1 || e2)
```

is a better choice than

```
if (e2 || e1)
```

There's similar logic for logical AND expressions like

```
if (e1 && e2)
```

Given the case in which the whole expression evaluates to `false`, we would like it to fail as early as possible without having to evaluate all subexpressions. The definition of the probability in this case is slightly different:

$p1 =$ the conditional probability that `e1` is `false`, given that (`e1 && e2`) is `false`

Again, we want to order the subexpressions in ascending order of weight.

You can easily encounter such decisions in practice. The specifications might require an implementation to check and handle some rare combination of events like:

```
if ( rareCondition_1() && rareCondition_2() ) {
    // Handle it
}
```

Since this combination is rare, the check will fail most of the time. We'd like for it to fail quickly on the first subexpression. This is, by the way, the reason why HTTP 1.1 compliant servers are somewhat slower than HTTP 1.0 implementations. The 1.1 specifications are much more complex and force the server to perform many checks for all kinds of esoteric scenarios that rarely happen. But you still have to perform the test to be 1.1 compliant. For example, an HTTP 1.1 compliant browser may ask for a portion of a large document instead of the complete document. In practice, the browsers ask for complete documents in the vast majority of requests. The server, however, must still check for a partial document request and handle it properly.

Optimization 16: Purge Obsolete Code ∎

This is another one of those tips that sounds silly but actually happens in practice quite often. We are talking about code that no longer serves a purpose but remains on the execution path. This is not likely to happen on a school programming assignment or a small prototype. It happens on large-scale programming efforts. The requirements that drive a software implementation present a moving target. They tend to evolve from one release to the next. New features are added and support for old features may be dropped. The implementation itself keeps shifting underneath your feet with bug fixes and enhancements. This constant movement of requirements and implementation creates bubbles of dead (never executed) and obsolete (executed but not necessary) code.

Let's go back to the trenches of one HTTP server for a concrete example. This server was not written in Java, but the point we are making here transcends language boundaries. This is a software engineering issue.

The initial crop of web servers supported both HTTP and the Secure-HTTP (S-HTTP) protocols. Shortly thereafter SSL has emerged as a replacement for S-HTTP. For a while our implementation supported all three. Then SSL took off and knocked S-HTTP into oblivion. Naturally, we followed the market trend and dropped support for S-HTTP.

In the early days of the WWW craze, product release cycles were reduced from 1–2 years to 2–3 months. Consequently, even though S-HTTP support was disabled, nobody bothered to clean out the source code. S-HTTP code was all over, and removing all traces of it was an error-prone, tedious, and time-consuming job. Obsolete code due to S-HTTP was taking a toll on performance in several major ways. First, there were many occurrences of data members introduced by S-HTTP into various objects. Those members were initialized and destroyed, unnecessarily, consuming CPU cycles because their values were essentially dead. Moreover, there were plenty of `if then else` decision points to separate S-HTTP execution flow from HTTP:

```
if (/* HTTP */) {
    ...
}
else {  /* S-HTTP */
    ...
}
```

Those extraneous branch points hurt performance by adding cycles as well as introducing bubbles into the processor's instruction pipeline.

Other minor damages inflicted by obsolete code are increased executable size, memory footprint, and source code. Source code that contains obsolete and dead code is harder to understand, maintain, and extend. For all those reasons, removing dead and obsolete code is highly recommended as routine source-code maintenance.

Key Points

- Don't perform premature computations. Defer computations to the point where you actually need them. Otherwise, you may find yourself exerting substantial computational energy just to throw the results away.

- Define your objects in the scope that uses them.

- If you choose to add tracing to your application, don't pour it blindly on every method in the execution path. You ought to skip tracing trivial methods that are called frequently. Any additions of code to such functions (tracing or other) could negatively impact performance.

- Member objects that are initialized to a default value in their definition are silently rolled into the constructor body. It is wasteful to initialize them again in the constructor, or subsequently.

- If you consider the set of all possible input data, 20 percent of it shows up 80 percent of the time. Speed up the processing of typical input at the expense of other scenarios.

- Large-scale software often tends towards chaos. One by-product of chaotic software is the execution of obsolete code, code that once served a purpose but no longer does. Periodic purges of obsolete code and other useless computations will boost performance as well as overall software hygiene.

3

Vectors and Hashtables

I originally intended to write a chapter on the collection framework discussing each and every collection. However, I could not get away from the 80–20 principle: 20 percent of the available data structures will be used 80 percent of the time. Since your time is valuable, I wanted to get straight to the point and discuss the two collections that I see most often in commercial code. These are `Vector` and `Hashtable`. I don't doubt that people are also using `Stack` and `ArrayList` and other fine collections, but the discussion of `Vector` and `Hashtable` performance issues will capture many of the generic principles underlying the other collections as well.

Optimization 17: Vector Add and Remove

The `Vector` public interface provides you with multiple ways to add an element to a `Vector`. You could do any one of the following (as of Java 2):

- `insertElementAt(e, index)`
- `addElement(e)`
- `add(e)`
- `add(index,e)`

This is an opportunity for us to shoot ourselves in the foot. Those insert methods are not exactly the same, and their performance characteristics could vary significantly. The `addElement(e)` and `add(e)` methods will add the element to the end of the `Vector`. The other two methods are capable of inserting the element anywhere you like in the `Vector`. Since vector elements are held in contiguous memory, adding an element to a `Vector` requires shifting all elements between the insertion point and the end of the `Vector`. This shift is necessary to make room for the new element. It follows that the best place to insert an element is at the end of a `Vector` and the worst place, from a performance perspective, is at the beginning. If you find yourself inserting elements anywhere other than the Vector end, you probably chose the wrong container to work with.

Let's put some numbers up for comparison. The first method below adds 1,000 elements to the end:

```
public void add1000(Vector v, String s) {
    for (int i = 0; i < 1000; i++) {
        v.addElement(s);
    }
}
```

I chose addElement(e) as opposed to add(e) because the latter returns a boolean while the former returns a void. They are identical otherwise; that should make addElement(e) slightly faster since it can skip the overhead of a return value.

The second method adds 1,000 elements to the beginning of the Vector:

```
public void add1000AtFront(Vector v, String s) {
    for (int i = 0; i < 1000; i++) {
        v.insertElementAt(s,0);
    }
}
```

A thousand invocations of those two methods exhibit our point. Additions at the end are far superior to additions at the front. See Figure 3.1.

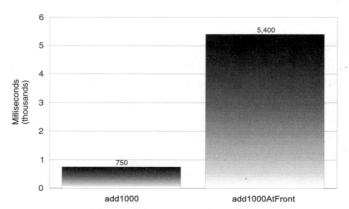

Figure 3.1.   Vector insertion

The same exact point holds true for element removal. The cheapest element to remove is at the end of the Vector. Removing elements in the middle gets progressively more expensive as you move towards the front. Removing an element from the front of a Vector gives the worst performance. If you find yourself frequently removing elements from anywhere other than the end of a Vector, you have got the wrong data structure.

Optimization 18: Vector Capacity ∎

A newly created Vector is initially empty because it has no elements. The initial size of the Vector is therefore 0. The capacity, however, is typically larger than 0. By default, the Vector constructor creates an array large enough to hold 10 objects, its initial capacity. The Vector object's capacity is the largest number of elements it can hold (its size) before an expansion must take place. Expansion involves allocating a larger array and copying the contents of the old array to the new one. Eventually, the old array object gets reclaimed by the garbage collector. Vector expansion is an expensive operation. This is not something you want to do on a regular basis. When you use the default constructor

```
Vector v = new Vector();
```

the initial capacity is set to 10. Future expansions will (roughly) double the capacity every time. Alternatively, you could specify the initial capacity, as in

```
Vector v = new Vector(100);
```

The initial capacity is set to 100 in this case and, as with the default constructor, capacity will double with every expansion. The third option you have is to specify both the initial capacity and the magnitude of the capacity increment:

```
Vector v = new Vector(100, 25);
```

This gives you a Vector whose initial capacity is 100 and will grow capacity by increments of 25 elements per expansion.

From a performance perspective, there are two issues to consider: initial capacity and increment. The goal is to minimize the need for expansion. It would be ideal if the initial capacity were sufficient for the life of the Vector

and no expansions were ever required. For that reason, using the default Vector constructor could get you in trouble. It is often the case that a 10-element
capacity is not enough. Often, you may have a pretty good guess for the
expected size of your Vector. You can use such an estimate to specify the initial capacity upon Vector construction.

The next question is, Should you also specify a capacity increment value? The
short answer is: no. If you leave the capacity increment unspecified, then the
Vector capacity will double every time an expansion is required, as opposed to
adding a fixed number of element slots. Exponential expansion will get you
faster to your required capacity. For that reason I prefer

```
Vector v1 = new Vector();
```

to

```
Vector v2 = new Vector(10,10);
```

Both v1 and v2 start with initial capacity of 10, but whereas v1 grows from 10
to 1280 in seven expansions, it will take 100 expansions to get v2 to capacity
of 1,000. We measured the insertion of 1,000 String objects to v1 and v2 as
well as v3 given by

```
Vector v3 = new Vector(1000);
```

We used the method add1000() to do the insertion for the various vectors:

```
public void add1000(Vector v, String s) {
    for (int i = 0; i < 1000; i++) {
        v.addElement(s);
}
```

The results of 1,000 invocations of add1000() are given by Figure 3.2.

As expected, Vector v3 performed the best since its final capacity was known
in advance and no expansions were ever necessary. Object v1 was next on the
performance chart since its capacity grew faster than that of v2.

The moral of the story is, if you have an intelligent guess for the size of your
Vector, use it to specify the initial capacity. Leave the capacity increment
alone. Exponential growth is likely to result in fewer expansion steps.

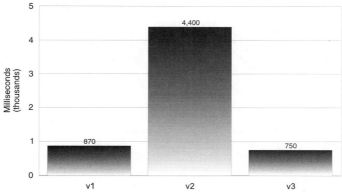

Figure 3.2. Performance and capacity

Optimization 19: `Vector` Enumeration ■

When you want to iterate over the elements of a `Vector`, you have another
choice to make. You can iterate the old-fashioned way by determining the size
of the `Vector` upfront:

```
int size = v.size();
for (int i = 0; i < size; i++) {      // v is a vector ...
    s = (String) v.elementAt(i);      // ...of String objects
    // do something
}
```

Or, you could use an `Enumeration` object:

```
for (Enumeration enum = v.elements();
    enum.hasMoreElements();
    ) {
    s = (String) enum.nextElement();
    // Do something
}
```

We don't really have to measure anything to conclude that using `Enumeration`
will be slower. You can tell by looking at the `Vector.java` source code. The
`elements()` method creates a brand new `Enumeration` object and returns it to
the caller. Constructing an `Enumeration` object is not particularly expensive,
but it is definitely not free. The `Enumeration` object has a private `int` member
(`count`) that must be initialized. Although there is no explicit constructor given

for the `Enumeration` class, the compiler will synthesize one to initialize the `count` member. It will be equivalent to

```
public Enumeration() {
    super();
    count = 0;
}
```

Looking back at our iteration choices, setting

```
i = 0
```

in the first `for` loop is superior to

```
enum = v.elements()
```

in the second. The `elements()` method creates a brand new `Enumeration` object. That `Enumeration` object must set the `count` member to 0 so it is already doing at least as much work as setting the index `i` to 0. All the work involved in creating and later destroying the `Enumeration` object is now pure overhead.

The next step is checking the termination condition. Here

```
i < size
```

is faster than

```
enum.hasMoreElements()
```

Both compare the counter against the number of elements in the `Vector`, but the method invocation requires more work. The third step is to fetch the next element. Doing it using the old-fashioned indexing, as in

```
s = v.elementAt(i);
i++;
```

is equivalent to

```
s = enum.nextElement();
```

The implementation of `nextElement()` has to retrieve the element at the current position and bump up the counter, just as the indexing scheme must do.

So iterating using `Enumeration` should be slower. There is one more twist to consider. The `nextElement()` method (as well as `elementAt()`) throws an exception when it falls off the `Vector` boundary. We can use that to terminate the loop, as in:

```
try {
    for (Enumeration enum = v.elements();
        ;
        ) {
        s = (String) enum.nextElement();
        // Do something
    }
} catch (NoSuchElementException e) {}
```

This could be faster because we skip the loop termination test.

In Java 2, the `Vector` class became part of a hierarchy of container classes. As part of that hierarchy, yet another way of iterating over a `Vector` is now available. We can use an iterator object

```
try {
    for (Iteration it = v.iterator(); ; ) {
        s = (String) it.next();
    }
} catch { (Exception e) {}
```

Now we have four iteration options to consider. Let's add a measurement to the discussion. We used a `Vector` object containing 1,000 `String` elements and we invoked each loop 1,000 times. The execution speed is given by Figure 3.3.

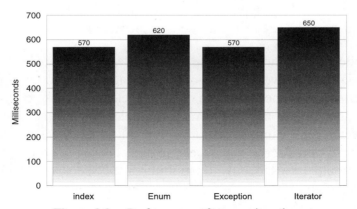

Figure 3.3. Performance of `Vector` iterations

As we predicted, indexing was best. It performed an implicit range-check one time only by determining the Vector size upfront. The other two schemes using Enumeration had to check the range every iteration. Having to create an Enumeration object did not help, either.

Looking at Figure 3.3, you can see that there are no dramatic performance gaps among the various forms of iterations. It is very likely that, in practice, with moderate computation performed per iteration, the performance distinctions will vanish. You may want to save your optimization energy for bigger and better things.

Optimization 20: Efficient Vector Class ∎

In Optimization 6 we discussed the fact that character access for String and StringBuffer objects was suboptimal. The charAt() method was checking the validity of the given index and the method for StringBuffer was even synchronized. The same issue also applies to the Vector implementation. If performance had been the only consideration in Vector.java, then the elementAt() implementation would have been something like

```
public Object elementAt(int index) {
    return elementData[index];
}
```

The two tasks of checking the validity of the index and ensuring synchronization would have been left as an exercise for the caller. In reality, the elementAt() method explicitly verifies that the index parameter does not fall out of bounds. (See Vector.java implementation of your favorite JVM.)

If the caller knows the size of the Vector, then the range-check in elementAt() is redundant. Moreover, if the Vector is not accessible to multiple threads, then synchronization is another waste of CPU cycles. For those cases for which synchronization is not needed, Java 2 provides an escape. The ArrayList is basically a Vector minus synchronization. As a result, we should use an Array-List instead of a Vector whenever the object is confined to a single thread. A Vector should be used only in multithreaded scenarios. That takes care of synchronization overhead. We still have the cost of range-checking. It is performed by the ArrayList as well.

Java 2 introduced another performance wrinkle into the Vector class. It is the modCount member. This is a member of the AbstractList, which the Vector class extends. This modCount member keeps track of the number of structural modifications of the collection (addition, deletion, and capacity expansion). It is necessary to ensure the validity of collection iterators. For example, the addElement() must update modCount, which is an additional cost. This is an example in which expansion of an interface to support additional functionality (iterators) has made some frequently called methods a little less efficient.

An additional hazard lurking in the Vector code is that quite a few methods must perform a sequential walk down the Vector elements, methods such as

- contains()
- indexOf()
- lastIndexOf()
- removeElement()
- remove()

These are all expensive. Their cost is proportional to the size of the Vector. There are other, obvious ones that were not mentioned in the list above. It will not surprise anybody that removeAllElements() and clear() must touch every element in the Vector. On the other hand, I have recently discovered the following in commercial code:

```
e = v.elementAt(v.size() - 1);
v.remove(e);
```

This remove() method traverses the Vector, visiting every element and searching for the given element. Unfortunately, that element happens to be the last one. As this code snippet shows, not all Java programmers are paying close attention to the performance characteristics of the methods they use.

The rich interface of the Vector class provides plenty of opportunities for programmers to misuse. Would it be better if we had a narrow interface where inefficient operations are not provided? It's a tough call. A rich interface provides a value-add in programming convenience and does not pose a problem to the segment of the development community that understands the performance characteristics of the various methods. In addition, the 80–20 principle tells us that performance considerations are irrelevant in 80 percent of our code.

Classes such as `Vector` were designed for use everywhere in our application's code. Designing a class for that 20 percent of performance-critical code would result in a different interface and implementation. It would also be less useful outside the performance-critical path. Next, we develop such a narrowly focused `Vector` for performance only.

The `PVector` class is making performance the highest priority. (It is pretty much the only consideration.) It is not concerned at all with programming and notational convenience. It provides a minimal interface, with no redundancy. `PVector` provides the basic services that we need a vector to provide: efficient addition, removal, access and update of a contained element. This is reflecting the usage pattern of many programmers. They usually use a `Vector` as an array that can grow itself, if necessary. In the case of `PVector`, the responsibility for range-checking and synchronization is passed on to the caller. That enables the extreme efficiency of `PVector`.

```java
public class PVector  {

    protected Object elementData[];
    protected int elementCount;

    public PVector(int initialCapacity) {
        elementData = new Object[initialCapacity];
    }

    private void ensureCapacity(int minCapacity) {
        int oldCapacity = elementData.length;
        if (minCapacity > oldCapacity) {
            Object oldData[] = elementData;
            int newCapacity = oldCapacity * 2;
            if (newCapacity < minCapacity) {
                newCapacity = minCapacity;
            }
            elementData = new Object[newCapacity];
            System.arraycopy(oldData, 0, elementData, 0, elementCount);
        }
    }

    public int size() {
        return elementCount;
    }
    public Object elementAt(int index) {
        return elementData[index];
    }
```

```
    public void setElementAt(Object obj, int index) {
        elementData[index] = obj;
    }

    public void addElement(Object obj) {
        ensureCapacity(elementCount + 1);
        elementData[elementCount++] = obj;
    }

    public void removeAllElements() {
        for (int i = 0; i < elementCount; i++)
            elementData[i] = null;

        elementCount = 0;
    }

    public Object remove() {
        Object oldValue = elementData[--elementCount];
        elementData[elementCount] = null; // Let gc do its work

        return oldValue;
    }

    public String toString() {
        int max = elementCount -1;
        StringBuffer buf = new StringBuffer();
        buf.append("[");

        for (int i = 0 ; i < elementCount ; i++) {
            String s = elementData[i].toString();
            buf.append(s);
            if (i < max) {
                buf.append(", ");
            }
        }
        buf.append("]");

        return buf.toString();
    }

}
```

In comparison to the Vector implementation, we have made quite a few changes to the PVector. Here's what we did and why we did it:

- We have eliminated the default constructor that initializes capacity to 10 elements. You have to provide an initial capacity. This will force you to think about the expected size of the vector. The idea is that we want to have zero capacity expansions in the life of this vector.

- We have also eliminated the `capacity()` method and made `ensureCapacity()` private. Capacity-expansion issues are handled by the class itself, under the covers. The only time the user interferes with capacity is upon construction of the vector.

- We have eliminated a bunch of redundant services such as `firstElement()` and `lastElement()`. If you want the first element, `elementAt(0)` will do just fine.

- Many methods that trigger sequential searches have been eliminated. These include methods such as `contains()` and `indexOf()` flavors. You should never perform a linear search in a performance critical path. There are other data structures more suitable for this job.

- Some methods of the `Vector` class that insert or remove an element other than the last one will trigger an expensive shift of elements. Those methods have been removed as well. Again, if you need to perform such operations, a `Vector` is not your data structure of choice.

- Of the methods we kept, we had removed all synchronization and range-checking as well as updates to the `modCount` member. Other than core methods, we have also kept `removeAllElements()` and `toString()`. At some point in the life of a vector, you are going to have to destroy its elements. Hopefully, you will do that outside the critical path. We also need the `removeAllElements()` method to recycle a vector into an object pool for later reuse.

Let's compare the performance of `Vector` to `PVector` on the core functions. We are interested in four core tests:

- *Addition*—Use `addElement()` to add 1,000 elements to an empty `Vector`. Do the same for `PVector`.

- *Deletion*—Start with a `Vector` containing 1,000 elements and delete them all, one at a time, using `remove()`. Do the same for `PVector`.

- *Access*—Use elementAt() to access all elements of a Vector (PVector) consisting of 1,000 elements.

- *Update*—Use setElementAt() to set all 1,000 elements of a Vector (PVector.)

Our measurement test cases consisted of 1,000 loop iterations over a core test. Take, for example, the addition test case for Vector. The heart of the test case is this:

```
v = new Vector(1000);
for (int j = 0; j < 1000; j++) {
   v.addElement(s);
}
```

We then wrap it in another for loop just to repeat it 1,000 times:

```
{
    String s = "HelloWorld";
    Vector v = null;

    long start = System.currentTimeMillis();  // <++++++++ Start timing here
    for (int i = 0; i < 1000; i++) {
       v = new Vector(1000);
       for (int j = 0; j < 1000; j++) {
          v.addElement(s);
       }
    }
    long stop = System.currentTimeMillis();  // <++++++++ Stop timing here
    ...
}
```

The test case for PVector was almost identical except for replacing the Vector object with a PVector. We used similar test cases to compare the performance of element removal, access, and update using remove(), elementAt(), and set-ElementAt(), respectively. The PVector class has outperformed the Vector class by a significant margin on all test cases. See Figure 3.4.

The PVector implementation is much faster than the Vector because it does not try to do as much. However, there's a deeper issue here that ought to be highlighted. The Vector implementation does not provide an atomic unit of

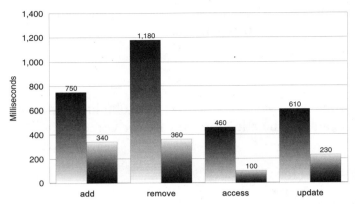

Figure 3.4.   Pvector is faster than Vector

functionality. It provides a molecule consisting of distinct particles of functionality. The Vector molecule contains the following computational atoms:

- A basic array providing access and update
- The ability to grow itself when capacity is exceeded
- Automatic range-checking
- Automatic synchronization
- Iterator support

Every Vector implementation would have to support the first atom, basic array functionality. The rest are optional. Four degrees of freedom give rise to 16 distinct implementations. The minimal implementation is the one provided by the built-in array. It supports the first atom only. The Vector implementation represents the maximal choice—it is a computational molecule containing all five atoms listed above. The maximal approach is best for programmer productivity. It provides the richest functionality. The problem, however, is that it is also the slowest. Optimal software is often associated with simplicity, not rich functionality. On the performance-critical path you often can ill-afford to waste CPU cycles on functionality you don't need. If you know the size of a Vector, then you don't need range-checking. If you are confined to a single thread, you don't need synchronization.

Now, in no way am I advocating that we should develop 16 versions of the Vector class. Some degree of suboptimality may be tolerable. It is also not worth spending lots of time and effort for minimal gains. However, if pro-filing indicates that your computational molecule is a performance hot spot, you may want to break off that molecule into smaller particles and use only those that you really depend on. That's what we did with the PVector.

The success of higher-level languages comes from increased developer produc-tivity. These languages achieve their productivity by providing computational molecules, not atoms. This idea is worth remembering because in a perfor-mance hot spot, it is sometimes necessary to reverse that trend. This approach is counterintuitive to a generation of object-oriented programmers that have been told to use and reuse software black-boxes and discouraged from looking under the hood.

Optimization 21: Using the API Wisely

When rich interfaces are available, it is often the case that you can accomplish a computational goal in several distinct ways. Some are better than others. One popular technique to pop an element from a Vector is given by

```
index = v.size() -1;
e = v.elementAt(index);
v.removeElementAt(index);
```

This works, but there's a faster way:

```
e = v.remove(v.size() -1);
```

The remove() method returns the element at the specified index and removes it from the Vector. We measured 1,000 invocations of these code fragments. The heart of the first test case was

```
for (int size = v.size(); size > 0; ) {   // Vector v contains 1000
                                           // String elements
    String s2 = (String) v.elementAt(size-1);
    v.removeElementAt(--size);
}
```

Again, we wrapped this test in a for loop and repeated it 1,000 times:

```
{
    String s1 = "HelloWorld";
    Vector v = new Vector(1000);

    long start = System.currentTimeMillis(); // <++++++++ Start timing here
    for (int i = 0; i < 1000; i++) {
        for (int j = 0; j < 1000; j++) { // Populate vector with 1,000 elements
            v.addElement(s1);
        }

        for (int size = v.size(); size > 0; ) {
            String s2 = (String) v.elementAt(size-1);
            v.removeElementAt(--size);
        }
    }
    long stop = System.currentTimeMillis(); // <++++++++ Stop timing here
    ...
}
```

The second test case was similar, with the exception that we replaced

```
for (int size = v.size(); size > 0; ) {
    String s2 = (String) v.elementAt(size-1);
    v.removeElementAt(--size);
}
```

with

```
for (int size = v.size(); size > 0; size--) {
    String s2 = (String) v.remove(size);
}
```

The superiority of the single remove() call is exhibited by Figure 3.5.

The remove() method was faster because it combined the work of both ele-mentAt() and removeElementAt() into a single call. Such misuse of the interface is not confined to the Vector class alone. I've discovered another one involving the Hashtable class. It would never occur to me that people would actually do this until I saw it in product code.

Here's the idea: We maintained a Hashtable of servlet data keyed by servlet name (a String.) When we were given a servlet name, we wanted to retrieve its related data from the table. If the servlet was not found, we created an entry for it and put it in the table for future access. The implementation was some-thing along the lines of the following:

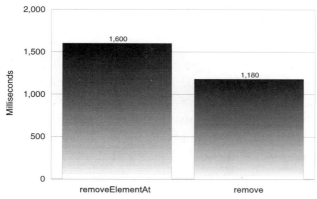

Figure 3.5.   Two ways to pop an element

```
if (table.containsKey(servletName)) {
    return table.get(servletName);
}
else {
    ServletEntry se = createEntry(servletName);
    table.put(servletName, se);
    return se;
}
```

What were they thinking? That the program will explode if they got a null back from the get() method? We are performing a completely redundant computation here. The containsKey() and get() methods are essentially identical except for having containsKey() return true/false, whereas get() returns the entry value or null. Other than that, these two are identical. A much better way to structure the code is to skip the call to containsKey(), as in

```
if ( (se = (ServletEntry) table.get(servletName)) != null) {
    return se;
}
else {
    ...    // as before
}
```

Other than being twice as fast, this code accomplishes the same exact task as the original one.

The same issue has another manifestation. It has to do with adding objects to a Hashtable:

```
if (!table.containsKey(key)) {
    table.put(key, value);
}
```

In this example the programmer was trying to avoid adding a key-value pair to the table if the key is already present. However, there is a redundant computation here under the surface. The `put()` method already checks for the existence of the key and will guard against duplicate keys. The same search logic that is in `containsKey()` is duplicated inside `put()`. In the likely case where the key is not present, we essentially determine it twice, once in `containsKey()` and once more in `put()`. The following statement is equivalent and more efficient:

```
table.put(key, value);
```

Optimization 22: `Hashtable` Parameters ■

A `Hashtable` is an array of "buckets," each of which contains a linked list of key-value pairs. When a key-value pair is inserted to the `Hashtable`, it is mapped to a specific bucket according to the key's `hashCode()`. It is then added to the linked list of key-value pairs rooted at that bucket. Similarly, when you want to retrieve a value corresponding to a given key, the key's `hashCode()` is computed to determine the bucket index and then a linear search is performed on this bucket's linked list in order to locate a matching key. The given key is compared to the keys of the linked list using the key's `equals()` method. When a match is found, the corresponding value is returned.

We are now in position to make a few observations on the factors influencing `Hahstable` performance.

- The linear search is crucial. We would like the linked lists to be as short as possible; ideally, none will be longer than one element.

- Anytime you want to `put()` or `get()` a value, the key's `hashCode()` will be computed. The performance of the key's `hashCode()` is important.

- The key's `equals()` method is called when searching the linked list. This `equals()` implementation better be efficient.

The topic of length (of the linked list) is, again, divided into two subtopics. First, the key's `hashCode()` should provide a reasonable distribution of the keys over the Hashtable buckets. You don't want a set of keys to cluster in a small number of buckets because of a poor hashCode() implementation. What would be a poor implementation? Imagine if the String hashCode() only looked at the first four characters to produce the hash index. In that case, all String objects with the same four-character prefix would be mapped to the same bucket. For that reason, the String.hashCode() implementation looks at every character in the String.

The other subtopic controlling the length of the linked list is the capacity and the load factor. The Hashtable initial capacity is the number of buckets in the table. The load factor is an indicator of how full the table can get before the number of buckets is doubled (rehashing.) For example, if you use the default constructor

```
Hashtable ht = new Hashtable();
```

the initial capacity is 101 and the load factor is 0.75. The rehash threshold is then set to

```
threshold = 101*0.75;   // initial_capacity * load_factor
```

Whenever the table element count goes above the threshold, a rehash will occur, doubling the number of buckets and redistributing the keys. In general, the load factor should be less than 1.0 so that you don't have more elements than buckets. If the number of elements exceeds the buckets, some linked lists will have to be larger than one. The default of 0.75 looks reasonable, and I don't see a reason to modify it.

Before we even get to search the linked list, we must find the bucket index by calling the key's hashCode(). We already mentioned that hashCode() should provide good distribution. It is also important that it provides a good distribution fast. It may be the case that we are better off with a less then perfect distribution if the hashCode() computation is orders of magnitude faster. Take a Vector.hashCode(), for example. (Why anybody would want to use a Vector as a key is beyond me, but, hey, it serves as a poster-child for a slow hash-Code().) The Vector computes its own hashCode() by calling the hashCode() method on each one of its contained elements. Anytime the Vector size exceeds four or five elements, it is calling for a performance disaster. Quite a few studies have claimed that random algorithms can sometimes come within a few percentage points of the accuracy of "perfect" algorithms. In this case, if it were up to me, I would compute the Vector.hashCode() by picking a random element and computing its hashCode(). That would divorce the hashCode() execution time from dependency on the length of the Vector. It is also very likely that the resulting distribution will be good enough.

The third issue is the performance of the equals() method when applied to the key object. When searching the linked list, we call the equals() method on each key in the list. A real slow equals() method could be punishing even if the length of the list is one.

Lastly, we go back to the first issue of minimizing the size of the lists. The default load factor (0.75) will take care of that via rehashing. The point is that the rehash operation itself is very costly. We have seen a similar issue before when the capacity of a Vector is insufficient. In the case of the Hashtable, we must allocate a new larger array of buckets, recompute the bucket distribution, and copy all the key-value pairs to the new array of linked lists. This rehash() is expensive; it is something to avoid on a performance-critical path. Ideally, you never want rehash() to occur on a performance-critical path. You can help the performance cause by specifying an initial capacity large enough to ever need a rehash(). You can specify an initial capacity via

```
Hashtable ht = new Hashtable(initial_capacity);
```

The load factor will default to 0.75.

Optimization 23: Speed Up hashCode() ∎

The performance of many Hashtable methods is strongly dependent on the efficiency of the key's equals() and hashCode() methods. It is also the case that String objects make a very popular choice for keys in a Hashtable. These two observations put together lead us to turn the spotlight now to the efficiency of those two methods with respect to the String class implementation.

The hashCode() implementation in String.java scans every character in the String object in the course of producing an int value. The speed of the hashCode() implementation is in reverse proportion to the length of the String. The longer the String, the slower hashCode() is going to be. Intuitively, it sounds like a real good idea to replace the hashCode() implementation with one that is divorced from the length of the String, yet provides a good key distribution. Since most people are not comfortable modifying the JDK, the next best option is to create a String wrapper object. It should not come as a big surprise that we named it StringWrapper:

```java
class StringWrapper {

    private String string;
    private int hash;

    public StringWrapper (String s) {
        init(s);
    }

    public void init(String s) {
        string = s;

        int len = string.length();
        int c0 = string.charAt(0);
        int cn = string.charAt(len-1);

        hash = len*(31*c0 + cn);
    }

    public boolean equals(Object anObject) {
        if (this == anObject) {
            return true;
        }
        if ((anObject != null) && (anObject instanceof StringWrapper)) {
            StringWrapper p = (StringWrapper) anObject;
            return string.equals(p.getString());
        }

        return false;
    }

    public int hashCode() { return hash; }
    public String getString() { return string; }
}
```

The StringWrapper hashCode() looks only at the first and last characters in the String object. To provide another dimension of randomness, we added the String length as a factor in the final hash value. Notice that we perform this computation in the constructor and cache it for future reference. If the hashCode() on this object is called more than once, our method will be a performance win. Putting this computation in the constructor also indicates that we do not intend to use this class for anything other than a key. If it had any other use that did not necessitate hashing, the evaluation of the hash code in the constructor would have become automatic dead-weight. The performance of this implementation is independent of the length of the String object and should outperform the String hashCode(). That's the theory, at least. We ran a measurement to put the theory to the test. The following test case populates a Hashtable with a large number of (key-value) pairs where the keys are String objects.

```
String keyString = args[1]; // Will create keys based on this String

    Hashtable str = new Hashtable();    // Hashtable using String keys
    Hashtable strW = new Hashtable(); // Hashtable using StringWrapper keys
    Object o = new Object();

for (int i = 0; i < 100; i++) { // Populate the Hashtable objects
    str.put(keyString + i, o);
    strW.put(new StringWrapper(keyString + i), o);
}
...
```

If the keyString given as a command-line argument is "myKey", then the generated keys will be "myKey1", "myKey2", and so on. The first test case measures the speed of repeated get() calls on the generated Hashtable with the above String keys.

```
String key = keyString + 1; // Some key in the table

long start = System.currentTimeMillis();  // <+++ Start timing here
for (int i = 0; i < n; i++) {
    Object o1 = str.get(key);
}
long stop = System.currentTimeMillis();  // <+++ Stop timing here
```

We then repeat a very similar test case in which the String keys are replaced with the corresponding StringWrapper keys.

```
long start = System.currentTimeMillis();  // <+++ Start timing here
for (int i = 0; i < n; i++) {
    Object o1 = strW.get(new StringWrapper(key)); // Use StringWrapper instead
}
long stop = System.currentTimeMillis();  // <+++ Stop timing here
```

Surprisingly, the test case using plain String objects (with an inefficient hash-Code()) has outperformed the one using StringWrapper even when the underlying key string was relatively long at 32 characters. There's no doubt that eventually, if we keep increasing the length of the String, the StringWrapper version is going to catch up and become more efficient. When we increased the String length to 64, the gap was much narrower but still in favor of plain String keys. At 128, the StringWrapper performance finally took the lead. See Figure 3.6. The left-hand side of each pair is the version using String keys.

However, the crossover point arrived much further down (with respect to String size) than I expected. We can conclude that this attempted optimization could be impractical in most scenarios. The 32-character-long String we used was a fair representative (with respect to size) of String objects that we are likely to see in practice.

Why did this optimization fail for String objects of size 32? Because the cost of creating new StringWrapper object, overwhelmed the efficiency gained by the faster implementation of the StringWrapper hashCode(). We have two important lessons to take from this experiment

- The cost of object creation requires serious consideration. Keeping object creation to a minimum is important for the performance of Java code.

- Intuition is a bad guide when it comes to optimization decisions. Don't base such decisions on gut feelings or industry folklore. Base your decisions on profiling or timing evidence.

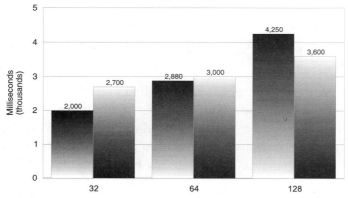

Figure 3.6. The cost of object creation competes with hashCode() gains

Our previous attempt at improving `hashCode()` performance came up short. We are not done yet. We have one more trick up our sleeve. Instead of creating a brand new `StringWrapper` object every time we want to access the `Hashtable`, we could easily recycle the same `StringWrapper` object by replacing its `String` member reference with a new reference. We do that by adding a `recycle()` method to the `StringWrapper` class:

```
public void recycle(String newStr) {
      init(newStr);
   }
```

The `recycle()` method simply re-initializes the `StringWrapper` object with a new `String` reference. Comparing the `recycle()` method to the `StringWrapper` constructor, we see that in both methods we must set the member references by calling `init()`. However, in the `recycle()` method, we don't have to allocate memory for a new object (which happens implicitly when a constructor is invoked). That should make the `recycle()` method superior to the constructor in performance.

We already measured a million iterations of

```
Object o1 = str.get(key); // Using String keys
```

and

```
Object o1 = strW.get(new StringWrapper(key));   // Using StringWrapperr keys
```

for a `String` key of length 32. We now add a third version using `StringWrapper` recycling:

```
sw.recycle(key); // sw is a reference to a StringWrapper object
Object o1 = strW.get(sw);
```

The last version using `recycle()` has vaulted to the top of the performance heap, leaping over the other two. Not only does it apply a more efficient `hashCode()` method but it also circumvented the need to create a new `StringWrapper` object. That creation has previously doomed the performance of the second technique using the `StringWrapper` constructor. See Figure 3.7.

The issue of object recycling is crucial for high-performance Java. We will revisit it in Chapter 6.

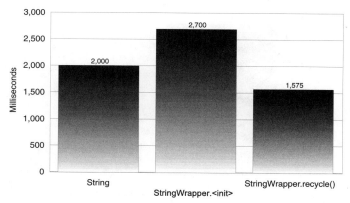

Figure 3.7. Recycling the StringWrapper provides a performance boost

Optimization 24: Speed Up equals() ∎

Another important aspect of using String objects as keys is manifested in String equals(). There are times where we may consider two keys equal even though they differ in case. For example, you may use a HashSet to store HTML or XML tags. Since the String equals() method insists on a case-sensitive match, we have two ways to proceed:

- We could agree that we keep all table keys in uppercase. Given a key, we will first convert it to uppercase before storing it. The same applies for searching. We will uppercase the search key prior to searching the table.

- The second option is to override the String equals() method. Instead of using String keys, we could use StringWrapper objects and redefine the StringWrapper equals() to perform a case-insensitive String comparison.

  To implement the second idea, we need to slightly modify the String-Wrapper equals() method. Inside the equals() implementation for StringWrapper, instead of calling

  ```
  return string.equals(p.getString()); // See Optimization 23
  ```

  we will call

  ```
  return string.equalsIgnoreCase(p.getString());
  ```

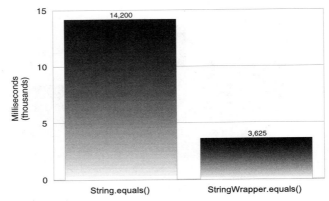

Figure 3.8.   The cost of `String.toUppercase()` was overwhelming

The test itself compares a million iterations using `String` keys,

```
String ucKey = key.toUpperCase();
Object o1 = str.get(ucKey);
```

to the same number of iterations using `StringWrapper` with the modified `equals()` method that ignores case,

```
Object o1 = strW.get(new StringWrapper(key));
```

Now both techniques are saddled with having to create a new object. The first one must create a new uppercase `String` whereas the second must create a new `String-Wrapper`. This time the `StringWrapper` provides a dramatic boost. See Figure 3.8.

Of course, our `StringWrapper` version would have been even faster if we recycled the `StringWrapper` object from one iteration to the next (as we did in Optimization 23.) Even so, with one hand tied behind our back, we still managed to beat the naive `String` technique of converting all `String` objects to uppercase.

Key Points

- The `Vector` class provides us more than one method to add elements to the `Vector`. Those insert methods could vary significantly in performance. The methods `addElement(e)` and `add(e)` are best, as they append the element to the back of the `Vector`. The same point holds for element removal. If you find yourself adding or deleting `Vector` elements anywhere other than the back, you have chosen the wrong data structure.

- The initial capacity of a `Vector` object is fairly low. Since `Vector` expansions are expensive and memory is cheap, you should specify a larger initial capacity in the `Vector` constructor.

- By default, a `Vector` doubles its capacity every expansion. Do not override this.

- Iterating over a `Vector` using a running index is faster than using an `Enumeration` or `Iterator` objects.

- If a `Vector` is confined to a single thread, you should use an `ArrayList` instead. The `ArrayList` is not synchronized.

- It is possible to manipulate Java collections in extremely inefficient ways. Watch your step and investigate the performance characteristics of your calls.

- To make your `Hashtable` more efficient, you must choose a large enough initial capacity such that you never need to `rehash()`. In addition, make sure that the key's `hashCode()` is fast and generates a good distribution over the `Hashtable` buckets. Also, the key's `equals()` method should be fast.

- The performance of the key's `equals()` and `hashCode()` methods significantly impacts the performance of a `Hashtable` and other collections built around it. In the popular case of a `String` key, you could gain significant speed by overriding those methods with a `String` object wrapper.

4

Caching

When you are faced with a performance hot spot, you have basically two options. You could delve into the nitty-gritty details of the computation or find a clever way to avoid the computation altogether. The latter option is the preferred way to go since avoiding a costly computation is likely to be much faster than optimizing it. Computational values tend to fall into three categories according to their expected lifetimes:

- *Static*—These values do not change at all during the life of the application. For example, a Web server returns its own name on every response header. The name of the server will not change for the duration of server execution.

- *Pure dynamic*—These values could change at any point in time and must be recomputed every time. They make very poor candidates for caching. For example, computing the balance on a checking account produces this type of values.

- *Semidynamic*—These values could change but have a relatively long lifetime. For example, if you browse the catalog in an e-commerce site, the prices don't change very often. Having to go and fetch the prices from a database would be unnecessarily expensive. Those prices could be cached and periodically refreshed.

Static and semidynamic values present a rich set of optimization opportunities. In this chapter we will discuss various manifestations of these optimizations, otherwise known as caching. Caching has been long known as one of the primary ways to improve efficiency.

Optimization 25: Cache File Contents

A large portion of HTTP requests are targeted at files containing static HTML and images. In that respect, the Web server is acting as a file server. It is possible for those files to be modified on the fly, and it is expected that the Web server will detect modifications and deliver fresh copies. However, static files don't change that often and serve as a model for the semidynamic category of computational values. A Web server that goes to the file system for every static file is going to suffer a substantial performance penalty caused by excessive file I/O. Most commercial Web servers perform content caching in one form or another. Here's one way to do it in Java.

The `FileInfo` class encapsulates the file information we want to capture. To make life simple, we'll pretend that the only thing we care about right now is the file contents:

```java
class FileInfo {
    private String content;
    private long lastUpdate;

    FileInfo (String c, long lu) {
        content = c;
        lastUpdate = lu;
    }

    public void setContent(String c) {
        content = c;
    }

    public void setLastUpdate(long lu) {
        lastUpdate = lu;
    }

    public String getContent() {
        return content;
    }

    public long getLastUpdate() {
        return lastUpdate;
    }

}
```

The cache itself is a Hashtable wrapper. It stores a FileInfo object in a Hashtable using the file name itself as a key. The first time the server gets a request for file x.html, it does not know anything about it. So the server reads the file contents from the file system and creates a new FileInfo object where the contents of x.html are stored. The FileInfo object is inserted into the file cache for subsequent use. The file cache object itself is given by

```
class FileCache {
    private Hashtable ht = new Hashtable(1001);
    private long cacheRefresh = 1000; // 1000 milliseconds == 1 second

    FileCache() {}  // Default cache refresh

    FileCache(long refresh) {
        cacheRefresh = refresh;
    }

    public void put(File file, FileInfo fi) {
        ht.put(file.getName(), fi);
    }

public FileInfo get(File file) {
    FileInfo fi = (FileInfo) ht.get(file.getName());
    if (fi == null) {
        return null;
    }

    long now = System.currentTimeMillis();
    if ((now-fi.getLastUpdate()) > cacheRefresh ) {
        ht.remove(file.getName());
        return null;
        }

    return fi;
    }

}
```

Subsequent requests for the same file will find its contents already in the cache so that a costly file-system I/O can be avoided. This caching scheme still has to guard against file modifications. Our solution is to refresh the cache periodically. You can pass in the refresh rate as a constructor argument, or you could default it to a reasonable value. In our code we chose a default of one second. This is a good enough granularity for this domain. The FileInfo object has a timestamp associated with it. If more than one second has elapsed, the FileCache will return a null that will force the server to recompute the file contents. Doing periodic I/O is far better than doing it 1,000 times per second.

As much as I like the above implementation, I must confess that it is not yet ready for prime time. It completely avoids some important considerations such as capacity and overflow. Still, it is effective in driving home the point on the benefits of caching.

Optimization 26: Design Caching into Your API ∎

As a developer you may find yourself in situations in which you are either a provider or a consumer of an Application Programming Interface (API). As an API consumer, you may be locked into a situation in which redundant computations are performed by the API calls you are making and there is nothing you can do about it. I was in this situation not long ago with event logging API that was developed by another group. We were keeping track of how many distinct servlets were active as well as the total number of requests targeted at each servlet:

```java
public void servletActive() {
    long time = System.currentTimeMillis()
    ...
}

public void incTotalRequests() {
    long time = System.currentTimeMillis()
    ...
}
```

For some statistical reasons, those event-logging methods needed to get a timestamp. They acquired the timestamp via System.currentTimeMillis() on every event-logging method (there were many more than the two shown above). The problem with this design is twofold.

- System.currentTimeMillis() is not a free call. It is expensive. Since Java relies on the system clock, there has got to be a native call involved. Crossing from Java to Java Native Interface (JNI) has a cost associated with it, so calls to System.currentTimeMillis() should not be taken lightly.

- The client code was often calling multiple event-logging methods one after the other and suffering needless redundant calls to `System.currentTimeMillis()`.

For example, upon receiving a servlet request, we often performed both of the following:

```
servletData.servletActive();
servletData.incTotalRequests();
```

We were in perfect position here to get a single timestamp and reuse it, but we could not because the API designers did not expose the timestamp as a possible input argument. It is your responsibility as an API provider to anticipate the usage pattern of your API and provide caching and other performance opportunities. For example, in the case of the event-logging API, the previous methods should have taken a timestamp argument, as in

```
public void servletActive(long time) {
    ...
}

public void incTotalRequests(long time) {
    ...
}
```

We opened up the opportunity for the client code to cache and reuse the timestamp:

```
long time = System.currentTimeMillis()

servletData.servletActive(time);
servletData.incTotalRequests(time);
```

Optimization 27: Precompute ∎

Eliminating loop invariants is one of the familiar classic optimizations [BEN 82]. This belongs in the category of caching static values, in which the value remains constant for the duration of loop execution. Take this loop, for example:

```
for (int i = 0; i < 100; i++) {
    a[i] = m*n;
}
```

The product m*n is a loop invariant. It is independent of the iteration index and its value remains unchanged from one iteration to the next. Computing the product m*n every iteration is therefore inefficient. The obvious optimization here is to lift m*n out of the loop:

```
int p = m*n;
for (int i = 0; i < 100; i++) {
    a[i] = p;
}
```

This same optimization opportunity may present itself in other scenarios but in a less obvious form. Take servlets for example. When a servlet is requested for the very first time, it is loaded and initialized via the servlet's init() method. It is followed by execution of the servlet's service() method that is in charge of generating the servlet response. Subsequent requests to this servlet will trigger the execution of the service() method only. The init() method is executed only once in the lifetime of the servlet. Some computations performed inside of the service() method produce a constant result on every service() call. I call these values service invariants.

```
public class PingServlet extends HttpServlet {
    ...
    public void service      (HttpServletRequest request,
                              HttpServletResponse response)
            throws ServletException, IOException  {

        response.setContentType("text/html");
        ServletOutputStream out = response.getOutputStream();
        String msg = "<html><head><title>" +
                     "Ping Servlet </title></head>" +
                     "<body><h1>Ping Servlet " +
                     "</h1></body></html>";
        out.println(msg);
    }
    ...
}
```

Let's take a close look at that service() method. The request and response objects given to it are going to be different from one invocation of service() to the next. The String msg object, on the other hand, is going to evaluate to the same value on every iteration of service(). It is a service invariant. Just as with loop invariants, we can improve performance by computing the msg String once in the init() method and reuse it in the service() call:

```
public class PingServlet extends HttpServlet {
    ...

    // We make this String a member of the servlet object
    private static final String msg = null;

    public void init() {
        msg = "<html><head><title>" +
              "Ping Servlet </title></head>" +
              "<body><h1>Ping Servlet " +
              "</h1></body></html>";
    }

    public void service       (HttpServletRequest request,
                               HttpServletResponse response)
            throws ServletException, IOException {

        response.setContentType("text/html");
        ServletOutputStream out = response.getOutputStream();
        out.println(msg);
    }
    ...
}
```

Now this is only half the story, and not even the significant one, since a decent compiler could perform the `msg` construction at compile time when all the constituent parts of the `String` are already available. What is much more significant is happening under the surface as character-to-byte conversion. Our `msg` is made of two-byte characters. What goes out on the wire is a stream of single bytes. Somewhere along the line, somebody must convert those characters to bytes; and this is not cheap. Again, this is a service-invariant computation, so why don't we do it in the `init()` method?

```
public class PingServlet extends HttpServlet {
    ...

    private static final String msg = null;
    private static final byte[] bytes;

    public void init() {
        msg = "<html><head><title>" +
              "Ping Servlet </title></head>" +
              "<body><h1>Ping Servlet " +
              "</h1></body></html>";
```

```
        bytes = msg.getBytes();
    }

    public void service    (HttpServletRequest request,
                            HttpServletResponse response)
            throws ServletException, IOException {

        response.setContentType("text/html");
        ServletOutputStream out = response.getOutputStream();
        out.write(bytes);
    }
    ...
}
```

This is essentially the same as optimizing loop invariants. We have taken a repetitive computation whose result is always the same and reduced it to a single computation whose value gets cached and reused on subsequent iterations.

Optimization 28: Relax Granularity ■

When I normally think of program correctness, I tend to think in binary terms—the program is either correct or faulty, with nothing in the middle. If you think about it, correctness is often not as rigid as zero or one. If I asked you what time it was and you responded with 3:47 P.M., that would be good enough for me even if the actual time were 3:46 and 59 seconds. Just because you do not specify nanosecond granularity does not mean your answer is wrong. There are many scenarios in which a correct computation can tolerate coarse-grain accuracy. In general, the finer the granularity, the more expensive the computation. You should refine a computation only to the point of acceptable accuracy and no more. Going beyond that point could result in dramatic performance penalties. In practice, you will often be working in reverse; starting with an overly granular computation, you will optimize expensive code by relaxing the degree of accuracy this code produces.

Take the Date class, for example. It is very expensive to compute the date regardless of language, and it is expensive even in C++. Starting from the system's representation, which is the number of seconds since 1.1.1970, the implementation must convert it into a string such as

```
Fri Jul 02 16:38:41 PDT 1999
```

This is a complex computation. It is even more complex in Java where the Date class is locale-sensitive. Different cultures (locales) may represent dates in slightly different formats. The Java Date implementation accommodates that requirement. This flexibility is partly why we like Java so much; it does so much of the routine work, making programmers so much more productive. That productivity boost, however, has a performance price tag. On a performance-critical path, therefore, you should work hard to avoid costly date computations. I will show you how to do that by relaxing the degree of accuracy.

When a Web server sends an HTTP response, it also attaches the current date to the response header. A naive implementation would compute the current date on every request, as in:

```
String dateHeader = "Date: " + (new Date());
```

It is very common for busy Web servers to process thousands of requests per second. Our naive implementation above is going to force our server to compute the current date thousands of times per second. It will perform the same computation, producing identical results, over and over.

A more performance-friendly implementation could boost efficiency by computing the date periodically (as in once per second) as opposed to once per request. That way the cost of the date computation is spread over hundreds (or even thousands) of requests as opposed to penalizing each and every one with the full cost of date computation. The worst outcome of this relaxed accuracy is that the HTTP date header could be off by 1 second. That's okay, the browser doesn't really care. The HTTP response generated by the server is still valid.

The following class performs an efficient coarse-grain evaluation of the current date. It only performs a real evaluation once per second. Otherwise, it returns a cached value that could be off by a second:

```java
class LazyDate {

    private long lastCheck = 0; // Never checked before
    private String today;
    private long cacheRefresh = 1000; // 1 second

    public LazyDate() {} // Default cache refresh
```

```
    public LazyDate(long refresh) {
        cacheRefresh = refresh;
        update();
    }

    public String todaysDate() {
        long now = System.currentTimeMillis();
        if ((now-lastCheck) > cacheRefresh) {
            update();
        }

        return today;
    }

    private void update() {
        lastCheck = System.currentTimeMillis();
        today = (new Date()).toString();
    }
}
```

The LazyDate constructor takes an argument, specifying how often we should perform the actual date evaluation. In other words, it specifies how long it has been before our cached value has gotten stale. The LazyDate constructor calls update() to compute the date, cache it, and store the time in which this evaluation took place. Future requests for the date will go through the todaysDate() method. If the cached value is still fresh, it will be served. Otherwise, a brand new value is computed by calling update().

In the Web server code, a single instance of LazyDate is constructed. It will provide the current date on future requests:

```
LazyDate today = new LazyDate(1000); // 1 second refresh time
...
while (true) { // While server is active
    ...
    String dateHeader = "Date: " + today.todaysDate();
    ...
}
```

How does the performance of LazyDate compare to that of the greedy evaluation of the Date class? The code fragment that follows measures the speed of 100,000 iterations, generating the current date as a String object:

```
String date = null;
start = System.currentTimeMillis();

for (int i = 0; i < 100000; i++) {
   date = (new Date()).toString();
   }

stop = System.currentTimeMillis();
```

The for loop above executed in 28,000 milliseconds, otherwise known as 28 seconds. I repeated a similar measurement with a LazyDate object:

```
String date = null;
LazyDate today = new LazyDate();
start = System.currentTimeMillis();

for (int i = 0; i < 100000; i++) {
   date = today.todaysDate();
   }

stop = System.currentTimeMillis();
```

The loop using the LazyDate object has executed 100,000 iterations in 40 milliseconds. The result was 40 ms compared to 28,000 ms of the plain Date object. That's three orders of magnitude faster. This ought to give you a feel for the gigantic overhead of creating a new Date object. It looks very easy, as in

```
Date today = new Date();
```

but it harbors a substantial amount of overhead. Somebody has got to do it; and just because you don't see it, does not mean you are not going to pay for it.

LazyDate is providing us two big advantages over Date. First, it saves the excruciating conversion from a long integer to a locale-sensitive String format. Secondly, it saves us the need to create (and eventually destroy) a brand new date object on each iteration. The more objects you create, the more work you are generating for the garbage collector. Object allocation and deallocation is not free. It is just done behind your back.

Optimization 29: Inheritance ■

Object-oriented designs involving complex inheritance hierarchies are often blamed for the poor performance of the resulting software [BM99]. Object-oriented designs in general and inheritance in particular are neither good nor bad for performance. It simply depends on how you use them. There are times where an inheritance-based design will exhibit superior performance in comparison to its procedural counterpart.

Take, for example, a simple scenario involving a human-resources application that wants to distinguish female from male employees. The application already has a class to represent an employee:

```
class Employee {
   ...
}
```

If you want to make a distinction according to gender, you have two design options [BM97]. You can add a boolean flag to the Employee class, as in

```
class Employee {
   boolean isFemale;
   ...
}
```

or you can choose to extend the Employee class, as in

```
class Female_Employee extends Employee {
   ...
}

class Male_Employee extends Employee {
   ...
}
```

Recently, I ran into this situation on a Web application server. The server provided an API to allow servlets to maintain HTTP session-state. In the case where the server ran in a standalone mode, it had a SessionMgr object that managed information associated with each and every session created by this server. Session information was kept in memory. Things got a little more complex when you ran a Web farm consisting of a cluster of application servers running in distinct JVMs. The farm had a front-end load-balancer box that sprayed requests to the clustered servers at the back. A session started on server X could easily end up on server Y on subsequent requests. We needed to modify the standalone design to allow sharing of session data in a cluster. What we came up with was a centralized session server that acted as repository for session data. An application server in a clustered environment accessed session data via RMI calls to the session server.

This support for clustered environments forced the `SessionMgr` class to have a split personality. It could be in one of three modes, determined during application server initialization. It could be running as one of the following:

- Standalone server

- Cluster session server

- Cluster session client

That split personality was implemented by adding two boolean flags to determine the mode of operation:

```
class SessionMgr {
    boolean isCluster; // Am I running in a cluster?
    boolean isServer;  // Am I the cluster session server?
    ...
}
```

This design choice feels more natural for programmers with heavy procedural background (which is almost all of us). It is bad for performance, however. It forced us to pollute the `SessionMgr` methods with conditional branches like

```
public void X() {
    if (isCluster) {
        if (isServer) {
            // I am a cluster server
            ...
        }
        else {
            // I am a cluster client
            ..
        }
    else {
        // I'm running standalone
    }
    ...  // Some common code for all environments
}
```

Every method of the `SessionMgr` class had to revisit this decision point and recompute something that was essentially known at initialization time. Moreover, once the application server is launched, its session mode cannot change without a shutdown. This information is static. A much better idea would be to use inheritance to capture the commonality between the modes:

```
class SessionMgr {
    ... // Common behavior
}

class SessionMgr_Standalone extends SessionMgr {
    ...
    public void X() { // specific implementation for this mode
        ...
    }
}

class SessionMgr_ClusterClient extends SessionMgr {
    ...
    public void X() { // specific implementation for this mode
        ...
    }
}
```

With this design, the application server works with the interface of the `SessionMgr` base class. When the server is initialized, it will determine its mode of operation and instantiate the appropriate subclass of `SessionMgr`. From this point on, we never have to revisit this decision. The `X()` method of the subclass already "knows" what type it is and does not have to perform those costly branch conditions over and over. Inheritance and polymorphism are used in this case to cache the class type.

Key Points

- Computational results that remain valid for some time present caching opportunities. Caching would allow us to skip expensive computations in favor of a cached result.

- You can extend the validity of a computational result by relaxing the accuracy requirement.

- As an API designer, you should anticipate the usage pattern of your code and provide your consumers with caching opportunities.

- You could precompute expensive results by pushing them out of the performance-critical path and into application and object initialization time.

- Inheritance could help performance by "remembering" the object type and avoiding type computations that are necessary in procedural designs.

5

I/O Streams

Java I/O streams are capable of reading and writing data to and from a variety of end points. Sockets, files, strings, character arrays, and more. All these are fair game for the I/O machinery. We are not going to inspect each and every one. What we want to do is flush out the fundamental performance principles underlying this jungle of combinations of I/O devices and stream classes. We can get there by drilling into a single dimension of streaming file I/O. It will expose the fundamental issues. We will find out that the cost of writing and reading data to and from Java I/O streams boils down to two central issues: buffering and Unicode conversions. Every optimization discussed in this chapter will eventually be reduced to one of those two issues.

Example I/O Code

To facilitate the discussion I will develop two small Java programs that spend the bulk of their time reading or writing data to (from) I/O streams. To make it slightly more interesting, we'll pretend that we are recording all of our stock-market trades over the past year so we can compute our capital gains. One program is going to output all trades to a file, and the second will read them back. What information do we need to capture with regard to a particular trade? We need the following:

- The date of the transaction. We'll represent the date in a `String` format so that we don't lose efficiency to `Date` computations. This chapter is about I/O, not `Date` nor `String` efficiency. We want to keep it focused on I/O.

- An indication of whether the trade was a "Buy" or a "Sell"

- Stock symbol

- Number of shares traded

- Price of the share

The `Trade` object captures the required information:

```
class Trade {
    String date;
    boolean buy;
    String symbol;
    int numShares;
    float price;
    ...
}
```

When we write a `Trade` object to file, we could do something like

```
Trade buy = new Trade ("01-01-99", true, 100, "IBM", 140);
fw.println(buy);    //  fw is a FileWriter
```

or

```
fos.write(buy.toString().getBytes());    //  fos is a FileOutputStream
```

The `println()` will trigger a call to `Trade.toString()`. The conversion of a `Trade` object to `String` is rather expensive. To keep this discussion focused on I/O performance, I wanted to eliminate costly `String` manipulations from the critical path that's being measured. Therefore, I computed the `Trade` `String` and `byte` representations in the `Trade` constructor so that I won't have to compute those representations on the fly. The `Trade` objects in my test program are constructed before entering the performance-critical path. The `Trade` class implementation is given below. Note that the `toString()` and `toByte()` methods are now extremely fast since they don't perform the actual computation. They just return a reference to an object constructed earlier.

```
class Trade {
    String date;
    boolean buy;
    String symbol;
    int numShares;
    float price;

    String stringRep;
    byte[] byteRep;

    public Trade (String d,
        boolean b,
        int n,
```

```java
            String s,
            float p) {

        symbol = s;
        numShares = n;
        buy = b;
        date = d;
        price = p;

        stringRep = privateToString();
        byteRep = stringRep.getBytes();
    }

    public Trade (String tr) {
        StringTokenizer st = new StringTokenizer(tr, " ");
        date = st.nextToken();

        if ("Buy".equals(st.nextToken())) {
            buy = true;
        }
        else {
            buy = false;
        }

        numShares = Integer.parseInt(st.nextToken());
        symbol = st.nextToken();
        price = Float.valueOf(st.nextToken()).floatValue();

        stringRep = privateToString();
        byteRep = stringRep.getBytes();
    }

    private String privateToString() {
        StringBuffer sb = new StringBuffer(128);

        sb.append(date).append(" ");

        if (buy) {
            sb.append("Buy ");
        }
        else {
            sb.append("Sell ");
        }

        sb.append(numShares).append(" ");
        sb.append(symbol).append(" ");
        sb.append(price).append(" ");
```

```
        return sb.toString();
    }

    public String toString() {
        return stringRep;
    }

    public byte[] toBytes() {
        return byteRep;
    }

}
```

I have used the StringTokenizer to parse a String back into a Trade object. You may recall that in Optimization 5 I blasted the StringTokenizer for lacking efficiency. The Trade constructor, however, is not going to be called on the performance-critical path, so we don't care about efficiency here. Where performance is not an issue, ease of programming rules.

With the Trade implementation tucked away, we are ready to go to work.

Optimization 30: Output Buffering ∎

Buffering is about minimizing the overhead per byte. If you send data one byte at a time, you'll have to traverse the whole output machinery for each byte. If you chunk the data into larger blocks, you can spread the fixed cost over a large number of bytes and minimize the amortized cost. This is nothing new; buffering output data enhances efficiency in all programming languages I have ever worked on. The Java I/O stream library makes buffering very easy. All you need to do is wrap a buffering stream around your intended output stream.

We will demonstrate the power of buffering by writing Trade records to a file using a FileOutputStream with and without buffering. The first version uses a FileOutputStream with no buffering:

```
private void out(int n)
    throws FileNotFoundException, IOException {

    Trade buy = new Trade ("01-01-99", true, 100, "IBM", 140);
    Trade sell = new Trade ("01-08-99", false, 100, "IBM", 150);

    FileOutputStream fos = new FileOutputStream("stock.dat");
```

```
    long start = System.currentTimeMillis(); // <+++ Start timing
    for (int i = 0; i < n; i++) {  // 1,000,000 iterations
        fos.write(buy.toBytes());
        fos.write(sell.toBytes());
    }
    long stop = System.currentTimeMillis(); // <+++ Stop timing

    System.out.println( " out time = " + (stop - start) );
    fos.close();
}
```

The loop under test iterates one million times, writing buy and sell Trade representations to file. I bought 100 shares and dumped them a week later for a hefty gain. They happen to be the same trades over and over, but that's okay. We are only trying to give the stream a workout. The test loop executed in 33 seconds. In the second test we simply decorated the FileOutputStream with a BufferedOutputStream, as in

```
BufferedOutputStream fos =
    new BufferedOutputStream(
        new FileOutputStream("stock.dat"));
```

That's it. The rest of the code remains the same. The execution time of the loop dropped to 19 seconds. Without buffering, every Trade was flushed out to file, roughly every 50 bytes. The default buffer size of BufferedOutputStream is 512, which allowed us to flush multiple Trade records at once and improve efficiency. Typically, flushing one byte at a time will be very costly. Efficiency will improve as the size of the buffer grows. At some point you reach optimal efficiency, and beyond that, you get diminishing returns or even a slight drop in efficiency. Trying to find that "sweet spot," we increased the buffer size from the default of 512 to 4,096:

```
BufferedOutputStream fos =
    new BufferedOutputStream(
        new FileOutputStream("stock.dat"), 4096);
```

We also reduced it to 64 to get the other extreme. It turns out that the default of 512 was close enough to the "sweet spot." See Figure 5.1 (measurements are in seconds; lower is better).

Note that a buffer size of 64 is not much larger than the size of our Trade representation, which forces a flush almost every Trade. The performance of that small buffer was closer to that of no buffering at all.

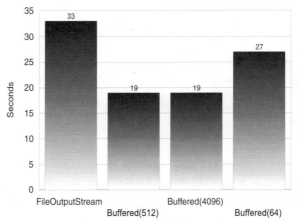

Figure 5.1.   The buffering impact

Optimization 31: Don't Flush Prematurely

Flushing output data should not be an automatic reflex. There are some subtle issues that ought to be considered. As a general rule, you are better off buffering your output data, and you must flush if the progress of the computation depends on it. For example, a socket client sending a request to a server must flush the request; otherwise, the data will get stuck in the output buffer and the client is hung. On the other hand, it would not be smart to flush bits and pieces of the request. The point with flushing is to find the right spot where flushing is necessary and to avoid doing it too often.

Take our application, for example. The only time you may consider flushing is at the end of a transaction. In our case, that occurs when you are done writing all the `Trade` objects. However, if the end of a transaction coincides with the closing of the stream, then you don't have to flush at all because the `close()` call will perform a `flush()` for you. I have seen such code in practice in which periodic flushes are performed unnecessarily. If the application produces enough data to exceed the buffer's capacity, you may want to leave flushing decisions to the buffered stream itself. Let's introduce premature flushing into our code and see what happens. We will use a `BufferedWriter` but will flush it after every `Trade` record:

```
private void out(int n)
      throws FileNotFoundException, IOException {

   Trade buy = new Trade ("01-01-99", true, 100, "IBM", 140);
   Trade sell = new Trade ("01-08-99", false, 100, "IBM", 150);

   BufferedOutputStream fos =
      new BufferedOutputStream(
         new FileOutputStream("stock.dat"));

   long start = System.currentTimeMillis(); // <+++ Start timing
   for (int i = 0; i < n; i++) {  // 1,000,000 iterations
      fos.write(buy.toBytes());
      fos.flush();
      fos.write(sell.toBytes());
      fos.flush();
   }
   long stop = System.currentTimeMillis(); // <+++ Stop timing

   System.out.println( " out time = " + (stop - start) );
   fos.close();
}
```

The million iterations we use to measure this code executed in 38 seconds. See Figure 5.2.

Frequent, periodic flushes completely undermine the buffering mechanism. In our example, it was actually worse than no buffering at all because we invested CPU cycles in copying the data into an intermediate buffer just to turn around

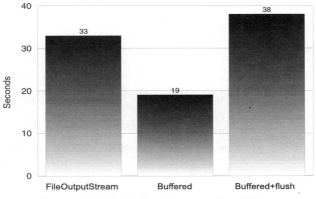

Figure 5.2.   Periodic flush() calls will hurt

and flush it immediately. If we wanted such frequent flushes, we could have chosen a nonbuffered stream instead.

There is one scenario in which you may end up having periodic flushes without calling them explicitly. The `PrintWriter` constructor allows you to specify a boolean argument to indicate your desire to have automatic flush whenever an end-of-line character is encountered:

```
PrintWriter pw =
   new PrintWriter(
      new BufferedWriter(
         new FileWriter("stock.dat")), true);    // autoFlush is turned on
...
long start = System.currentTimeMillis(); // <+++ Start timing
for (int i = 0; i < n; i++) {  // 1,000,000 iterations
   pw.println(buy);    // calls buy.toString() under the covers
   pw.println(sell);    // calls sell.toString() under the covers
}
longstop = System.currentTimeMillis(); // <+++ Stop timing
```

Since the `autoFlush` indicator is true, the `PrintWriter` object will inspect every character that goes through it. This is expensive in itself even if the end-of-line is not encountered. In the case of the `Trade` object representation, we did not include any end-of-line characters in it, but scanning the data for one has significantly slowed down execution of the above writer. A million iterations of the loop executed in 88 seconds. When we used the default `PrintWriter`, the `autoFlush` feature was turned off by default:

```
PrintWriter pw =
   new PrintWriter(
      new BufferedWriter(
         new FileWriter("stock.dat")));    // autoFlush defaults to off
...
```

Execution time of this `PrintWriter` improved to 42 seconds. See Figure 5.3.

Note that this gigantic loss of performance was not due to actual flushes because our `Trade` representation did not contain any new line characters. The drop in performance was purely because the `PrintWriter` had to scan our character stream one character at a time in search of a new line that never showed up.

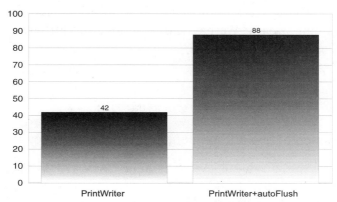

Figure 5.3. The autoFlush feature is a killer

Optimization 32: Prefer Byte Stream to Unicode

You could split the set of output streams to roughly two sets: Those who handle Unicode strings are called writers and the rest handle byte arrays. When you are sending Unicode characters down a writer stream, they eventually reach an underlying sink that may very well be a socket or a file. The problem with those end points is that they don't "talk" Unicode, they "talk" bytes. Somewhere along the way, your Unicode characters must be converted to a byte stream, and that conversion is expensive (see Optimization 4). The writers basically sit on top of more primitive byte streams. The OutputStreamWriter is the bridge class that glues the two sets together by converting a Unicode stream to a byte stream. When you define a FileWriter as in

```
FileWriter fw = new FileWriter;
```

what you really get is equivalent to

```
OutputStreamWriter osw =
   new OutputStreamWriter(
      new FileOutputStream);
```

The writer streams provide a more convenient interface to work with and, as often is the case, convenience trades off with efficiency. Somebody, some-where, has got to do the work on our behalf and it is usually not as fast as we could do ourselves. Let's compare the use of a buffered file writer to a buff-ered file output stream. We have already done the buffered `FileOutputStream` in the previous section. We used

```
BufferedOutputStream fos =
   new BufferedOutputStream(
      new FileOutputStream("stock.dat"));
```

in the execution of one million iterations of the loop below:

```
for (int i = 0; i < n; i++) {   // 1,000,000 iterations
   fos.write(buy.toBytes());
   fos.write(sell.toBytes());
}
```

This loop executed in 19 seconds. We now replace the stream with a writer:

```
BufferedWriter fw =
   new BufferedWriter(
      new FileWriter("stock.dat"));
```

We also have to modify the test loop to fit the `BufferedWriter` interface:

```
for (int i = 0; i < n; i++) {
   fw.write(buy.toString(), 0, buy.toString().length());
   fw.write(sell.toString(), 0, sell.toString().length());
}
```

With this writer, the loop execution time increased to 34 seconds. See Figure 5.4.

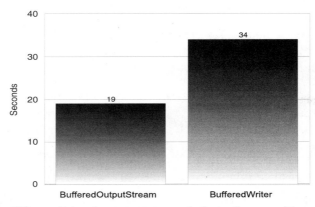

Figure 5.4.   An output stream is faster than a writer

The dramatic difference in performance is due to the char-to-byte conversion overhead incurred by the writer. The `FileOutputStream` skips that step because the output data is already in a byte-stream format. The moral of the story is that, if you have a choice in the matter, you should perform the char-to-byte conversion outside the performance-critical path and then just send a byte array down the stream.

Optimization 33: Input Buffering ∎

We reverse direction now from output to input streams. The issues are analogous, although with a different twist. The most important issue is still buffering. We'll continue driving the discussion with the same program we used earlier only this time instead of writing `Trade` records to file, we will read them in from a file. The code for reading `Trade` records back in is given by

```
private void in() throws IOException {
    Trade buy = null;
    Trade sell = null;
    String line = null;

    DataInputStream dis =
        new DataInputStream(
            new FileInputStream("stock.dat"));

    long start = System.currentTimeMillis(); // <+++ Start timing
    while ((line = dis.readLine()) != null) {    // 100,000 iterations
    }
    long stop = System.currentTimeMillis(); // <+++ Stop timing

    System.out.println( " in time = " + (stop - start) );
    dis.close();
}
```

When we created this file, we used the `println()` method such that `Trade` records are separated by a new line character. Therefore, we need to use an input stream that provides us the ability to read in one line at a time. The `DataInputStream` is one such stream. Notice that the `in()` method as it stands above does not perform any buffering. Using this method to read in a file consisting of 100,000 `Trade` records has taken 40 seconds. (Don't compare this directly to our previous output measurement. Our output tests have written a million records out to file, while here we are only reading 100,000 records.)

This is pretty slow. It is about 10 times slower than it has taken us to write the same number of records out to file. The problem with our code above is that it truly reads in one byte at a time. It is not the fault of the `readLine()` method. The `readLine()` method must inspect every character for line termination, but that does not mean that characters must be read one at a time. The real problem is that the `DataInputStream` is wrapped directly around a nonbuffered input stream such as `FileInputStream`. The `FileInputStream` is simple and stupid—if you ask for a single byte, a physical read of a single byte will take place. What we really want to have is a logical read of a single byte but physical reads of large chunks so that we minimize the overhead per byte. You can get exactly this result if you insert a `BufferedInputStream` between your `DataInputStream` and the `FileInputStream`. So, let's do that:

```
DataInputStream dis =
    new DataInputStream(
        new BufferedInputStream(
            new FileInputStream("stock.dat")));
```

That's a one-line change. The rest of the code remains intact, demonstrating the beauty of the Java I/O library design. Performance of this version improved by almost a whopping 9×, from 40 seconds to 4.7 seconds. See Figure 5.5.

The `readLine()` method still reads one byte at a time, but this time it is not read from an outside source. It is coming from the `BufferedInputStream` object's internal buffer.

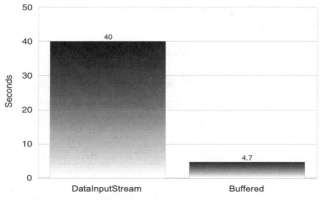

Figure 5.5. Input buffering is highly recommended

We can see the same lesson when we compare

```
FileReader fr = new FileReader("stock.dat");
```

to

```
BufferedReader fr =
    new BufferedReader(
        new FileReader("stock.dat"));
```

This comparison is obvious. In general, we have to strongly consider wrapping our byte streams, readers, and writers with the appropriate buffered one.

Optimization 34: Byte-to-Char Conversions ■

Previously, we saw the way converting Unicode characters to a byte stream could take a toll on performance. A similar issue exists in the reverse direction if a byte stream needs to be converted into Unicode characters. We have already encountered this issue in Optimization 4. There we recommended the use of a deprecated method to do the conversion when ASCII strings are involved. The politically correct way to convert a byte stream into a Unicode stream is by use of the FileReader, as in

```
BufferedReader fr =
    new BufferedReader(
        new FileReader("filename"));
String line = fr.readLine();
```

We tried this approach on our test loop by replacing the FileInputStream with a FileReader:

```
BufferedReader fr =
    new BufferedReader(
        new FileReader("stock.dat"));
String line = null;

long start = System.currentTimeMillis(); // <+++ Start timing
while ((line = fr.readLine()) != null) {  // 100,000 iterations
}
long stop = System.currentTimeMillis();// <+++ Stop timing
```

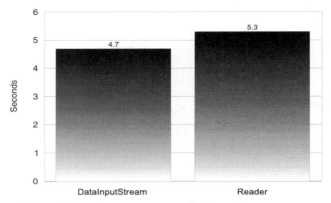

Figure 5.6.   An InputStream is faster than a Reader

Execution time using the FileReader increased to 5.3 seconds. Recall from Optimization 33 that the very same code using a DataInputStream took only 4.7 seconds. See Figure 5.6.

The difference is due to the fact that the DataInputStream readLine() method is "cheating" by blindly casting a byte into a Unicode char. This step works only if the byte represents an ASCII character, but it is fast. If you know that your input byte stream is an ASCII stream, there's no harm in taking this shortcut. Once again, simplifying assumptions and narrowing the computational focus can lead to significant gains in speed. When you need to drill a hole in a brick wall, a narrowly focused laser beam is much more effective than a 60 Watt lightbulb.

Optimization 35: Binary I/O ∎

Up to this point we have focused all our attention on the performance aspects of producing and consuming human-readable I/O. Towards that goal we have stripped away all other computations that might have consumed our precious CPU cycles and clouded the I/O performance picture we were trying to highlight. For example, we constructed the String representation of a Trade object right in the Trade constructor so as to take this computation outside the performance-critical path of our specific test program. There are two major drawbacks to that approach.

- First, this approach is not very realistic. When we read a Trade String representation from the input file, we never bothered to reconstruct the underlying Trade object. We simply tossed away the line we read—not a very realistic solution.

- Second, we have committed a performance sin by computing the Trade String representation inside its constructors. This is a very bad idea. An object, in general, may be used in many different ways without ever needing to call its toString() method. If we call such an expensive method in the object constructor, we are penalizing all users of the class, whether they need this computation or not. One of the points we try to stress in this book is that you need to defer costly computations to the point at which you actually need them (Optimization 12). We have violated this principle in order to drive the I/O performance story.

So let's put the discussion back on more realistic grounds. We will modify the Trade class by taking the String computation out of the constructors and into toString() where it belongs:

```
class Trade implements Serializable {
    String date;
    boolean buy;
    String symbol;
    int numShares;
    float price;

    public Trade (String d,
            boolean b,
            int n,
            String s,
            float p) {
    symbol = s;
    numShares = n;
    buy = b;
    date = d;
    price = p;
}

public Trade (String tr) {
    StringTokenizer st = new StringTokenizer(tr, " ");
    date = st.nextToken();
    if ("Buy".equals(st.nextToken())) {
        buy = true;
    }
```

```
        else {
            buy = false;
        }
        numShares = Integer.parseInt(st.nextToken());
        symbol = st.nextToken();
        price = Float.valueOf(st.nextToken()).floatValue();
    }

    private String privateToString() {
        StringBuffer sb = new StringBuffer(128);

        sb.append(date).append(" ");
        if (buy) {
            sb.append("Buy ");
        }
        else {
            sb.append("Sell ");
        }
        sb.append(numShares).append(" ");
        sb.append(symbol).append(" ");
        sb.append(price).append(" ");

        return sb.toString();
    }

    public String toString() {
        return privateToString();
        }
}
```

Now, whenever we write a Trade object to our human-readable file, we will have to perform the toString() call on the fly, inside the performance-critical path. This will become part of the measurement, as shown by

```
private void out(int n)
            throws FileNotFoundException, IOException {

Trade buy = new Trade ("01-01-99", true, 100, "IBM", 140);
Trade sell = new Trade ("01-08-99", false, 100, "IBM", 150);

BufferedOutputStream fos =
    new BufferedOutputStream (
        new FileOutputStream("stock.dat"));

long start = System.currentTimeMillis();// <+++ Start timing
for (int i = 0; i < n; i++) {  // 1,000,000 iterations
    fos.write(MyGetBytes.asciiGetBytes(buy.toString())); // fast char-to-byte...
```

```
                                               // ...see Optimization 4
    fos.write(MyGetBytes.asciiGetBytes(sell.toString()));  //  fast char-to-byte...
                                               // ...see Optimization 4
    }
    long stop = System.currentTimeMillis();// <+++ Stop timing

    System.out.println( " out time = " + (stop - start) );
    fos.close();
}
```

This time, the conversion of a `Trade` object into a `String` really took place during the measurement. We threw in our ASCII-to-byte converter (`MyGetBytes`) from Optimization 4 trying to help out, to no avail. A million iterations of this loop executed in 94 seconds. Recall that when we "cheated" and precomputed `toString()` ahead of time, execution time was only 19 seconds. The difference between these two resulted from the inclusion of the `Trade.toString()` computation in the new measurement. See Figure 5.7.

This result also explains why we previously had to eliminate this `String` computation. Otherwise, the I/O performance measurement would have been skewed. Important issues such as buffering would seem unimportant by comparison.

In any event, what we have done up to this point is to invent a proprietary `String` representation for `Trade` objects. This would be fine if we have to produce human-readable format. In many instances, though, that's unnecessary. For example, if all the program intends to do is compute capital gains (or losses), then a binary representation of `Trade` objects will do just fine. The

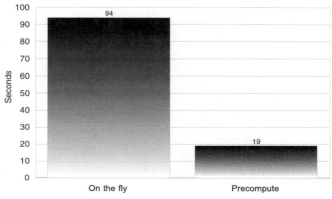

Figure 5.7. The cost of `Trade.toString()`

beauty of it is that we don't have to invent a binary representation for our
`Trade` objects. Java already knows how to represent Java objects in a binary
format: by serialization. The `ObjectOutputStream` and `ObjectInputStream` are
doing all the routine work for us. They make it extremely easy for us users to
serialize and deserialize Java objects. Serializing our `Trade` objects to a file is
as simple as

```
private void out(int n)
        throws FileNotFoundException, IOException {

Trade buy = new Trade ("01-01-99", true, 100, "IBM", 140);
Trade sell = new Trade ("01-08-99", false, 100, "IBM", 150);

ObjectOutputStream oos =
    new ObjectOutputStream(
        new BufferedOutputStream (
            new FileOutputStream("stock.dat")));

    long start = System.currentTimeMillis(); // <+++ Start timing
    for (int i = 0; i < n; i++) {   // 1,000,000 iterations
        oos.writeObject(buy);  //  Magic
        oos.writeObject(sell);  //  Magic
    }
    long stop = System.currentTimeMillis(); // <+++ Stop timing

    System.out.println( " out time = " + (stop - start) );
    oos.close();
}
```

We repeated our test of iterating one million times over the loop, and execution time dropped from 94 seconds for the ASCII representation to 6 seconds
for the binary one. This is more than 15× speedup. See Figure 5.8.

Why is the difference in speed so dramatic? In the first scenario we bounced
the `Trade` objects around from one representation to another. All those transformations were costly. We started with a binary representation of a `Trade`
object in the JVM, then converted it to a Unicode `String`, and then went
through one more transformation to a byte stream representation. In the binary
scenario we have transformed the `Trade` object from a binary JVM format
directly to a byte stream that is essentially another binary format. We skipped
the costly transformations to and from Unicode format.

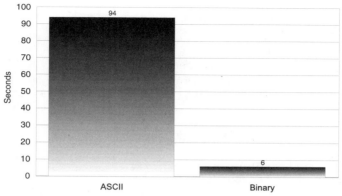

Figure 5.8. Transformations to and from Unicode are expensive

Of course, we have an analogous input story. This time, we are not going to toss away the `String` we read from the input stream. We are going to reconstruct the `Trade` object it stands for. First, the ASCII format:

```
private void in() throws IOException {
    Trade tr = null;
    String line = null;
    DataInputStream dis =
        new DataInputStream(
            new BufferedInputStream(
                new FileInputStream("stock.dat")));

    long start = System.currentTimeMillis(); // <+++ Start timing
    while ((line = dis.readLine()) != null) {
        tr = new Trade(line);  // Reconstruct the Trade object
    }
    long stop = System.currentTimeMillis(); // <+++ Stop timing

    System.out.println( " in time = " + (stop - start) );
    dis.close();
}
```

One hundred thousand iterations of the loop executed in 9.8 seconds. The corresponding code for reading in a 100,000 serialized `Trade` objects in binary format (serialized) is only slightly different. It is given by

```
private void in()
        throws IOException, ClassNotFoundException {
```

```
Trade tr = null;
String line = null;
ObjectInputStream ois =
    new ObjectInputStream(
        new BufferedInputStream(
            new FileInputStream("stock.dat")));
long start = System.currentTimeMillis(); // <+++ Start timing
try {
    while (true) {
        tr = (Trade) ois.readObject();
    }
} catch (EOFException e) { }
long stop = System.currentTimeMillis(); // <+++ Stop timing

System.out.println( " in time = " + (stop - start) );
ois.close();
}
```

One-hundred thousand iterations of this loop executed in 0.9 seconds, an order of magnitude faster than the ASCII format. See Figure 5.9.

The rationale is the same. When we use an ObjectInputStream, the Trade object goes from one binary state (serialized) to another (JVM format). When using a DataInputStream, we go from an ASCII byte-stream format, to Unicode String, and finally to a binary JVM format for a Trade object. Those extra transformations between radically distinct formats take a severe toll on performance.

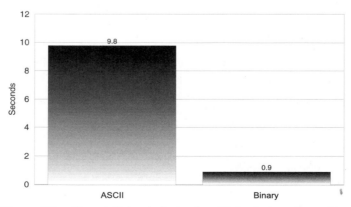

Figure 5.9. Deserializing is faster than Unicode transformations

Key Points

- Output buffering is one of the two big issues with stream output performance. Buffering spreads the fixed cost of an I/O call over a large number of bytes and reduces the cost per byte. There's no need to write any buffering code yourself. The I/O library is already equipped with buffered streams. Just use them.

- Buffering efficiency is sensitive to the size of the underlying buffer. The default sizes seem to be okay. If you choose to conserve memory and lower the size of the buffer, remember that as the size of the buffer decreases, performance gains slowly evaporate.

- Frequent, periodic flushes may undermine the buffering mechanism. Pick your flushing spots carefully.

- If you turn on the `autoFlush` feature of the `PrintWriter`, you can forget about efficiency.

- Conversion of Unicode characters to bytes is expensive. Consequently, it is faster to send a byte array down a stream than a Unicode `String` through a writer.

- Failure to buffer input data will result in physical reads of a single byte at a time. It could degrade performance by an order of magnitude. This loss is worse than a failure to buffer output because your typical output calls will attempt to write more than a single byte.

- The `DataInputStream` will outperform input readers when ASCII streams are being read. The `DataInputStream` performs a proper byte-to-Unicode conversion for ASCII streams only. This is the classic tradeoff between speed and flexibility.

- Not surprisingly, reading and writing binary data is vastly superior (in performance) to reading and writing Unicode characters.

6

Recycling

Regardless of continuous improvements in memory management speed, allocating and eventually discarding objects (via garbage collection) will always impose a nontrivial performance cost on Java programs. Moreover, object creation itself imposes an additional cost of properly setting the initial state of the constructed object via a constructor invocation. Object construction triggers the following steps [LY97]:

- Sufficient memory is allocated to hold all instance variables (object members) as well as those of each superclass.

- All instance variables of this class and those of each superclass are initialized to their default values (numeric variables to 0, boolean to false, reference types to null.)

- Proper values are assigned to the constructor arguments.

- If the constructor starts with an explicit invocation of another constructor of the same class (using this), then that constructor is invoked after evaluation of its arguments.

- Otherwise, implicitly or explicitly, the superclass constructor (super) is invoked after evaluation of its arguments, if any.

- Instance variable initializers are executed for this class as they appear in the source code.

- The rest of the constructor body is executed.

As you can tell, object creation can get expensive very quickly. The cost is proportional to the number of instance variables, the depth of the inheritance chain for the constructed class instance itself, as well as to the complexity of any member object references that are initialized to anything other than null.

The least expensive objects are those that are never constructed. This chapter presents a few optimizations that try to circumvent the whole issue of object construction and destruction by recycling old ones.

Optimization 36: Object Recycling

In general, when faced with an expensive computation, my first question is not How can I speed up this computation?, but rather Can I modify my design to get rid of this computation altogether? It is better to avoid a difficult situation in the first place rather than to find a clever way to get out. The same applies to object creation and garbage collection. It is preferred to restrict the proliferation of objects in Java code rather than to rely on the latest and greatest improvements in the garbage-collection subsystem. One way to limit the creation of new objects is to recycle old ones.

Suppose you have a servlet that uses a Vector object in its response generation. Since a servlet is intended to serve repeated requests in its lifetime, you must decide what to do with this Vector object as it goes from one request to the next. You have a couple options:

One, you could create a new Vector object for every request. Old Vector objects used by earlier requests are going to be garbage collected at some later point.

The second option is to make it a member of the servlet object and recycle it from one invocation to the next. At the end of one request you reset the Vector member and reuse it for the next request. Of course, reseting an object often replicates much of the constructor code, but it avoids memory allocation and therefore should always be faster than new object construction. Consequently, recycling an object is the preferred way to go. It is faster and it reduces the memory footprint, a double bonus. Reduction in memory footprint could help application speed by increasing the effectiveness of the processor cache [BM99].

To quantify the performance win, we tested one million iterations of a loop in which a new Vector object was created every time:

```
String s = "HelloWorld";
String p = null;

long start = System.currentTimeMillis();  // <+++ Start timing
```

```
for (int i = 0; i < n; i++) {
    Vector v = new Vector();
    v.addElement(s);
    v.addElement(s);
    v.addElement(s);
    p = (String) v.elementAt(0);
}
long stop = System.currentTimeMillis();  // <+++ Stop timing
```

We compared it to a second version that recycles the same Vector object from
one iteration to the next:

```
Vector v = new Vector();

long start = System.currentTimeMillis();  // <+++ Start timing

for (int i = 0; i < n; i++) {
    v.clear();                            // Reset the Vector to an initial state
    v.addElement(s);
    v.addElement(s);
    v.addElement(s);
    p = (String) v.elementAt(0);
}

    long stop = System.currentTimeMillis();  // <+++ Stop timing
```

Recycling the Vector object between iterations was faster than creating a new
one every time. See Figure 6.1.

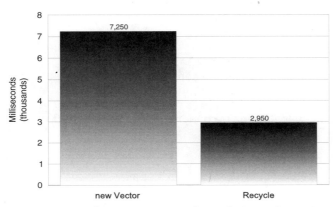

Figure 6.1.   Recycling a Vector was faster than creating a new one

Optimization 37: Object Pools ∎

The previous optimization was made simple by the fact that we knew in advance that we needed only a single Vector object in the course of the computation. If you know in advance that you need only one instance of a resource that is used repeatedly, you could recycle and reuse that same instance over and over. This is actually a degenerate case in which the pool size is 1. In the more general scenario, you don't necessarily have advance knowledge of how many instances are required. It could be 0, 1, or many. In that case, you may have to acquire the resources on the fly but you still want to avoid the cost of creating and destroying expensive resources on a regular basis. The answer here is pooling. After a brief transient state of populating the pool, acquiring and releasing the pooled resource is significantly cheaper because acquire and release operations do not really equate to expensive create and destroy. We merely put and get to and from the pool. Resources that often get pooled are threads, JDBC connections, persistent sockets, as well as other user-defined heavyweight objects.

The following code is a rudimentary object pool:

```
public class ObjectPool {
    protected Object   objects[];
    protected Class    cls;
    protected int      head;

public ObjectPool(String className, int size)
    throws ClassNotFoundException, IllegalArgumentException {

    this(Class.forName(className), size);
}

private ObjectPool(Class p_class, int size)
    throws IllegalArgumentException {

    if((null == p_class) || (size <= 0)) {
        throw new IllegalArgumentException("Invalid arguments");
    }

    head = 0;
    cls = p_class;
    objects = new Object[size];
}
```

```
public Object getObjectFromPool()
    throws InstantiationException, IllegalAccessException {

    Object obj = null;

    synchronized(this) {
    // If there is an available object in
    // the pool, then return it. Else, create
    // a new instance of the class and return it.
        if (head > 0) {
        head--;
        obj = objects[head];
        objects[head] = null;
    }
    else {
        obj = (Object)cls.newInstance();
    }
}

    return obj;
}

public void returnObjectToPool(Object p_object) {
    synchronized(this) {

    // If the size of the pool is large enough to
    // fit the returned object, then add it.
    // Else, increase the size of the pool then
    // add the object.
        if(objects.length > head) {
        objects[head] = p_object;
        head++;
    }
    else {
        expandObjectPool();
        objects[head] = p_object;
        head++;
        }
    }
}

/*
 * By default, double the size of the object pool.
 */
public synchronized void expandObjectPool() {
    Object  newObjectPool[];
```

```
      // Allocate a new object array.
      newObjectPool = new Object[objects.length * 2];

      // Copy objects from original array to the new array.
      System.arraycopy(objects, 0, newObjectPool, 0, objects.length);

      // Make the new array current.
      objects = newObjectPool;

   }
}
```

In Optimization 36 we tested two versions. One did not recycle at all and simply created a brand new Vector object every iteration. The second version recycled the same object. We now extend the recycling notion from a single object to a pool of objects. The test case is very similar to the one used in Optimization 36:

```
private void recycleUsingPool (int n) throws Exception {

   // Create a Vector pool of size 10
   ObjectPool pool = new ObjectPool("java.util.Vector", 10);

   String s = "HelloWorld";
   String p = null;
   Vector v = null;

   long start = System.currentTimeMillis();   // <+++ Start timing

   for (int i = 0; i < n; i++) {
      v = (Vector) pool.getObjectFromPool();

      v.addElement(s);
      v.addElement(s);
      v.addElement(s);
      p = (String) v.elementAt(0);

      v.clear();            // Reset the Vector to an initial state
      pool.returnObjectToPool(v);
   }

   long stop = System.currentTimeMillis();   // <+++ Stop timing
   System.out.println( " time = " + (stop - start) );
}
```

Notice that it is the client's responsibility to reset the Vector via

```
v.clear();
```

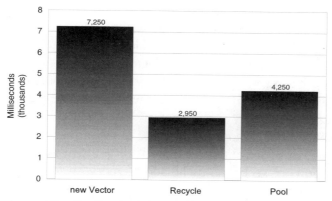

Figure 6.2. Pooling is understandably slower than recycling

prior to freeing it back to the pool. The pool itself, being a container of undetermined objects, does not know how to reset an object to an initial state. Only the caller knows. A million iterations of the loop in `recycleUsingPool()` executed in 4,250 ms. Figure 6.2 compares pooling to the other two variations of recycling a single object and creating one from scratch every time.

As you can tell from Figure 6.2, creating a new object every time is very wasteful. If you are going to need only one object, then you ought to recycle it. If the number of necessary objects is not known in advance, you ought to use object pooling. It beats reliance on the garbage-collection subsystem.

On the downside, keep in mind that pooling is a typical optimization in which speed is gained at the expense of some other software metric. Although pooling could provide a substantial performance kick, it is often more complex than simply creating a new object when you need one. Also, the extra code necessary for proper recycling is error-prone. You must remember to release an object back to the pool and reset it to a proper state. These are some issues you don't have to worry about with automatic garbage collection.

Optimization 38: Last In, First Out

On multithreaded servers you will often encounter a performance requirement to pool server threads. Threads are expensive to create and destroy and therefore are ideally suited for object pooling. This is, however, a special pool with additional performance nuances.

A Java thread can easily drag with it one MB of memory dedicated to required JVM data structures, as well as additional user-defined data. The last thread to hold the CPU has already gone through the work of loading its pages onto memory and a significant portion of its data and code segments onto the instruction and data cache. It would be foolish to throw all this work away. The thread pool should dole out threads in a last in, first out (LIFO) order. That way, we can have lots of threads in the pool (for a rainy day) but only a few that are truly active and using the CPU. This approach makes a much more effective use of the limited cache and memory space. A smaller number of active threads may fit all of their data and code into the cache. A LIFO thread pool keeps the cache and memory "warm." Otherwise, if the pool gives equal opportunity to all its threads, we are likely to have a "cold start" for each thread from a caching and paging perspective. Some containers, such as a `Stack` and `Vector`, automatically lend themselves to the LIFO policy. The `Stack` won't let you do it any other way, and the `Vector` should have elements added and removed from the back only (see Optimization 17). In a linked list, on the other hand, you could erroneously attach your threads to the end of the pool and remove from the front. That would be a costly caching and paging mistake.

Key Points

- Object creation could be expensive. It includes the cost of memory allocation and initialization of the object's direct instance variables as well as those instance variables inherited from each and every superclass.

- Object destruction is performed implicitly as part of garbage collection. Like creation, object destruction is not free. It contributes to the overall cost of garbage collection.

- Many class implementations provide a reset operation to restore an object to its initial state. Often, this is much more economical than polluting the code with new objects. It also lightens the load on garbage collection.

- Recycling a single object is a special case of an object pool of size 1. It is the simplest and fastest recycling mechanism. Otherwise, if you cannot tell in advance how many objects are required during execution, you can still tap into the benefits of recycling by using object pools.

- In the special case of a thread pool, it is more efficient to enforce a LIFO policy to better utilize the system's limited cache and memory space.

7

Scalability and Multithreading

As a server-side programmer, my picture of the world is somewhat distorted by my experience. I have never worked on software that was single-threaded. Multithreaded design and implementation is the backbone of server-side programming, but they are definitely not limited to the server alone. Multithreading comes in handy on the client side as well. Why would you want to multithread your software? Three good reasons immediately come to mind:

- Increased throughput
- Reduced response time
- Better CPU utilization

Take a Web server, for example. Practically all of the dominant Web servers are multithreaded. Each incoming HTTP request is assigned to a server thread that will "escort" the request from its arrival until its departure in the form of a response. That thread could easily get blocked waiting on a page-fault, disk I/O (while reading a file), or socket I/O (waiting to receive data from a CGI script or a database.) If a Web-server thread gets blocked, there are usually plenty of other threads that can step up and continue serving other requests and keep the server cruising at full speed. This is where increased throughput comes into play on the server side. Multithreading also improves CPU utilization because there's usually some thread ready to make productive use of the CPU.

As mentioned earlier, multithreading is not limited to the server side; it also plays a major role on the client side. When you want to bail out of a very slow browser download, you hit the cancel button and the download aborts. If the browser is single-threaded, it isn't very responsive. That single thread becomes tied up with the document download and ignores your plea to abort. Multithreaded programming is what makes the clients appear so responsive.

Multithreaded programming has a special role in Java. When it comes to raw speed, Java programs are slower than C and C++ programs, and that is not going to change any time soon. In theory, you would expect this to be a show-stopper on the server side. In practice, however, Java is now carving itself a significant territory as a viable server-side programming language. This is not just because Java is so portable and its programmers so productive. It is also not because customers all of a sudden abandoned their obsession with perfor-mance. It is, to a large extent, because hardware is cheap and you could always throw in a 12-way SMP monster to elevate Java application performance to the required level. On the other hand, a powerful SMP machine does not guaran-tee improved performance. A serious programming challenge is still facing the Java developers: to design and implement our software in a scalable fashion.

Faced with the task of speeding up a Java application, you generally have the following options:

- *Tune your application.* Reduce the application's pathlength by optimiz-ing the code. This approach has been the focus of our discussion up to this point: speeding up a single thread of execution regardless of the underlying machine architecture (UP or SMP.)

- *Upgrade processing speed.* A faster CPU should result in faster execu-tion for CPU-bound workloads.

- *Add processors.* A multiprocessor machine consists of multiple CPUs. In theory, multiple CPUs should outperform a single CPU of identical speed. This is what scalability is all about.

The challenge in scalability for an application code is to keep up with the addi-tional processing power. When you move an application from a uniprocessor to a two-way multiprocessor, it would be nice if you could double execution speed. Would your application run four times as fast on a four-way multipro-cessor? Most applications will not exhibit such perfect linear scaling, but the goal is to get as close as you can.

Scalability Basics

To understand software performance and scalability issues on a multiproces-sor, we have to have a rudimentary grasp of the underlying architecture. Since multiprocessors evolved out of uniprocessors, let's step back and start with a quick overview of the uniprocessor computer architecture. The mainstream uniprocessor architecture consists of a single CPU and a single main memory module. Program data and instructions reside in main memory. Since CPU speed is at least an order of magnitude faster than memory, we also have an additional (very) fast memory inserted between the processor (= CPU) and main memory. This fast memory is also known as the cache. The cache provides faster access to program data and instructions. The cache may be split into two physical units, one for data and another for instructions. We'll ignore that distinction and refer to it as a single logical entity. The processor needs at least one memory access per instruction in order to retrieve the instruction itself. On most instructions the processor may need additional memory references for data. When the processor needs memory access, it looks in the cache first. Since cache hit-ratios are upwards of 90 percent, slow trips to main memory are infrequent. This whole story is summarized in Figure 7.1.

An application is a single process or a set of cooperating processes. Each process consists of one or more threads. The scheduling entity on modern operating systems is a thread. The operating system does not execute a process, it executes a thread. Threads that are ready to execute are placed on the system's run queue. The thread at the front of the queue is next in line for execution (Figure 7.2).

Modern uniprocessor machines are controlled by preemptive multitasking operating systems. An operating system of that type creates the illusion of

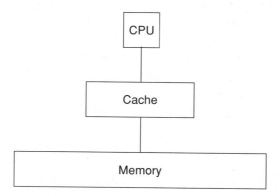

Figure 7.1. The Uniprocessor architecture

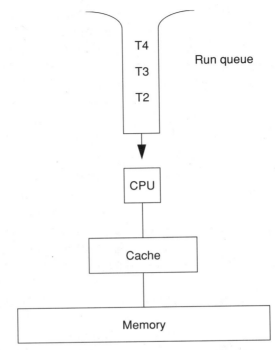

Figure 7.2.   Threads are the scheduling entities

concurrent program execution. From the user's point of view, multiple programs appear to be executing simultaneously. As you know, this is not the case. At the hardware level, there's only one CPU and only one thread of execution at any one time. Multitasking on a uniprocessor is accomplished by having threads take turns using the CPU, frequently switching between threads to maintain the illusion of true parallel execution.

With this picture of a uniprocessor architecture tucked away, we are now ready to move on to multiprocessors. Faithful to our 80–20 principle, we will focus the discussion on the dominant multiprocessor architecture. This is the symmetric multiprocessor, otherwise known as SMP.

The SMP Architecture

The name SMP already describes its characteristics:

- It is a multiprocessor (MP). The system consists of multiple identical CPUs.

- It is symmetric. All processors have an identical view of the system. They all have the same capabilities. For example, they have identical access to any location in memory as well as to any I/O device.

- Everything else is single. It has a single memory system, a single copy of the operating system, a single run queue.

Figure 7.3 depicts the architecture.

Unless your application code bends over backwards, threads have no affinity to any particular CPU. The same thread may execute on CPU_1 in one particular time-slice and CPU_2 on the next time-slice. Another idea shown in Figure 7.3 is that multiple threads really do execute simultaneously. While thread T1 executes on CPU_1, thread T2 may very well execute on CPU_2. Since the scheduling entity is a thread, there's nothing to prevent threads T1 and T2 from belonging to the same process. In this case, it is very likely that they will access the same memory locations on a regular basis. That brings us to the next issue: There is only one bus connecting the processors to the memory system. The bus is the major bottleneck in SMP systems and the chief reason why 256-way SMP machines are not commonplace. Bus contention would bring them to a grinding halt.

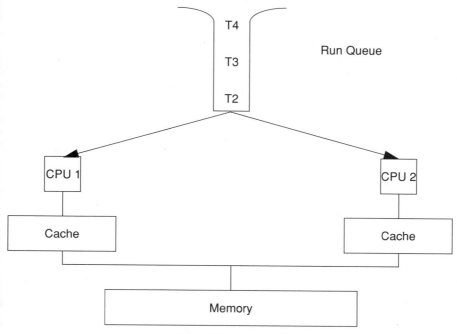

Figure 7.3. The SMP architecture

The solution to bus contention is large on-chip caches—one per processor. A large on-chip cache would make bus trips infrequent, but would raise a new problem: What if two distinct caches both have a copy of a variable, x, and one of the processors updates its private copy? The other cache might have a stale, incorrect, value for x; we hate when that happens. This is the *cache consistency* problem. The SMP architecture provides a hardware solution for it. The details are not terribly important; all we need to know is that when variable x gets updated, all of its other cache copies eventually get updated, as well as the main memory master copy. The cache-consistency hardware solution is completely invisible to the application software.

The SMP architecture offers potential scalability. Obviously, the number of processors presents an easy upper bound. Typically, you cannot get more than 8× speedup on an eight-way SMP. The practical scalability limit may be even tighter than that. We explore that practical limit next.

Amdahl's Law

Amdhal's law quantifies the fact that the sequential portion of an application will put a lid on its potential scalability. This law is best illustrated by a matrix multiplication example that consists of three stages:

- Initialization—read in the matrices data values.
- Multiplication—multiply the two matrices.
- Presentation—present the resulting matrix.

Let's assume further that the whole computation takes 10 ms, broken down as follows (these numbers are completely fictitious but help illustrate the point):

- Initialization—2 ms
- Multiplication—6 ms
- Presentation—2 ms

Over the years, many clever parallel algorithms have been developed to exploit multiprocessor architectures to speed up the second phase, that of matrix multiplication. The initialization and presentation phases are a different story. Practically, these two stages in the computation are sequential. In the ideal

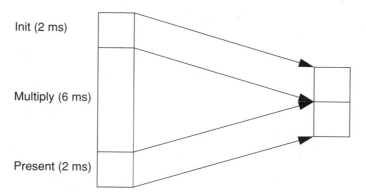

Init (2 ms)

Multiply (6 ms)

Present (2 ms)

Figure 7.4. Potential speedup is limited

world, an unlimited number of parallel processors could, in theory, reduce the multiplication stage to 0 ms. But they would not help at all with the other two sequential stages, as shown by Figure 7.4.

In the figure, an unlimited number of parallel processors has only reduced a 10 ms computation to 4 ms. The multiplication phase has been reduced to 0 ms but the initialization and presentation stages still take 2 ms each. Looks as if 2.5× is the speedup limit for this particular application on any SMP system regardless of the number of processors.

Sequential computations are the major roadblock on the way to scalability. In the following sections we will enumerate ways to eliminate or at least minimize sequential computations. Before we go there, we need to briefly clarify some terminology.

Multithreaded and Synchronization Terminology

This is not the first time that we have run into synchronization terminology. We have already used terms such as synchronization, critical sections, race condition, and locks. We never really explained them, and it is time to step back now and clarify the terminology.

Take a simple code statement such as

```
x = x + 1;
```

If two threads execute this statement, we expect the resulting value stored in x
to be x+2. Any other value would be incorrect. The problem with this code
statement is that it is not executed atomically. After compiling it into the
native machine assembler instructions, it is actually broken into a small number of instructions:

```
load    x, r5 // load the value of x into register r5
add     r5, 1 // add 1 to register r5
store   r5, x // store the value of register r5 into x
```

If two threads execute the above code at roughly the same time, their instruction execution could interleave in a way that would result in x+1 stored as the
new value of x instead of x+2. That unfortunate interleaving of thread execution is called a race condition. The solution to this race condition is to guarantee that this block of assembler statements executes atomically. We call that
block a critical section. Once a thread enters a critical section, no other thread
can enter until the first one leaves. In that case, we say that the two threads are
synchronized and that the critical section is mutually exclusive. Because the
variable x is accessed by more than a single thread, it is considered shared
data. Critical sections always revolve around access to shared data. To guarantee safe access to shared data (and correct execution), we use a synchronized
block or a synchronized method. To protect the variable x in

```
x = x+1;
```

we could use one of three options. The first is a synchronized method:

```
class C {
   private int x;
   ...
   public synchronized void plusOne() {
      x = x+1;
   }
}
```

The second option is a synchronized block:

```
class C {
   private int x;
   ...
   public void someMethod() {
```

```
    ...
    synchronized (this) {
        x = x+1;
    }
    ...
    }
}
```

Both options above are using the same lock to protect concurrent access to member x. Every Java object has an associated lock. When you invoke

```
cObject.someMethod()
```

or

```
cObject.plusOne()
```

both methods use the lock associated with cObject in order to lock the shared resource. Alternatively, we could use an entirely different object to lock on:

```
class C {
    private int x;
    private Object myLock = new Object();
    ...
    public void someMethod() {
        ...
        synchronized (myLock) {
            x = x+1;
        }
        ...
    }
}
```

This time, the synchronized block uses the lock associated with the member object myLock to protect concurrent access to member x. This ability to lock on an external object can be used to improve scalabilty. We will elaborate on this point later.

A thread must check the state of the lock prior to entering the synchronized region. If the lock is off, no other thread is currently executing in the synchronized region, nor any other code fragment synchronized on the object. Consequently, access permission is granted and the state of the lock status is changed to reflect it. If the lock is on, the thread must wait until the lock status is turned off by the thread currently executing the synchronized code. When a code segment is protected by a lock, we often say that its execution is sequential. Multiple threads wanting to enter the synchronized code have to line up and enter one at a time.

With this terminology out of the way, we move on to discuss ways to alleviate the scalability bottlenecks inherent in sequential execution.

The Cost of Synchronization

Multithreaded programming is a tricky business and if you don't watch your step you could get into trouble with race conditions, deadlock, starvation, and other landmines associated with concurrency. Defects resulting from race conditions are particularly difficult to debug. If concurrency is so delicate, why don't we just synchronize everything and be done with it? From a performance standpoint, there are at least two good reasons why we should use synchronization very sparingly. First is the overhead of the synchronization mechanism itself. Somewhere, a lock must be acquired and released before and after the synchronized code. For instance, take the simple operation of integer increment. We will measure its speed with and without synchronization:

```
class Counter {

private long counter;
private static long sharedCounter;

public static void main(String args[]) {

    int n = Integer.parseInt(args[0]);
    Counter c = new Counter();

    long start = System.currentTimeMillis();  // <+++ Start timing
    for (int i = 0; i < n; i++) {
        c.bumpCounter();
    }
    long stop = System.currentTimeMillis();  // <+++ Stop timing

    System.out.println("Execution time = " + (stop - start));
}
```

```
public void bumpCounter() {
    counter++;
}

public static synchronized void bumpSharedCounter() {
    sharedCounter++;
    }
}
```

We invoked this program using

```
Java Counter 1000000
```

to execute one million iterations of the loop

```
for (int i = 0; i < n; i++) {
    c.bumpCounter();
}
```

where `bumpCounter()` is unsynchronized. We then replaced `bumpCounter()` with its synchronized counterpart `bumpSharedCounter()`

```
for (int i = 0; i < n; i++) {
    c.bumpSharedCounter();
}
```

The unsynchronized method ran almost two orders of magnitude faster than the synchronized one. See Figure 7.5.

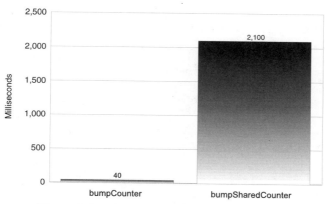

Figure 7.5.   Synchronized methods are slower

The gap here is exaggerated by the fact that we make frequent calls to the synchronized method. The method itself does very little, and this highlights the synchronization overhead.

Let's get a little more realistic. We need a comparison in which the measured code tries to perform some work other than just pounding on the shared lock. We have a perfect example in the JDK itself—a comparison of `ArrayList` to `Vector`. One of the user complaints against the JDK implementation of the `Vector` class was originally that all access methods were synchronized, penalizing those who wanted to use a `Vector` object whose manipulation was confined to a single thread. The solution arrived in Java 2 in the form of an `ArrayList`. The `ArrayList` is essentially an unsynchronized `Vector`. If we give those two classes a workout, we'll have another data point for the overhead of synchronization.

Our test case will perform repeated traversal of a 1,000-element `Vector` and `ArrayList`. The `Vector` version is shown first:

```
private void vectorIterate(int n) {
String s = "HelloWorld";

Vector v = new Vector(1000);
for (int i = 0; i < 1000; i++) {  // Populate the vector
   v.addElement(s);
}

long start = System.currentTimeMillis();  // <+++ Start timing
for (int j = 0; j < n; j++) {
   for (int i = 0;i < v.size();i++) {
      s = (String) v.elementAt(i);
   }
}
long stop = System.currentTimeMillis();  // <+++ Stop timing

   System.out.println(" time = " + (stop - start) );
}
```

The corresponding version for `ArrayList` is similar:

```
private void ArrayListIterate(int n) {
   String s = "HelloWorld";
```

```
ArrayList al = new ArrayList(1000);
for (int i = 0; i < 1000; i++) {  // Populate the ArrayList
    al.add(s);
}

long start = System.currentTimeMillis();  // <+++ Start timing
for (int j = 0; j < n; j++) {
    for (int i = 0;i<al.size();i++) {
        s = (String) al.get(i);
    }
}
long stop = System.currentTimeMillis();   // <+++ Start timing

System.out.println(" time = " + (stop - start) );
}
```

The code for the ArrayList has executed faster than the one for Vector. See Figure 7.6. This is not surprising. The overhead of synchronization is weighing down on Vector speed. However, the gap was not as drastic as in our first example. The magnitude of the synchronization penalty will vary among applications. The fact remains, however, that synchronization itself imposes some additional cost. Unsynchronized code will always be somewhat faster in a straight-line execution.

The cost of executing the synchronization instructions is actually the less important issue. The major issue with careless synchronization is the impact of thread contention on performance. Frequent contention for locks will prevent a thread

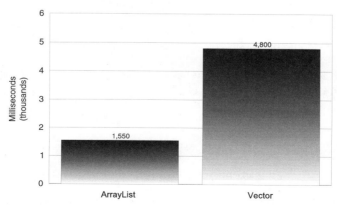

Figure 7.6. ArrayList is unsynchronized and consequently faster

from having a smooth ride through its CPU time-slice. It will force frequent context switches when the executing thread fails to acquire the lock used by the synchronized method or block. Context switches are expensive and, if they happen too often, performance will suffer. The following program moves the Counter class above into a multithreaded arena. We will let multiple threads contend for access to the counter.

```java
class MtCounter {
    public static void main(String args[]) {
        try {
            if(args.length != 2) {
                System.out.println("Usage java MtCounter" +
                                    " <count> <numThreads>");
                return;
            }

            int count = Integer.parseInt(args[0]);
            int numThreads = Integer.parseInt(args[1]);

            WorkerThread mc[] = new WorkerThread[numThreads];

            for(int i = 0; i < numThreads; i++) {
                mc[i] = new WorkerThread(count,i);  // Create the threads
            }

            long start = System.currentTimeMillis();  // <+++ Start timing
            for(int i = 0; i < numThreads; i++) {
                mc[i].start();  // Launch the threads
            }

            for(int i = 0; i < numThreads; i++) {
                mc[i].join();
            }
            long stop = System.currentTimeMillis();  // <+++ Start timing

            System.out.println("Execution time = " + (stop - start));
        } catch(Exception e) {
            System.err.println(e);
        }
    }
}

class WorkerThread extends Thread {
    private int iter;
    private int tid;
    private static long sharedCounter;
```

```
public WorkerThread(int iterationCount, int id) {
    this.iter = iterationCount;
    this.tid = id;
}

public void run() {
    for(int i = 0; i < iter; i++) {
        bumpSharedCounter();
    }
}

public synchronized static void bumpSharedCounter() {
    sharedCounter++;
}

}
```

The `MtCounter` `main()` method takes two arguments specifying the number of iterations per thread and the number of threads, as in

```
java MtCounter <count> <numThreads>
```

I decided that the overall "task" for this program would be to bump the `sharedCounter` from 0 to 1,000,000. This task is going to be accomplished collectively by a number of parallel threads. If I invoke

```
java MtCounter 1000000 1
```

then a single thread is going to do the whole task. Alternatively, I could divide the work among two threads:

```
java MtCounter 500000 2
```

In this invocation, each thread will do half the work, bumping the counter 500,000 times each. Even though I increase the level of concurrency, I keep the total amount of work constant. Figure 7.7 displays the result of our experiment relating the number of threads to the execution time of the program. This experiment was executed on a 12-way AIX SMP server (12X166 MHz.)

As you can tell from Figure 7.7, as we increased the contention level for the synchronization lock of this class, performance went down. It wasn't so bad going from no contention (single thread) to light contention (two threads), but execu-

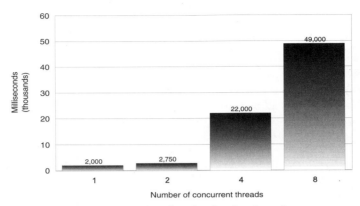

Figure 7.7. Synchronization bottlenecks

tion time took a severe hit when we increased the number of concurrent threads to 4. But don't be scared away from using multiple threads. In practice, you are not likely to see a large number of threads doing nothing other than pound relentlessly on a single lock. Realize, however, that high-contention locks will impact performance negatively. This chapter has tried to help you in developing effective techniques to achieve the computational tasks facing a multithreaded application while keeping the levels of thread contention under control.

Optimization 39: Parallel Subtasks ■

In order to unleash potential scalability, your application must divide its computational task into multiple subtasks that could be executed in parallel. A Web server is a good example. The computational task is to service multiple client requests as they arrive on a designated HTTP port. If your Web server is single-threaded, it can perform only one request at a time. All other requests have to queue up. To enable scalability we must break up the service task. The task of servicing all the requests on the queue is split into smaller subtasks of serving a single request. By unleashing multiple threads on the smaller subtasks, we can achieve true parallelism and scalability. Breaking up the Web service into parallel subtasks improves several performance indicators:

- Response time of an individual request
- Server throughput in requests per second
- Server CPU utilization

A Web server performs frequent blocking I/O operations. If the server consists of a single thread, no work is performed while waiting on I/O completion. A multithreaded server would just switch over to perform other tasks and keep the processors humming. The result is better throughput and higher CPU utilization. One thing that could certainly make customers unhappy is seeing their 12-way SMP server at 25 percent CPU utilization.

Starting from a single-threaded application, you are likely to see throughput rise significantly as you move into multithreaded territory and increase the number of concurrent threads. As you increase the level of concurreny, you will eventually reach a point of peak throughput. If you continue to increase the number of threads beyond this "sweet spot," you are not going to see any more gains in performance. If you keep on going, eventually throughput and other performance measures are going to plummet. Multithreading is like sugar. It could get to the point where it is just too much. Too many threads create higher contention for resources, and they eat up cache and memory space. Shortage of cache and memory space lead to costly cache misses and page faults. This could degrade performance by an order of magnitude.

In Chapter 11 we develop a scalable multithreaded Java Web server. We control the number of server threads via a configuration property. We experimented with various levels of multithreading to exhibit the interaction between concurrency and throughput. We ran the Java Web server on a four-way SMP (Pentium-II, 4X200 MHz) running NT. Figure 7.8 charts the mapping from number of concurrent threads to server throughput measured by requests per second.

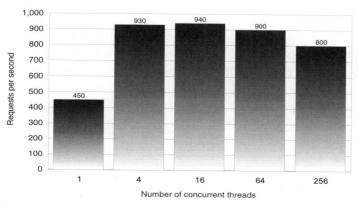

Figure 7.8. The relationship between concurrency and throughput

Optimization 40: Synchronization False Sharing ■

Every Java object and class has a single lock associated with it. If you synchronize on an object via a synchronized method or block, you are locking up the object. If two synchronized methods in the same object try to access completely unrelated resources, they will lock each other out. This is a case of false sharing, where two logically unrelated operations are forced to physically share the object's lock. The same point applies to the class lock in the case of static shared resources.

Take, for instance, a multithreaded Web server listening on both HTTP and HTTPS (otherwise known as SSL) ports. Most reasonable implementations of a Web server will make some rudimentary statistics available to the Webmaster. At the very least, they will keep track of the number of HTTP and HTTPS requests:

```
class HTStats {
    private static int httpReqs;
    private static int sslReqs;
    ...
};
```

Since multiple threads may try to manipulate the statistics concurrently, such manipulations must be synchronized:

```
public synchronized static void addHttpReq() {
    httpReqs++;  // Increment the counter for HTTP requests.
}

public synchronized static void addSslReq() {
    sslReqs++;  // incement the counter for HTTPS requests.
}
```

The HTStats class uses a single lock to protect the manipulation of all of its static counters. Fusing multiple unrelated shared resources under the umbrella of a single lock is normally a bad idea. It widens the scope of the synchronized regions and creates friction among otherwise independent threads. The only possible exception to this rule is when both of the following two conditions are satisfied:

- All of the shared resources are always manipulated together.

- None of the manipulations of the shared resources consume significant CPU cycles.

In the case of counting HTTP and SSL requests, the second condition was satisfied (shared counters; updates are fast) but the first condition was broken: A thread that updated one counter did not access the other. An SSL thread might update the SSL counter but have no interest in the state of the HTTP counter. The preferred solution is to have two distinct locks protecting two unrelated counters so that the contention for each lock is reduced by half:

```
class HTStats {
   private static int httpReqs;
   private static Object lockHttp = new Object();
   private static int sslReqs;
   private static Object lockSsl = new Object();
   ...
   public static void addHttpReq() {
      synchronized (lockHttp) {
         httpReqs++;  // Increment the counter for HTTP requests.
      }
   }

   public static void addSslReq() {
      synchronized(lockSsl) {
         sslReqs++;  // incement the counter for HTTPS requests.
      }
   }
};
```

The updates for HTTP and SSL counters will now use two distinct locks belonging to the objects lockSsl and lockHttp. The above implementation increases scalability. It prevents the sets of SSL and HTTP threads from getting in each other's way.

Let's put up some numbers in support of this theory. MtTwoCounters.java is a multithreaded program that updates two independent shared counters. Half the threads will update one counter, and the other half will update the second. The code is given by

```
class MtTwoCounters {
   public static void main(String args[]) {
      try {
         if(args.length != 2) {
            System.out.println("Usage java MtTwoCounters <count> <numThreads>");
            return;
         }
         int count = Integer.parseInt(args[0]);
```

```java
            int numThreads = Integer.parseInt(args[1]);
            WorkerThread mc[] = new WorkerThread[numThreads];
            for(int i = 0; i < numThreads; i++) {
                mc[i] = new WorkerThread(count,i);
            }
            long start = System.currentTimeMillis();   // <++++ Start timing
            for(int i = 0; i < numThreads; i++) {
                mc[i].start();
            }
            for(int i = 0; i < numThreads; i++) {
                mc[i].join();
            }
            long stop = System.currentTimeMillis();   // <++++ Stop timing

            System.out.println("Execution time = " + (stop - start));
        { catch(Exception e) {
            System.err.println(e);
        }
    }
}

class WorkerThread extends Thread {

    private int iter;
    private int tid;
    private static long counter1;
    private static long counter2;
    private static Object lock = new Object();

    public WorkerThread(int iterationCount, int id) {
        this.iter=iterationCount;
        this.tid = id;
    }

    public void run() {
        if ((tid % 2) == 0) {
            for (int i = 0; i < iter; i++) {
                bumpCounter1();
                }
        }
        else {
            for (int i = 0; i < iter; i++) {
                bumpCounter2();
            }
        }
    }
```

```
public static void bumpCounter1() {
    synchronized(lock) {
        counter1++;
    }
}

public static void bumpCounter2() {
    synchronized(lock) {
        counter2++;
    }
}
}
```

The way this code is structured right now, both methods bumpCounter1() and bumpCounter2() are synchronized on the same lock object. Invoking

```
java MtTwoCounters 1000000 4
```

creates four threads, each of which, bumps its target counter one million times. Execution time for this version was 85 seconds on a 12-way AIX SMP server. We then replaced the single lock object with two independent locks:

```
class WorkerThread extends Thread {
    ...
    private static Object lock1 = new Object();
    private static Object lock2 = new Object();
    ...
    public void bumpCounter1() {
        synchronized(lock1) {
            counter1++;
        }
    }

    public void bumpCounter2() {
        synchronized(lock2) {
            counter2++;
        }
    }
    ...
}
```

Introducing two lock objects in place of one has cut the contention by a half. The new execution time has dropped dramatically, from 85 to 18 seconds. See Figure 7.9.

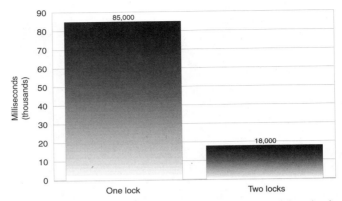

Figure 7.9. Fixing lock contention resulting from false sharing

Notice that the impact of lock contention on performance is not linear. Cutting lock contention by 2× has resulted in 5× speedup.

Optimization 41: Lock Fusion

In the previous optimization we lobbied in favor of splitting two unrelated updates under the protection of two independent lock objects. On the other extreme, if two shared resources are related to one another and their updates seem to happen in tandem, it does make sense to fuse those two updates under the protection of a single object lock. Let's continue along the lines of a Web-server implementation. Suppose that the server not only records the number of HTTP and SSL requests, but also the number of bytes served for each protocol. The class keeping track of those statistics is HTStats:

```
class HTStats {
    private static int httpReqs;  //  Number of requests.
    private static Object lockHttpReqs = new Object();
    private static int httpBytes;  //  Number of bytes served.
    private static Object lockHttpBytes = new Object();
    ...
    public static void updateHttpStats(int bytes) {
        addHttpReq();
        addHttpBytes(bytes);
    }

    public static void addHttpReq() {
    synchronized (lockHttpReqs) {
```

```
            httpReqs++;  // Increment the counter for HTTP requests.
        }
    }

    public static void addHttpBytes(int bytes) {
        synchronized (lockHttpBytes) {
            httpBytes += bytes;  // Increment the counter for HTTP bytes.
        }
    }

};
```

As is stands, the methods for updating the HTTP requests and byte counters are
using distinct objects to provide synchronization. The updateHttpStats(), however, always updates those two counters together. It seems to make more sense to
fuse those two counters under the same synchronized block. That's the theoretical
solution. Let's see what happens in practice. We develop a test case that closely
mimics the above scenario. The scaffolding of the test is pretty much the same as
previous tests: We launch a few threads, give them something to do and measure it:

```
class MtFusion {
    public static void main(String args[]) {
        try {
            if(args.length != 2) {
                System.out.println("Usage java MtFusion <count> <numThreads>");
                return;
            }

            int count = Integer.parseInt(args[0]);
            int numThreads = Integer.parseInt(args[1]);

            WorkerThread mc[] = new WorkerThread[numThreads];

            for(int i = 0; i < numThreads; i++) {
                mc[i] = new WorkerThread(count,i); // Create the threads
            }

            long start = System.currentTimeMillis(); // <++++ Start timing
            for(int i = 0; i < numThreads; i++) {
                mc[i].start(); // Threads get going here
            }

            for(int i = 0; i < numThreads; i++) {
                mc[i].join(); // Wait for threads to finish
            }
            long stop = System.currentTimeMillis(); // <++++ Stop timing
```

```
                System.out.println("Execution time = " + (stop - start));
        } catch(Exception e) {
            System.err.println(e);
        }
    }
}
```

What dominates the execution time is the run() method of the WorkerThread objects:

```
class WorkerThread extends Thread {

    private int iter;
    private int tid;
    private static long counter1;
    private static long counter2;
    private static Object lock = new Object();
    private static Object lock1 = new Object();
    private static Object lock2 = new Object();

    public WorkerThread(int iterationCount, int id) {
        this.iter=iterationCount;
        this.tid = id;
    }

    public void run() {
        for (int i = 0; i < iter; i++) {
            bumpCounter1();
            bumpCounter2();

        }
    }

    public static void bumpCounter1() {
        synchronized(lock1) {
            counter1++;
        }
    }

    public static void bumpCounter2() {
        synchronized(lock2) {
            counter2++;
        }
    }

}
```

In the first scenario we made two distinct calls to bump `counter1` and `counter2`. Each counter was protected by a distinct lock. We invoked this test by

```
java MtFusion 1000000 4
```

which launched four threads. Each of these threads executed one million iterations of the loop in `run()`. Execution time for this version was 22,000 milliseconds (22 seconds). We then modified the `run()` method to fuse the two synchronized blocks into a single block under the protection of a single lock:

```
public void run() {
    for (int i = 0; i < iter; i++) {
        bumpBothCounters();
        }
    }
}

public static void bumpBothCounters() {
    synchronized(lock) {
        counter1++;
        counter2++;
    }
}
```

We traded two "thin" blocks for a single "fat" block. The experimental data supported that decision. The second version (employing lock fusion) has improved execution time from 22,000 milliseconds to 12,500. See Figure 7.10.

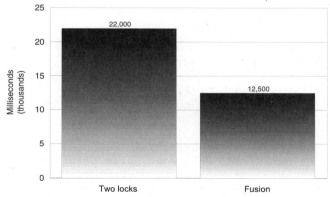

Figure 7.10. Lock fusion may be helpful

Optimization 42: Code Motion ∎

Splitting a sequential task into parallel subtasks is just the first step. Beyond that we must structure our multithreaded code to allow the subtasks to execute independently and minimize friction among the threads executing those parallel subtasks. The most common friction among threads is the contention for shared resources. When a thread acquires exclusive access to a shared resource, all other threads that want access to that resource must wait. We therefore must speed up execution inside the synchronized blocks and methods and release shared resources as fast as possible.

Code motion is often associated with loop optimization [BEN82]. A computation whose value is constant across loop iterations should not be performed inside a loop. It ought to be computed once before entering the loop. Similarly, the critical section should only contain critical computations. The critical computations are those that directly manipulate shared resources. All other computations ought to be performed outside the critical section. We discuss an example of code motion below.

Imagine a multithreaded application that must log some data to a shared file (a Web server must log every request, for example). We will mimic such an application with the code below. The main program creates a number of parallel threads whose run() method attempts to log data to the shared file. The shared file itself is created and closed by the main program. An output stream reference is provided to the threads as a constructor argument:

```
import java.io.*;

class CodeMotion {
    public static void main(String args[]) {
        try {
            if(args.length != 2) {
                System.out.println("Usage java CodeMotion <count> <numThreads>");
                return;
            }
            int count = Integer.parseInt(args[0]);
            int numThreads = Integer.parseInt(args[1]);
            WorkerThread mc[] = new WorkerThread[numThreads];
            BufferedOutputStream fos =
                new BufferedOutputStream (
```

```
                    new FileOutputStream("print.out"));
            for(int i = 0; i < numThreads; i++) {
                mc[i] = new WorkerThread(count,i,fos);
            }
            long start = System.currentTimeMillis();  // <++++ Start timing
            for(int i = 0; i < numThreads; i++) {
                mc[i].start();
            }
            for(int i = 0; i < numThreads; i++) {
                mc[i].join();
            }
            long stop = System.currentTimeMillis();  // <++++ Stop timing

            fos.close();
            System.out.println("Execution time = " + (stop - start));
        } catch(Exception e) {
            System.err.println(e);
        }
    }
}

class WorkerThread extends Thread {
    private int iter;
    private int tid;
    private BufferedOutputStream fos;
    private static Object lock = new Object();

    public WorkerThread(int iterationCount,
                                int id,
                                BufferedOutputStream fos ) {
        this.iter=iterationCount;
        this.tid = id;
        this.fos = fos;
    }

    public void run() {
        try {
            for (int i = 0; i < iter; i++) {
                log("a", i, "c");
            }
        } catch (IOException e) {
            System.out.println(e);
        }
    }

    public void log(String part1,
                    int part2,
                    String part3) throws IOException {
```

```
        synchronized(lock) {
            fos.write((part1+part2+part3).getBytes());
        }
    }
}
```

The threads are using `log()` to write data to the shared file. This method receives two `String` objects and an `int` as input parameters. It then uses these parameters to construct a `String` and convert it into a byte array inside of the synchronized block. Invocation of

```
java CodeMotion 10000 32
```

triggers the launching of 32 threads, each writing 10,000 messages to the shared file. On a four-way NT SMP server (Pentium-II, 4X200 MHz) we achieved 23 seconds execution time. We then modified the implementation of `log()` to compute the `String` and the byte array before entering the synchronized block:

```
public void log(String part1,
                int part2,
                String part3) throws IOException {
    byte[] bytes = (part1+part2+part3).getBytes();
    synchronized(lock) {
        fos.write(bytes);
    }
}
```

With this modification, execution time dropped from 23 seconds to 8. Notice that we did not cut down on the amount of work performed by each thread. We simply moved some of it outside the synchronized block. See Figure 7.11.

It is generally important to keep synchronized code as small as you can. The only code that goes inside a synchronized region is code that directly manipulates a shared resource. In our previous example, writing to a file counted as manipulating a shared resource, but creating the `String` object and converting it into a byte array did not. They could have been safely done outside the synchronized code since those `String` objects were not shared. The significant boost in performance was due to the fact that we drastically narrowed the time each thread spent in the synchronized block. Smaller, faster, synchronized code improves chances for multiple threads to move through the critical sections without colliding.

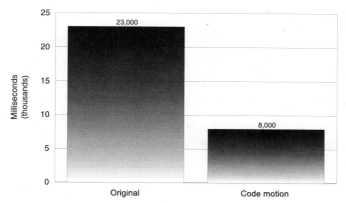

Figure 7.11. Code motion reduces lock contention

Optimization 43: Share Nothing

In the previous section (Optimization 42) we established the validity of the principle calling for a reduction in the amount of computation (and hence CPU cycles) executed inside synchronized code. In the most extreme form of this principle we eliminate sharing altogether, leading to the elimination of the synchronized code. In this chapter we introduce various techniques to minimize time spent in synchronized code, but erasing it altogether is even better. Your first question when faced with a synchronization hot spot should be: Can I restructure my design so as to eliminate the need for synchronization?

Let's look at a concrete example involving a Web-server implementation. In Chapter 11 we develop a multithreaded Web server. One type of Web server is a file server for HTML documents. A Web server that does not perform file caching (such as in the early releases of the popular Apache server) will be slowed down by file I/O. The typical solution employed by many Web-server implementations is to cache HTML documents in a memory-resident cache managed by the server. There's typically a single cache object shared by all threads of the multithreaded server. This shared cache is often the place where all server threads collide, competing for exclusive access. Since the cache is a dynamic object from which files come and go, access to it must be synchronized. There are quite a few potential solutions to this contention hot spot:

- *Private file chaches.* Give each thread a private file cache, independent of the other threads. The need for synchronization is removed along with the lock contention.

- *Partial sharing.* Find a middle ground between having a single server-wide cache on one extreme and providing a cache per thread on the other. We discuss this further in Optimization 44.

- *Read/write locks.* The file cache is read-mostly. Updating (write) the cache is relatively infrequent. See Optimization 45 for further details.

The scalability upside of eliminating shared resources is clear. There's a downside, as well. Providing each server thread with its own copy of the cache leads to a drastic increase in the memory footprint of the server. What if each cache grows to 10 MB and we have 500 active threads? Such a design choice will have to be compensated for by either restricting cache size, limiting the number of concurrent threads, or some combination of both.

This design choice is available in many multithreaded applications and it does not always come bundled with a footprint penalty. It should find a place in your bag of tricks.

Optimization 44: Partial Sharing

Optimization 43 discussed the various design options for providing concurrent access to an HTML document cache. This is a particular instance of a more generic issue, that of resource pooling. When a particular resource is expensive to acquire and release, we want to spread the cost by recycling the resource many times before we let go of it (Optimizations 36, 37, and 38.) Examples of such resources you are likely to encounter are file contents, JDBC connections, threads, and more. A pooled resource may often be some user-defined object that is frequently used by your application, and pooling it may be more efficient than relying on the garbage-collection subsystem.

We have already mentioned the two opposite extremes of resource sharing: the publicly shared resource pool and the thread-private instance of a resource.

Between these two extremes lies the sharing middle ground of the partial-sharing resource pool.

When each thread requires a single instance of a resource, you can easily eliminate contention by making it thread-private (Optimization 36). If the required number of instances cannot be determined in advance, or if the side effects of maintaining thread-private resources are too severe, you need to use a resource pool that is shared among all threads (Optimization 37). Such shared resources often become a thread contention hot spot that severely degrades performance and scalability. Threads spend significant cycles spinning idle. Partial sharing of resource pools offers a way out of a hotly contended resource pool without paying a heavy toll for side effects such as memory and cache consumption.

On one extreme you can have a single resource pool serving all threads as in Figure 7.12.

Our goal was to reduce thread contention by reducing the number of threads competing for a resource. Towards that goal we converted the single resource pool above into multiple identical subpools. We preferred two pools (Figure 7.13) with half the contention, or four pools with one-fourth contention, over a single pool that draws all the activity.

The threads that formerly all ganged up on a single pool are now distributed over multiple subpools. Distributing the thread requests over separate pools

Threads

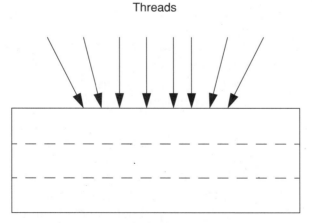

Figure 7.12.   A single shared resource pool

Threads

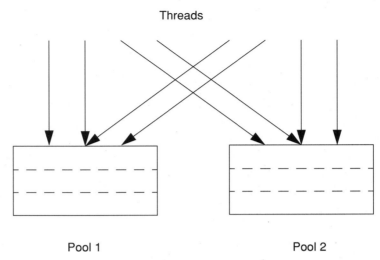

Pool 1   Pool 2

Figure 7.13.   Spreading the contention over two pools

could be achieved by using a precomputed thread ID or any other trick for fast random distribution. Each subpool must still be protected for mutual exclusion, but the thread contention has been reduced to a fraction of its previous level.

As you increase the number of subpools, contention among threads decreases. Eventually, you may end up reaching the extreme where the number of pools roughly equals the number of threads. In that case, it is almost like having a thread-private resource with no contention.

We speculate that in most practical scenarios, splitting a single pool into two, four, or even eight subpools will suffice to reduce contention to negligible levels. There's a point of diminishing returns. The ultimate judge is empirical data, which is application-dependent.

Optimization 45: Read/Write Locks ∎

Another way to ease the pain of synchronization is to relax the requirement that one and only one thread may have exclusive access to shared data. The need to synchronize access to shared data stems from the fact that the shared data may be modified by one of the threads accessing it. It follows that we must give exclusive access only to those threads aiming to modify shared data (writers). Conversely, threads that are merely interested in reading shared data (readers) could access shared data concurrently.

Reader/writer locks are those that allow multiple readers to access shared data instead of waiting for exclusive access. A thread trying to get read access to shared data will be granted read access in one of two cases:

- No other thread was granted access.
- The only threads granted access are readers.

If a writer thread has been granted access, all readers must wait for the writer thread to leave the critical section. A writer thread is granted access if and only if no other thread has been granted access to the shared resource.

Java does not provide built-in read/write synchronization, but you can build your own from the available synchronization primitive building blocks. See D. Lea, *Concurrent Programming in Java* [LEA97], for one such implementation.

If all your threads try to modify a shared resource, then reader/writer locks would not help. In fact, they would hurt performance because their implementation is by nature more complex and therefore slower than plain locks. If, however, your shared data is read-mostly, reader/writer locks will improve scalability by eliminating contention among reader threads.

Key Points

- SMP is currently the dominant MP architecture. It consists of multiple symmetric processors connected via a single bus to a single memory system. The bus is the scalability weak link in the SMP architecture. Large caches, one per processor, are meant to keep bus contention under control.
- Amdhal's law puts an upper limit on the potential scalability of an application. The scalability is limited by portions of the computation that are synchronized or otherwise single-threaded.
- The straight-line execution of unsynchronized code is faster than synchronized code, even without contention. Synchronized code hides the cost of acquiring and releasing a lock associated with a class or object.

- In the presence of thread contention, synchronized code could become a severe performance and scalability inhibitor.

The trick to scalability is to reduce and, if possible, eliminate synchronized code. Following are some steps you can take towards that goal:

- *Division of labor*. Split a monolithic task into multiple subtasks that are conducive to parallel execution by concurrent threads.

- *False sharing*. If two class (or object) members are logically unrelated, don't use the associated class (or object) lock to synchronize access. That will force the two unrelated data entities to share a lock, which increases contention. Protect access to those members using distinct locks.

- *Code motion*. Synchronized code should only contain access to shared data and nothing else. Code that does not directly manipulate shared resources should not reside within the scope of synchronization.

- *Share nothing*. If you need only a small, fixed number of resource instances, you should avoid the use of public resource pools. Make those instances private to the thread and recycle them.

- *Partial-sharing*. It is better to have two identical pools with half the contention.

- *Reader/writer locks*. Shared data that is read-mostly will benefit from these locks. They eliminate contention among reader threads.

8

JNI

You cannot dedicate a book to Java performance without addressing the issue of Java Native Interface (JNI.) After all, JNI is perceived by many to be the performance silver bullet when all else fails. Imagine working on a performance-challenged Java code, trying all the ideas set forth in earlier chapters and still falling short in achieving efficiency. You may be tempted, in desperation, to turn to JNI as a last resort. There are actually three popular scenarios for the use of native methods:

- You may have a complex, pre-existing software written in C/C++ and the conversion of this code to Java is not a practical option for some reason. You can hook this software into your Java code via JNI. In this case, JNI bails you out of a costly porting effort.

- You may need computational results that are simply not available in the Java environment and that necessitate the use of a system call. There are many such examples in the JDK that you may not be aware of. For example, `System.currentTimeMillis()` retrieves a timestamp from the underlying physical machine.

- You may want to speed up a slow computation, and you think JNI will help you via C/C++ execution.

In this chapter we will discuss the last (third) item only, as it is rooted in performance considerations that are up for debate. There's a popular misperception that JNI is always a performance winner. The reality is not that simple.

Optimization 46: JNI Surprise

We start with a counterintuitive example that will take most Java programmers by surprise. This is the case of a nontrivial task that is executed faster in

Java than JNI. A JNI call involves substantial work under the covers to cross from Java to the native environment and back. At the very least we must convert data structures from their JVM representation to the ones expected by C/C++. Take a String, for example. It is represented in Java as a sequence of Unicode characters in which each character is a two-byte entity. A String in C/C++ is a sequence of single-byte characters terminated by a null byte. There's some work involved in bouncing String objects back and forth across those two environments.

Take a concrete task of converting an ASCII String to uppercase. This is definitely faster in C/C++, as you can convert the individual characters in place. In Java, however, we must create a new String object to contain the corresponding uppercase string. The original (lowercase) string remains intact, as String objects in Java are immutable. Given that fact, I was surprised to find out that the Java version was faster than JNI. Both versions were tested with a string of length 128:

```
String s = "a";
for (i = 2; i < 8; i++) { // Build a String of 128 characters
    s += s;
}
```

The measurement consisted of 10,000 iterations of the Java version:

```
String p = s.toUpperCase();
```

as compared to a corresponding JNI version:

```
String p = jniToUpperCase(s);
```

The C++ implementation of jniToUpperCase() is given by

```
jstring JNICALL
Java_Jni_jniToUpperCase(JNIEnv *env, jclass thisClass, jstring s) {
    char *utf_string;
    jboolean isCopy;

    utf_string = (char*) env->GetStringUTFChars(s, &isCopy);
    for (char *p = utf_string;*p;p++) {
        *p = toupper(*p);
    }
```

```
jstring rs = env->NewStringUTF(utf_string);
if (isCopy == JNI_TRUE) {
    env->ReleaseStringUTFChars(s,utf_string);
}

return (rs);
}
```

The Java version was substantially faster. See Figure 8.1.

Although it is faster to convert a character sequence to uppercase in C++, the cost of bouncing String objects in and out of the native environment has swamped the little gain there was in the C++ processing. Processing larger strings resulted in the same conclusion: Java was faster. This result should alert us to the fact that JNI is not an automatic performance booster. We must have a large performance gain in the native language (C/C++) processing to compensate for the JNI call overhead. Clearly, this does not always happen.

Optimization 47: JNI to the Rescue

Software performance engineering is a delicate task. There are very few blanket statements that apply in all situations. Almost every performance principle depends on context and could easily backfire if applied out of context. The same holds for JNI. As demonstrated earlier, you cannot always trust that JNI execution speed is superior to Java. But you cannot claim the opposite, either,

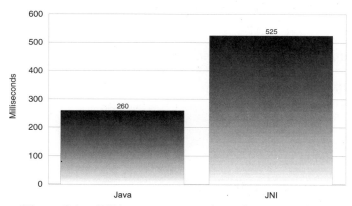

Figure 8.1. JNI is not an automatic performance winner

because there are plenty of computational scenarios in which JNI execution speed will leave Java in the dust. We will examine one such example next.

Whenever I search for a compute-intensive task in Java, the Date class immediately comes to mind. The conversion of a Date object to a String representation is expensive and slow:

```
Date date = new Date();
...
String p = date.toString();
```

This is why I sometimes refer to Java as a performance minefield. Some computations look and feel extremely simple, yet they may harbor a significant performance cost. In a statement as simple as the one-line Date statement above, there is a world of computational complexity. The visual correspondence between the complexity of the source code and its cost have been broken in higher level languages. An assembly-language programmer would know right away how expensive this computation is because it would take her hundreds of assembly-language instructions to perform this complex conversion from a timestamp to a String object representing a date.

This conversion looks pretty simple in C/C++, with the exception that it is a lot faster. Here's the JNI implementation using the ctime() call in C. First, the Java class definition:

```
class MyJni {
...
private static native String jctime(); // Native method
};
```

The native implementation is shown below:

```
jstring JNICALL Java_MyJni_jctime(JNIEnv *env, jclass thisClass) {
    time_t t;
    char *s;

    time(&t);
    s = ctime(&t);

    return (env->NewStringUTF(s));
}
```

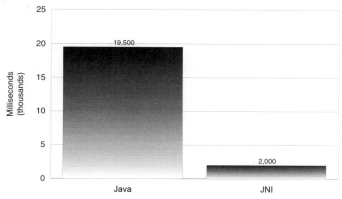

Figure 8.2.   JNI could provide performance relief for some tasks

The preceeding is the C/C++ implementation of a native method called `jctime()` declared for a class called `MyJni`. This is where the name `Java_MyJni_jctime()` comes from. If the class `MyClass` declares a native method `myMethod()`, the corresponding JNI function name would be `Java_MyClass_myMethod()`. We contrasted 100,000 iterations of

```
String p = date.ToString();
```

to the JNI call

```
String p = jctime(); // compute the String rep of (new Date())
```

The performance measurement was dramatically in favor of JNI. The JNI implementation was an order of magnitude faster. See Figure 8.2.

Optimization 48: Prefer `System.arraycopy()`   ■

In Optimizations 47 and 46 we established the potential upside and downside of using JNI. In a nutshell, JNI calls harbor two opposing performance forces:

- Setting up and tearing down the JNI call in terms of argument passing presents an overhead that must be taken into consideration.
- Some compute-intensive tasks execute much faster in C/C++.

A JNI call will be a good bet if the second force dominates the first. Some computations are faster in Java (Optimization 46); others are faster using JNI (Optimization 47.) Between those two extremes, there's a large set of computations that exhibit a crossover point depending on the size of the computation. If you want to copy a single byte, you are probably better off using the assignment statement in Java. If you want to copy 1,000 bytes, I'd speculate that using the System.arraycopy() call will be faster than executing 1,000 assignments. The question is, Where is the crossover point? To answer that question, we need a measurement.

The measurement consists of 10,000,000 iterations of copying a byte array. We built byte arrays of varying sizes (powers of 2) depending on the command-line argument:

```
String s = "X";
int n = Integer.parseInt(args[0]);
for (int i = 1; i < n; i++) { // Build a String whose length is a
                              // power of two
    s += s;
}

int size = s.length();
byte[] src = s.getBytes();
byte[] dst = new byte[size];
```

The first version used the assignment statement

```
for (int i = 0; i < 10000000; i++) {
    for (int j = 0; j < size; j++) dst[j] = src[j];  // Copy the array
}
```

While the second called System.arraycopy()

```
for (int i = 0; i < 10000000; i++) {
    System.arraycopy(src,0,dst,0,size);
}
```

For this particular platform[1] the crossover point arrived very early, at around 8 bytes. From that size and on, the version using arraycopy() was much superior to using Java assignments. It was 5× faster for byte arrays as small as 256 bytes.

---

[1] NT 4.0, Pentium II 366 MHz, Sun 1.2.2 JDK.

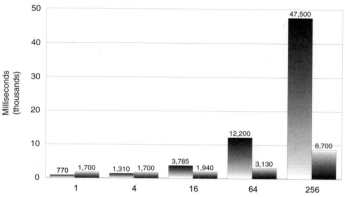

Figure 8.3. Often, the Java–JNI performance decision has a crossover point

See Figure 8.3. Each pair represents the execution time of Java assignments and `arraycopy()` for a fixed-size array. The one on the right corresponds to `arraycopy()`.

Using the Java assignment operator was faster for arrays of size 4 or less. At size 16, the JNI version has taken over the performance lead for good.

Key Points

- The use of JNI does not guarantee a performance gain.

- Some JNI calls will be dominated by the cost of shuttling arguments back and forth between Java and the native environment. Those computations should bypass JNI and stay in the Java environment.

- In many scenarios, the performance of C/C++ is superior to Java, and the performance gain will dwarf the JNI overhead. In those cases, JNI is a winner.

- Prefer `System.arraycopy()` to other methods of copying contiguous collections of objects.

9

RMI

Recent advances such as CORBA/IIOP, EJB, and RMI have made it easier than ever to develop distributed software solutions whose execution is no longer confined to a single physical machine. The adoption of these technologies is driven in part by the fact that they insulate the programmer from having to worry about the fine details of socket programming. Socket programming is the assembly language of distributed computing. It is the building block of higher-level protocols. Socket programmers typically need to invent a proprietary protocol that both client and server must adhere to. They need to marshal and demarshal parameters passed back and forth between client and server. Often, they must also deploy a pool of server threads to handle socket requests concurrently. This is tedious, complex, delicate, and error-prone work. RMI can do all that for you and protect you from the details of socket communication.

The evolution of programming languages has made it easier to develop complex solutions, but the advances typically come with a performance price tag. Lower-level languages allow you a finer level of control that makes those languages both more efficient from an execution perspective and less productive from a development effort standpoint. The move from sockets to RMI is no exception. RMI is a much more convenient programming layer, but sockets are likely to be more efficient. This is the theory, at least. In this chapter we will explore how well this theory holds up in practice.

The RMI Network Plumbing

We start with a simple program that sends two `String` objects from client to server. The server will return the result of concatenating these two `String` objects. This program doesn't do much, and so it is ideal for evaluating the cost of socket and RMI network plumbing. We will compare a socket version to an RMI version. Starting with sockets, the client side is shown by

```
import java.net.*;
import java.io.*;

public class SockClient {
    public static void main(String[] argv) {
        if (argv.length != 2) {
            System.out.println("java SockClient <host> <count>");
            return;
        }

        String host = argv[0];
        int count = Integer.parseInt(argv[1]);
        String z = null;
        Socket s = null;

        try {
            s = new Socket(host,8080);
            DataOutputStream dos =
                new DataOutputStream(
                    new BufferedOutputStream(s.getOutputStream()));
            DataInputStream dis =
                new DataInputStream(
                    new BufferedInputStream(s.getInputStream()));

            long start = System.currentTimeMillis(); // <+++ Start
                                                      // timing
            for (int i=0; i < count; i++) {
                dos.writeUTF("Hello");
                dos.writeUTF("There");
                dos.flush();
                z = dis.readUTF();
            }
            long stop = System.currentTimeMillis(); // <+++ Stop timing

            System.out.println("exec time = " + (stop-start));
            s.close();
        } catch (Exception e) {
            System.err.println("Close...");
            if (s != null) {
                try {s.close();} catch (Exception ex) {}
            }
        }
    }
}
```

The socket server is given next:

```
import java.net.*;
import java.io.*;

public class SockServer {
    public static void main(String[] argv) {
        ServerSocket ss = null;
        Socket s = null;

        try { ss = new ServerSocket(8080); }
        catch (Exception e) {
            System.err.println("could not create listen socket");
            return;
        }

        while (true) {
            try {
                System.out.println("Accept...");
                s = ss.accept();
                DataOutputStream dos =
                    new DataOutputStream(
                        new BufferedOutputStream(s.getOutputStream()));

                DataInputStream dis =
                    new DataInputStream(
                        new BufferedInputStream(s.getInputStream()));

                while (true) {
                    String x = dis.readUTF();
                    String y = dis.readUTF();
                    dos.writeUTF(x+y);
                    dos.flush();
                }
            } catch (Exception e) {
                System.err.println("Close...");
                if (s != null) {
                    try {s.close();} catch (Exception ex) {}
                }
            }
        }
    }
}
```

We measured the speed of this code by executing 10,000 client requests (iterations of the client-side loop). Both client and server executed on the same physical machine, a 4-way Netfinity server.[1] It executed in 5,500 milliseconds.

---

[1] 4-way Netfinity server (Pentium II, 4×200 MHz), running the NT 4.0 operating system with the IBM Win32 1.1.7 JVM.

Next we turn our attention to the equivalent RMI version. Starting with the RMI remote interface and followed by the server itself

```
import java.rmi.Remote;
import java.rmi.RemoteException;

public interface RemoteServer extends Remote {
    public abstract String hiThere(String x, String y)
            throws RemoteException;
}

import java.rmi.Naming;
import java.rmi.RemoteException;
import java.rmi.server.UnicastRemoteObject;

public class Server extends Thread implements RemoteServer {
    static public void main(String[] args) {
        try {
            Server server = new Server();
            Naming.rebind("Server", server);
            System.out.println("Server is ready...");
        }
        catch( Exception e ) {
            e.printStackTrace();
        }
    }

    public Server() throws RemoteException {
        super();
        UnicastRemoteObject.exportObject(this);
    }

    public String hiThere(String x, String y) {
        return x+y;
    }

}
```

The RMI client side is given by

```
import java.io.IOException;
import java.rmi.Naming;
import java.rmi.RemoteException;
import java.rmi.server.UnicastRemoteObject;
```

```
public class Client {
    static public void main(String[] args) {

        RemoteServer server;

        if( args.length != 2 ) {
            System.out.println("Syntax: java Client rmiHost count");
            return;
        }

        String rmiHost = args[0];
        System.out.println("RmiHost is " + rmiHost);
        String url = "rmi://" + rmiHost + "/Server";
        int count = Integer.parseInt(args[1]);

        try {
            System.out.println("Looking up: " + url);
            server = (RemoteServer)Naming.lookup(url);
            System.out.println("Lookup Done.");
        } catch( Exception e ) {
            e.printStackTrace();
            return;
        }

        long start = System.currentTimeMillis(); // <+++ Start timing
        for (int i = 0; i < count; i++ ) {
            try {
                server.hiThere("Hello", "There");
            } catch( RemoteException e ) {
                e.printStackTrace();
                return;
            }
        }
        long stop = System.currentTimeMillis(); // <+++ Stop timing

        System.out.println("exec time = " + (stop-start));
    }
}
```

Just as with the socket code, we measured 10,000 iterations of the RMI client loop. We used the same environment setup as in the earlier socket test. As expected, the RMI speed was significantly slower than the socket speed. It took 15,250 milliseconds. Although the RMI code was much simpler, it was slower by a factor of almost three. See Figure 9.1.

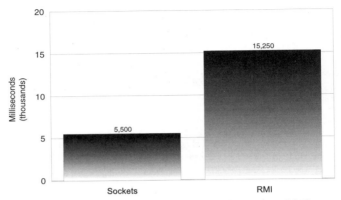

Figure 9.1. Sockets are obviously faster than RMI

A 3× degradation in speed seems like a hefty price to pay for the programming ease of RMI. This difference, however, is somewhat misleading. We could just as easily concoct a test case that would make the performance gap between sockets and RMI look negligible. It all depends on the amount of computation performed on the server, which is the topic of the next section.

Varying the Server Workload

The performance of a distributed application depends roughly on two cost factors:

- *The network I/O plumbing*—the cost of bouncing requests and response data among the various participants in the distributed computation. There may be several servers involved in a single distributed transaction. Servers such as HTTP, application servers, and database servers are a few that immediately come to mind.

- *Response data*—the cost of computing the response data on the server side, excluding the I/O cost mentioned above.

In our first test case, the production of the response data was relatively simple. It entailed a single operation of String concatenation, which paled in comparison to the network I/O effort. That test was therefore dominated by the first cost factor, that of the network I/O plumbing. Consequently, it made RMI look alarmingly expensive in comparison to sockets. In reality, however, the situation is not that bad. The computations performed on the server side are likely to be more complex and shift the costs from the network I/O arena to the response-generation effort. That would tend to diminish the perceived gap between RMI and sockets. We will make this point more concrete in the following test case. This time we are going to pass an integer array from client to server. The array contains 100 integers:

```
int[] x = new int[100];

for (int i = 0; i < 100; i++) {
    x[i] = i;
}
```

The server will take this array, convert each of its elements to a String, and write it out to file. In order to vary the amount of work performed on the server, we will introduce another test knob. We will pass an additional integer parameter telling the server how many repetitions to perform. For example, if we pass the parameters

```
(int 64, int[] x)
```

then the server will write the array x to file 64 times.

Let's look at the socket server first:

```
public class SockArrayServer {
    public static void main(String[] argv) {
        ... // As before
        while (true) {
            try {
                System.out.println("Accept...");
                s = ss.accept();
                DataOutputStream dos =
                    new DataOutputStream(
                        new BufferedOutputStream(s.getOutputStream()));

                ObjectInputStream ois =
                    new ObjectInputStream(
                        new BufferedInputStream(s.getInputStream()));

                while (true) {
                    PrintWriter pw =
```

```
            new PrintWriter(
                new BufferedWriter(
                    new FileWriter("array.out")));

        int serverReps = ois.readInt();
        int[] x = (int[]) ois.readObject();
        for (int i = 0; i < serverReps; i++) {
            printIt(pw,x);
        }
        dos.writeUTF("Done");
        dos.flush();
        pw.close();
      }
    } catch (Exception e) {
        ...  // Handle exceptions
      }
    }
  }

  // Print the array to the output stream
  private static void printIt(PrintWriter pw, int[] x) {
    int size = x.length;
    for (int i = 0; i < size; i ++) {
      pw.print(x[i]);
      if ((i%10) == 0) pw.println();
    }
  }
}
```

The corresponding client code is given by

```
public class SockArrayClient {
  public static void main(String[] argv) {
    if (argv.length != 3) {
      System.out.println("java SockClient <host>
                          "<cliReps> <ServReps>");

      return;
    }

    String host = argv[0];
    int clientReps = Integer.parseInt(argv[1]);
    int serverReps = Integer.parseInt(argv[2]);
    String z = null;
    Socket s = null;
    int[] x = new int[100];
```

```
for (int i = 0; i < 100; i++) {
   x[i] = i;
}

try {
   System.out.println("socket...");
   s = new Socket(host,8080);
   ObjectOutputStream oos =
      new ObjectOutputStream(
         new BufferedOutputStream(s.getOutputStream()));
   DataInputStream dis =
      new DataInputStream(
         new BufferedInputStream(s.getInputStream()));

   long start = System.currentTimeMillis(); // <+++ Start
                                            //         timing
   for (int i=0; i < clientReps; i++) {
      oos.writeInt(serverReps);
      oos.writeObject(x);
      oos.flush();
      z = dis.readUTF();
   }
   long stop = System.currentTimeMillis(); // <+++ Stop timing

   System.out.println("exec time = " + (stop-start));
   s.close();
} catch (Exception e) {
   // ... cleanup...
   }
  }
}
```

Our test consisted of a fixed amount of 100 client requests while varying the server repetitions from 1 to 256. By asking the server for increased repetitions, we were gradually shifting the computational center of gravity from the network I/O to the server task. The test was performed on a uniprocessor PC.[2] Figure 9.2 displays the timing results in milliseconds. It charts the response time as a function of server repetitions.

We then replaced the socket machinery with the equivalent RMI implementation. We modified the remote interface to accept the number of repetitions as well as the array itself:

---

[2] Uniprocessor, Celeron 366 MHz, running Windows 98 with the Sun 1.2.2 JDK.

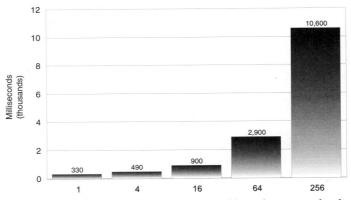

Figure 9.2. Response time increases with socket-server load

```
public interface RemoteRmiArrayServer extends Remote {
    public abstract String hiThere(int serverReps, int[] x)
        throws RemoteException;
}
```

The RMI server implements the remote call

```
public class RmiArrayServer extends Thread implements
RemoteRmiArrayServer {
    ... // As before

    public String hiThere(int serverReps, int[] x) {
        PrintWriter pw = null;
        try {
            pw =
                new PrintWriter(
                    new BufferedWriter(
                        new FileWriter("array.out")));
        } catch (IOException e) {}

        for (int i = 0; i < serverReps; i++) {
            printIt(pw,x);
        }
        pw.close();

        return ("Done");
    }

    private static void printIt(PrintWriter pw, int[] x) {
```

```
        int size = x.length;
        for (int i = 0; i < size; i ++) {
            pw.print(x[i]);
            if ((i%10) == 0) pw.println();
        }
    }
}
```

Finally, the RMI client drives the measurement:

```
public class RmiArrayClient {
    static public void main(String[] args) {
        if( args.length != 2 ) {
            System.out.println("Syntax: java Client " +
                               "clientReps serverReps");
            return;
        }

        ... // Read command line args followed by RMI server lookup

        int[] x = new int[100];

        for (int i = 0; i < 100; i++) {
            x[i] = i;
        }

        String z = null;
        long start = System.currentTimeMillis();  // <+++ Start timing
        for (int i = 0; i < clientReps; i++ ) {
            try {
                z = server.hiThere(serverReps, x);
            } catch( RemoteException e ) {
                ... // Handle exception...
            }

        }
        long stop = System.currentTimeMillis();  // <+++ Stop timing
        ...
    }
}
```

We repeated the equivalent measurement for the RMI implementation. See
Figure 9.3.

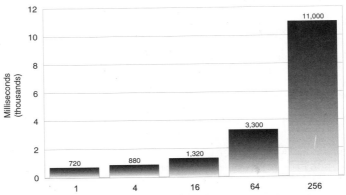

Figure 9.3. No surprise, RMI server response time degrades with higher load

Putting the socket and RMI numbers side by side on the same chart reveals that increasing the workload on the server side, tends to narrow the speed differential between sockets and RMI. If we keep increasing the load, eventually, the speed gap will become negligible. See Figure 9.4.

Notice also that when the server workload is light, quadrupling the workload does not result in a corresponding 4× speed degradation because the test is still dominated by network I/O (which remains fixed throughout).

In short, although sockets are more efficient, the choice between sockets and RMI is context-sensitive and highly dependent on server workload. The bene-

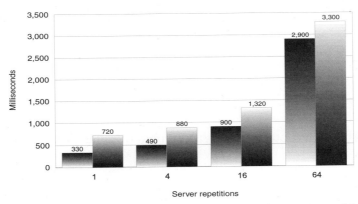

Figure 9.4. The RMI–sockets gap shrinks with higher server workloads

fits of RMI programming are significant and should not be abandoned unless you can make a very strong performance case for it, backed by empirical data.

RMI Server on Remote Machine

Up to this point, we deployed both client and server on the same physical machine. In practice, you are more likely to encounter designs that deploy the client and server on separate machines. From a performance standpoint, is it better to run the RMI server locally (client and server on same machine) or remotely? The definite answer is: It depends. There is a performance advantage and disadvantage to either choice. If you run the RMI server locally, you will be stealing precious CPU cycles from the client since both client and server are vying for the use of the same CPU(s). However, in the local scenario, the TCP/IP execution path is much shorter since both underlying sockets are on the same machine. There's no need to traverse the full IP stack and peripheral device-driver code. The exact opposite is the case for remote deployment. Both client and server have more CPU cycles for their own use but the TCP/IP and device-driver code execution are weighing down the computation. In Chapter 10, Servlets, we have speculated that those two competing factors may cancel each other out. Again, there is no one-size-fits-all answer here since the answer depends on the efficiency of the TCP/IP and device-driver implementations. It will also depend on the client and server computational load. Let's look at one particular example.

In the first example in this chapter we introduced an RMI server that took in two String objects and returned the result of their concatenation. Running 10,000 iterations took 15,250 milliseconds when both client and server were deployed on the same four-way Netfinity server. We then moved the server object to a 12-way AIX SMP machine.[3] The new execution time for 10,000 iterations was slightly better at 14,250, but not by much. See Figure 9.5.

The remote numbers might not have been that good had we run the RMI server object on a less powerful machine. Most people will find this result counterintuitive, as we usually tend to associate "local" with "faster." In any event, in this particular case, moving the server to a remote machine paid off.

---

[3] PowerPC, 12X166 MHz, IBM 1.1.6 JDK.

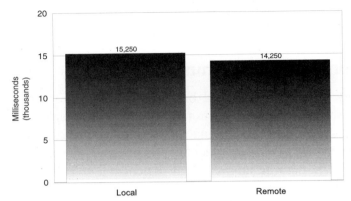

Figure 9.5. The local–remote RMI decision is not easy

Serializing Heavyweight Objects

In the same way that I/O performance is largely affected by the size of the data transferred, RMI speed is influenced by the complexity of the objects in transit. These are the remote method parameters and the return value, if any, of that method. These objects must be serialized over a socket connection and resurrected on the other side. Naturally, the speed of serialization will depend on the complexity of the object in terms of number of member fields, and it will depend recursively on the complexity of the member fields themselves. A primitive type member is easier to serialize than a reference to a compound object.

In the very first RMI example in this chapter we used `String` objects in the role of method parameters and return value. Our remote method was given by

```java
public String hiThere(String x, String y) {
    return x+y;
}
```

To make life slightly more interesting, let's replace the `String` objects with more complex objects. The `Z` class contains a `String` member, but we also add a few more object members:

```java
import java.io.*;

class Z implements Serializable {
```

```
    private String name;
    private Integer i;
    private Float f;
    private Double d;

    public Z(String n) {
        name = n;
        i = new Integer(1);
        f = new Float(1.0);
        d = new Double(1.0);
    }

    public String getName() {
        return name;
    }

    public void setName(String n) {
        name = n;
    }
}
```

Serializing a `Z` object requires the serialization of not only a `String` object but also an `Integer`, `Float`, and `Double`. This should make the serialization and resurrection of a `Z` object somewhat more expensive than for a `String` object. Let's go to the numbers. We compared 10,000 remote invocations of

```
public String hiThere(String x, String y) {
    return x+y;
}
```

to 10,000 remote invocations of

```
public Z hiThere(Z z1, Z z2) {
    Z z3 = new Z(z1.getName() + z2.getName());
    return z3;
}
```

As speculated above, the second test involving the `Z` object was slower. See Figure 9.6.

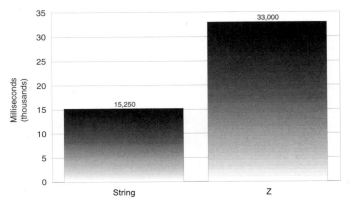

Figure 9.6.   Complex objects are more expensive to serialize

Key Points

- Sockets are the primitive building blocks for distributed computing. As such, they are more efficient than higher-layer protocols.

- The performance gap between RMI and sockets is more pronounced if the server's task is computationally light. As the server computation becomes more complex, the bottleneck shifts from network I/O to the response computation itself and helps to narrow the gap between RMI and sockets.

- From a pure performance standpoint, it is not clear whether the RMI server should be deployed locally or remotely. It depends on the computational context. It is not always the case that "local is faster."

- In the same way that data size impacts socket performance, RMI performance is strongly influenced by the complexity of serializing the remote method's parameters and return value. Complex objects are more expensive to serialize and will weigh down RMI speed.

10

Servlets

Data flowing on the WWW can vary significantly with regard to its life span. On one extreme is static data. Static data never changes, at least as long as the server is up and running. On the other extreme is dynamic data. Dynamic data could be instantaneously outdated, like stock market quotes. Other types of data fall somewhere in the middle between those two extremes. Whereas static data typically resides on the server's file system, dynamic data is typically generated by a server-side executable program. The de facto standard for dynamic data generation used to be the Common Gateway Interface, otherwise known as CGI. CGI was there first and it is still the dominant vehicle for dynamic data. The problem with CGI is that it was designed in the early days when the current success of the WWW was beyond anybody's wildest dreams. The CGI protocol was never meant to accommodate thousands of concurrent users. Each CGI request forces the server to spawn a new process to execute the CGI script (or executable). The proliferation of those processes and the cost of creating and destroying them is the Achilles heel of the CGI protocol.

Java servlets have emerged as a strong contender to replace CGI as a dominant generator of dynamic data. Servlets fix the most painful performance issue that is inherent in CGI, the need to create and destroy a process per request. All Java servlets may reside in a single JVM process that stays resident from one request to the next. For that reason, people often claim that servlets are faster than CGI. It is actually not that simple. The fact that servlets live in a persistent process gives them a huge initial advantage over CGI executables. If all you are doing is a very simple "Hello World" type application, then servlets could run as much as 10× faster on some platforms. However, real-life applications are much more complex than "Hello World," which is why benchmarks can be misleading. As the complexity of the Web application increases, performance will shift from the Web application server plumbing to the application's business logic. In that case, a CGI executable written in C, will start closing the gap on a servlet written in Java, because C is faster than Java. At some point you may cross a complexity threshold where a CGI may outperform a corresponding servlet. This is a rare occurence, but we should still be cautious when we brag that servlets are faster than CGI.

The optimizations provided in earlier chapters were meant to improve the efficiency of any Java code. As such they apply automatically to servlet performance. Especially important is the chapter on String performance because Web applications tend to work intensively with String objects. In this chapter we will highlight some optimization opportunities that seem to surface very often on the servlet scene. We will also cover the relative performance of typical servlet categories.

A word of caution: In earlier chapters our measurements were given in terms of response time, for which lower was better from a performance perspective. When it comes to Web servers, a more popular metric is requests-per-second, which is the measurement we use in this chapter. Bear in mind that with this metric, higher is better.

Servlets Using `PrintWriter`

Our first stab at a typical servlet is given by the Writer1 servlet. We did not want to overburden its performance with generating too much data or be unrealistic with too little data. So we repeated the message "<h1>Hello World 1</h1>" 10 times to generate a 100+ bytes of HTML output. This servlet uses the doGet() method, which is a reasonable choice for handling HTTP GET requests. It also uses the PrintWriter class as an output writer. The PrintWriter is capable of handling any character encoding, not just ASCII. As such, it is capable of converting the original output into any target encoding, and this capability makes it a popular choice for servlet writers. The code for Writer1 is given by

```
public class Writer1 extends HttpServlet {

public void doGet (HttpServletRequest req, HttpServletResponse res)
      throws ServletException, IOException {

   res.setContentType("text/html");
   PrintWriter out = res.getWriter();

      out.println("<html>");
      out.println("<head><title>Hello World</title></head>");
      out.println("<body>");
```

```
        for (int i = 0 ; i < 10; i++) {
            out.println("<h1>Hello World 1</h1>");
        }

        out.println("</body></html>");
    }
}
```

One minor issue that I would take with the above implementation is the use of `println()` instead of `print()`. A `println(s)` will follow the `String` s with the appropriate line-separator sequence. That line separator is meaningless for the HTML interpreter and is going to be ignored. It has absolutely no impact on the HTML display. The `println()` method, however, is more expensive than `print()`. Internally, `println()` is typically implemented as

```
public void println(String s) {
    ...
    print(s);
    println();
    ...
}
```

Since `println(s)` itself calls `print(s)`, it is obviously more expensive, and since it does not contribute any functionality whatsoever (in this case), it should be replaced by `print(s)`:

```
public class Writer1 extends HttpServlet {

public void doGet (HttpServletRequest req, HttpServletResponse res)
        throws ServletException, IOException {

        res.setContentType("text/html");
        PrintWriter out = res.getWriter();

        out.print("<html>");
        out.print("<head><title>Hello World</title></head>");
        out.print("<body>");

        for (int i = 0 ; i < 10; i++) {
            out.print("<h1>Hello World 1</h1>");
        }

        out.print("</body></html>");
    }
}
```

Most performance people automatically recoil when faced with multiple print() calls. They look like lots of I/O, and that sounds inefficient. One trick that I've seen used is to buffer the output data in a StringBuffer and then send it in a single print() call:

```
public class Writer2 extends HttpServlet {

public void doGet (HttpServletRequest req, HttpServletResponse res)
        throws ServletException, IOException {

    StringBuffer msg = new StringBuffer(1024);
    res.setContentType("text/html");

    msg.append("<html>");
    msg.append("<head><title>Hello World</title></head>");
    msg.append("<body>");

    for (int i = 0 ; i < 10; i++) {
        msg.append("<h1>Hello World 2</h1>");
    }

    msg.append("</body></html>");

    PrintWriter out = res.getWriter();
    out.print(msg.toString());
    }
}
```

We loaded those two servlets (Writer1 and Writer2) on an NT server.[1] We used a very powerful driver machine (12-way AIX) to bombard the Web application server (running on NT) with concurrent requests for those servlets. The AIX driver used 100 concurrent clients to generate requests. The throughput measurement (in requests per second) showed that Writer1 was actually slightly faster than Writer2 as shown by Figure 10.1 (higher is better).

Obviously, this buffering "trick" did not do us any good. Multiple print() calls do not really translate to multiple I/O operations. The Writer underneath the PrintWriter has the capability to buffer data until it reaches the buffer limit. For that reason, buffering the data yourself in a StringBuffer does not

---

[1] Four-way SMP, Pentium-II (4X200 MHz), NT 4.0, IBM Win32 1.1.7 JDK.

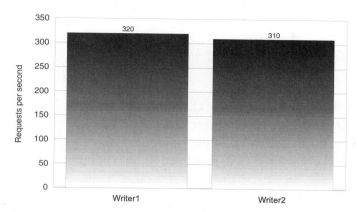

Figure 10.1.   Homegrown buffering did not work

really buy you anything. It actually makes the situation worse because it causes double-copy of the data, buffering it once in the `StringBuffer` and once again when the `Writer` itself has to copy the `String` characters into a char array:

```
public class OutputStreamWriter extends Writer {
    ...
    public void write(String str, int off, int len) throws IOException {
        char cbuf[] = new char[len];
        str.getChars(off, off + len, cbuf, 0);
        write(cbuf, 0, len);
    }
    ...
}
```

For that reason, `Writer2` was actually worse than `Writer1`. Unfortunately, buffering the data in a `StringBuffer` did not work, so let's move on and try something else.

Servlets Using `ServletOutputStream`

One of the recurrent themes in our discussion is that more generic and powerful software often translates into slower execution. We've emphasized this idea in many situations. The `PrintWriter` is a case in point. The ability of the `PrintWriter` to generate any target character encoding does not come without a price tag. The `PrintWriter` has an underlying character output stream as a protected member:

```
public class PrintWriter extends Writer {
    ...
    protected Writer out;
    ...
}
```

When the `PrintWriter` sends a character stream down the `Writer` object, that `Writer` must inspect each character and convert it into its target character encoding. That means that each two-byte Unicode character may end up going out as a one-, two- or even three-byte sequence. That character-to-byte conversion process is naturally very expensive. On the other hand, a simpler stream such as a `ServletOutputStream` assumes that the character stream is ASCII and the target character encoding is the same. A `ServletOutputStream` converts a character stream to a byte stream by simply dropping one byte of each two-byte character. This is exactly the same conversion mechanism we used in Optimization 4 when we developed a fast converter from an ASCII `String` to an ASCII byte array. That's a much faster conversion than the one performed by a `Writer`.

The moral of the story is that you should use `PrintWriter` only if a conversion from one encoding to another is necessary. There's a large segment of the population that uses `PrintWriter` even though a `ServletOutputStream` would do just fine and provide greater efficiency to boot. Our next version is `Stream3`. It replaces the `printWriter` with the more efficient `ServletOutputStream`. It differs from `Writer2` in a single line, as shown below:

```
public class Stream3 extends HttpServlet {

    public void doGet (HttpServletRequest req,
                       HttpServletResponse res)
        throws ServletException, IOException {

        ... // As before
        /**** PrintWriter out = res.getWriter(); ****/
        ServletOutputStream out = res.getOutputStream(); // The only change

        ... // As before
    }
}
```

A performance measurement confirmed, just as we expected, that `Stream3` is more efficient than its relatives that we already met. It clocked in at 354 requests per second. Figure 10.2 exhibits the evolving performance story (higher is better).

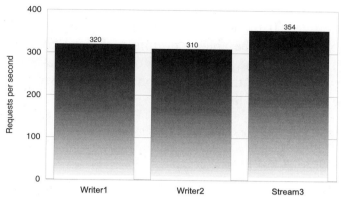

Figure 10.2. ServletOutputStream is faster than PrintWriter

One concern to keep in mind is that the use of ServletOutputStream for text data (ASCII or not) is deprecated. The officially recommended route for text data is by use of the PrintWriter class. In the future, the ServletOutput-Stream may drop out of the servlet API. As the Y2K bug has taught our generation, ignoring future considerations may come back to haunt us. On the other hand, migrating from a ServletOutputStream to a PrintWriter is as easy as a one-line change from

```
ServletOutputStream out = res.getOutputStream();
```

to

```
PrintWriter out = res.getWriter();
```

The rest of the code is intact.

Precomputing Message Bytes

The character-to-byte conversion performed by the ServletOutputStream is faster than the one performed by a PrintWriter. However, it does consume CPU cycles. You still have to "touch" every character and grab one of its two bytes. It would be even faster if we did not have to do that at all. We can push this conversion step out of the doGet() method and into the init() method of the servlet. The init() method is called only once when the servlet is loaded. The doGet() method is called every time the servlet is invoked with an HTTP GET request. Any time you can move computations from doGet(), doPost(), or service(), to the init() method, you are looking at a performance win (see Optimization 25). If the doGet() constructs its output on the fly from, say, a database, you will not be able to do this trick very effectively. You can only use init() to convert the portion of the output data that is known at that point. In our servlet example, the whole output data is known at initialization time, so we take advantage of that:

```
public class Stream4 extends HttpServlet {

byte [] msgBytes = null;

public void init(ServletConfig c) throws ServletException {

        super.init(c);
        String msg = "<html><head><title>Hello World</title></head><body>";
        for (int i = 0 ; i < 10; i++) {
            msg += "<h1>Hello World 4</h1>";
        }
        msg += "</body></html>";
        msgBytes = msg.getBytes();
    }


        public void doGet (HttpServletRequest req,
                        HttpServletResponse res)
            throws ServletException, IOException {

        res.setContentType("text/html");
        ServletOutputStream out = res.getOutputStream();
        out.write(msgBytes);
    }
}
```

Stream4 uses the init() method not only to construct the output data but also to convert it into a byte array. Notice that I'm using the slow getBytes() as opposed to the fast one we developed in Optimization 4. That's because I don't care about the performance of init(). It is only called once and considered to be outside the performance-critical path. In the doGet() method we just send the byte array down the stream skipping the character-to-byte conversion altogether. Figure 10.3 adds this new servlet to the performance mix.

I was a little miffed when this fine optimization did not translate into any detectable performance boost: 356 compared to 354 requests per second is not really a performance boost. It is just measurement "noise." I know this is more

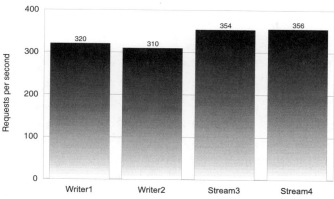

Figure 10.3.   Precomputing the message bytes

efficient because we have eliminated a nontrivial computation. However, it is tough to argue with facts. The reason this improvement was undetectable is twofold: First, when an HTTP request arrives at the server, it is first handled by the HTTP server and then by the Java Application Server. These two combine to have a significant instruction count. You have to really make a dent in the overall instruction count in order to get noticed. That leads to the second issue: We are not generating enough data in order for this optimization to make a difference. One hundred bytes of data (or so) is not much. We will do that next.

Pumping More Data

Converting characters to bytes ahead of time is a good idea, but we need to generate more data to see some results. We do that in servlet LotsOfData_W by using a Writer object:

```
public class LotsOfData_W extends HttpServlet {

    public void doGet (HttpServletRequest req,
                       HttpServletResponse res)
        throws ServletException, IOException {

        res.setContentType("text/html");
        PrintWriter out = res.getWriter();

        out.print("<html>");
        out.print("<head><title>Hello World</title></head>");
        out.print("<body>");
```

```
        for (int i = 0 ; i < 1000; i++) {
            out.print("<h1>Hello World 5</h1>");
        }

        out.print("</body></html>");
    }
}
```

LotsOfData_W servlet generates about 22 KB of data by repeating the string "<h1>Hello World 5</h1>" 1,000 times. It uses a PrintWriter object to send data back to the client. For comparison, we also coded an identical servlet that converts the data into bytes ahead of time and uses ServletOutputStream to send it out. We call that servlet LotsOfData_S:

```
public class LotsOfData_S extends HttpServlet {

    byte [] msgBytes = null;

    public void init(ServletConfig c) throws ServletException {

        super.init(c);
        String msg = "<html><head><title>Hello World</title></head><body>";
        for (int i = 0 ; i < 1000; i++) {
            msg += "<h1>Hello World 6</h1>";
        }
        msg += "</body></html>";
        msgBytes = msg.getBytes();
    }

    public void doGet (HttpServletRequest req,
                       HttpServletResponse res)
        throws ServletException, IOException {

        res.setContentType("text/html");

        ServletOutputStream out = res.getOutputStream();
        out.write(msgBytes);
    }
}
```

Now the performance results make a little more sense. The servlet that performs the character-to-byte conversion in the init() method is indeed noticeably more efficient. LotsOfData_S was measured at 80 requests per second whereas LotsOfData_W did only 70. See Figure 10.4 (higher is better).

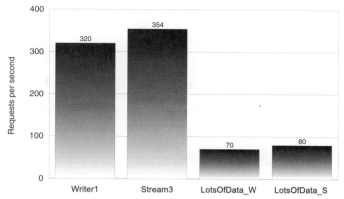

Figure 10.4. Precomputing the message bytes is more efficient

Figure 10.4 shows that one important factor that affects servlet performance is the amount of data generated. When we upped the amount of data from 220 bytes to 22 KB, servlet throughput took a severe beating. This is not just because I/O to a peripheral device is expensive. It is also because we copy the data from one buffer to another a few times along the way. In the case of the ServletOutputStream, I can think of three data movements:

- First we place the data into a byte array in the init() method. We'll consider this one to be free of charge.

- We then move the data to a buffer maintained by ServletOutputStream or a subclass extending it.

- From there, the data goes into a socket buffer maintained by the TCP/IP protocol stack.

- Finally, the data is copied into the device buffer, which is often a communication adapter of some sort.

In the case in which the data is generated on the fly in the service() (or doGet()) method, you'd also implicitly buffer the data in the character array internal to the String or StringBuffer objects.

Data moves consume CPU cycles, but worse than that, they eat up cache space. On a busy server, a large number of concurrent threads can easily overflow the cache. This overflow is directly proportional to the amount of data that each thread "touches." When the cache overflows, we are in trouble because accessing a byte in memory is an order of magnitude more expensive than accessing a byte present in the cache.

PingServlet—A Performance Upper Bound

Let's switch gears and turn our focus to the world's most efficient servlet. This is the Ping servlet:

```
public class Ping extends HttpServlet {

    static final String message = "<html>\n" +
        "<head><title>Ping</title></head>\n" +
        "<body>\n" +
        "<h1>Ping 7</h1>\n" +
        "</body></html>\n";
    static final byte[] bytes = message.getBytes();

    public void service(ServletRequest req,
                    ServletResponse res)
        throws ServletException, IOException {

        res.getOutputStream().write(bytes);
    }
}
```

Why is Ping the world's fastest servlet? Because it is the least common denominator of all servlets. It does the minimal amount of work that every servlet must do. As such, it serves as an upper-limit indicator for servlet performance. It just doesn't get any faster than that. These days, many people are coming out with a Web application server providing servlet support. The Ping servlet provides a good test case to evaluate the upper limit on the throughput of a Web application server under test. Of course, that limit will vary with the speed of the server hardware. On the particular four-way NT we were testing on, Ping servlet clocked in at 372 requests per second, as shown in Figure 10.5.

Some people consider Ping-type tests to be worthless because such do-nothing applications are not representative of any real-life workload. I, however, am not in that camp. Upper limits are important to know. They give meaning to the efficiency of real workloads. How would we know if a certain workload is executing efficiently if we had nothing to compare it against? Comparing it against the

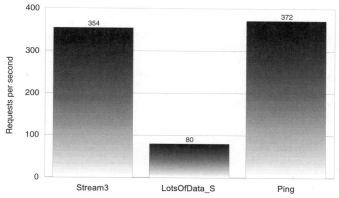

Figure 10.5.   `Ping` is a servlet performance upper bound

upper limit is a meaningful measure of relative efficiency. It could also help prevent excessive (and harmful) optimizations when the performance level is already close enough to being optimal. The importance of knowing the upper limit can hardly be overstated.

Extending `PingServlet`

Armed with an upper limit, we can extend `Ping` in various dimensions to make it a bit more realistic. Up until now we had knowledge of the complete servlet response right from the get-go of servlet loading. This is unrealistic. If the servlet response is of such static nature, it would have been a static HTML file, residing in the file system. If it is a servlet, then some of the response must be computed on the fly when the servlet request is handled. So we are in search of such dynamic content. How about counting the number of servlet invocations? The `PingCounter` servlet will maintain a counter that is bumped by one every time the servlet is invoked. Since multiple servlet requests may be handled concurrently, we must synchronize access to this counter. The code for `PingCounter` is given by

```
public class PingCounter extends HttpServlet {

    private static int counter;
    private static final String prefix =
            "<html>" +
            "<head><title>Hello World</title></head>" +
            "<body><h1>Counter = ";
    private static final String suffix = " </h1></body></html>";
    private static final byte[] prefixBytes = prefix.getBytes();
    private static final byte[] suffixBytes = suffix.getBytes();
```

```
public void service (HttpServletRequest req,
                     HttpServletResponse res)
    throws ServletException, IOException {

    res.setContentType("text/html");
    ServletOutputStream out = res.getOutputStream();
    String countString = null;

    synchronized (this) {
        counter++;
        countString = String.valueOf(counter);
    }

    out.write(prefixBytes);
    out.print(countString);
    out.write(suffixBytes);
    }
}
```

PingCounter is doing slightly more work than Ping did. It writes the data out in three steps instead of one, the countString must be converted to bytes on the fly and it also has to maintain a synchronized integer counter. Naturally, it is a little slower, as shown in Figure 10.6.

Session State

It is good to see that the performance of PingCounter is not too far off of that upper limit established by Ping. Let's move on and add some more complex-

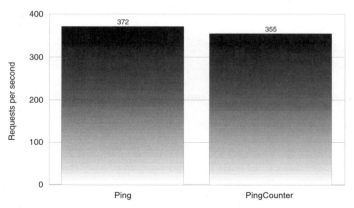

Figure 10.6. PingCounter trades some throughput for function

ity. PingCounter maintains a form of servlet state but it does not record any HTTP session state. HTTP session state is maintained by being able to correlate a sequence of HTTP requests originating from the same client. For example, if you buy books online, you'd be pretty annoyed if you were asked for your identity every time you add a book to your shopping cart. The fact that the server "remembers" who you are is the magic of session state. To learn more about session state, see *Java Servlet Programming* by Hunter and Crawford [JH98]. The PingSession servlet maintains a distinct counter for every user. For any user X, it knows how many times has X requested the invocation of PingSession:

```java
public class PingSession extends HttpServlet {

    private static final String prefix =
                "<html><head><title>Ping Session" +
                "</title></head><body><h1>" +
                "Ping Session</h1>" +
                "You have hit this page ";

    private static final String suffix = " times</body></html>";

    private static final byte[] prefixBytes = prefix.getBytes();
    private static final byte[] suffixBytes = suffix.getBytes();

    public void service (HttpServletRequest request,
                                    HttpServletResponse response)
                throws ServletException, IOException {

        HttpSession session = null;

        try {
            session = request.getSession(true);
        }
        catch (Exception e) {
            e.printStackTrace();
        }

        // Get the session data value
        Integer ival = (Integer)
            session.getValue ("sessiontest.counter");
        if (ival == null) ival = new Integer (1);
        else ival = new Integer (ival.intValue () + 1);
        session.putValue ("sessiontest.counter", ival);

        response.setContentType("text/html");
```

```
            ServletOutputStream out = response.getOutputStream();

            out.write(prefixBytes);
            out.print(ival.toString());
            out.write(suffixBytes);
        }
}
```

You can already see the emerging efficiency pattern. Some portions of the request are static and known in advance. Those portions are converted into bytes in the `init()` method. Only the session counter has to be created on the fly. Despite our heroic efforts, the throughput of the `PingSession` servlet has dropped significantly. See Figure 10.7.

The most popular technique for maintenance of session state is via cookie exchange between the client and server. The cookie is a string ID that the server creates to associate a particular user with an HTTP request. It is attached to the server's response. Subsequent requests from this particular client to that same server will include the cookie, which will identify the client to the server. Cookie handling forces the application server into significant amount of `String` crunching. Since most application servers do not utilize the `String` manipulation tricks we discussed in Chapter 1, session state takes a toll on performance.

PingJdbc

We are trying to evolve our servlet examples into more realistic scenarios. One of the building blocks of a realistic servlet is the fact that data often comes

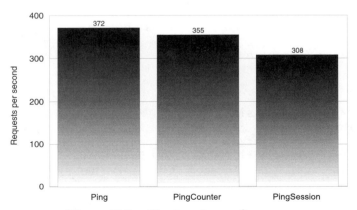

Figure 10.7. `PingSession` performance

from an outside source. So far, the servlet never had to leave the Java process in order to get the data. That is not a very practical scenario. In reality, the servlet is going to get its data from an outside source such as a database or RMI server. Those outside sources will often reside on remote physical servers. Next we will throw in database connectivity into the mix. The servlet will extract its data from a database via the JDBC interface:

```java
import java.io.*;
import java.sql.*;
import javax.servlet.*;
import javax.servlet.http.*;

public class PingJdbc extends HttpServlet {

    static {
        try {
            Class.forName("COM.ibm.db2.jdbc.app.DB2Driver");
        } catch (Exception e) {
            e.printStackTrace();
        }
    }

    private static final String prefix =
                "<html>" +
                "<head><title>Ping Jdbc</title></head>" +
                "<body><h1>";
    private static final String suffix =
                " </h1></body></html>";

    private static final byte[] prefixBytes = prefix.getBytes();
    private static final byte[] suffixBytes = suffix.getBytes();

    private static final String url = "jdbc:db2:sample";
    private static final String query =
                    "SELECT FIRSTNME from employee " +
                    "where LASTNAME = 'PARKER'" ;

    public void service(HttpServletRequest req,
                                    HttpServletResponse res)
            throws ServletException, IOException {

        try {
            // Get user and password
            String user = req.getParameter("user");
            String pw = req.getParameter("pw");
```

```
            // Connect using user/password
            Connection con = DriverManager.getConnection(url,user,pw);

            res.setContentType("text/html");

            // Next three lines prevent dynamic...
            // ... content from being cached on browsers.
            res.setHeader("Pragma", "no-cache");
            res.setHeader("Cache-Control", "no-cache");
            res.setDateHeader("Expires", 0);

            ServletOutputStream out = res.getOutputStream();
            out.write(prefixBytes);

            // Retrieve data from the database
            Statement stmt = con.createStatement();

            ResultSet rs = stmt.executeQuery(query);

            // Display the result set
            while (rs.next()) {
                String firstName = rs.getString(1);

                // The following is supposed to be
                // slightly faster than
                // out.print(" Hello " + firstName + " Parker");
                // although not as readable...
                StringBuffer buf = new StringBuffer(128);
              buf.append(" Hello " ).append(firstName).append(" Parker");
                out.print(buf.toString());
            }

            out.write(suffixBytes);

            rs.close();
            stmt.close();
            con.close();

        } catch( Exception e ) {
            e.printStackTrace();
        }
    }
}
```

On the performance front, we got hammered. Throughput has plummeted to 42 requests per second. See Figure 10.8.

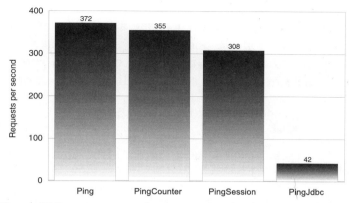

Figure 10.8. `PingJdbc`—database action dominates performance

We have bent over backwards to try and boost the performance of `PingJdbc`. For example, instead of executing

```
out.print(" Hello " + firstName + " Parker");
```

we have followed the advice given in Optimization 1 and used the more efficient equivalent,

```
StringBuffer buf = new StringBuffer(128);
buf.append(hello).append(firstName).append(parker);
out.print(buf.toString());
```

It didn't help. The performance of `PingJdbc` is dominated by the creation and destruction of a database connection per request. All of our efficiency tricks got overwhelmed by the cost of connection setup and teardown.

Caching JDBC Connections

As far as the database connections go, we must find a way to reuse connections if we have any chance at good throughput. Fortunately, connection pooling is offered by many vendors, including application server providers that bundle database connection pooling with the server. We are even providing one for free in Appendix A. This fine connection-pooling code was provided by Chet Murthy from IBM research [CM98]. It is provided in Appendix A for your hacking pleasure. Connection-pooling code maintains persistent connections to a database. When you close a connection, the connection pool does not really close it, it just puts it back in the pool. Similarly, when you request a new connection, the pool does not create a new one. It simply gives you an available connection from the pool. We only need to make two slight modifications to `PingJdbc` to allow it to use Chet's connection pooling code. First we have to load Chet's driver in the static initializer of the servlet class:

```
public class PingJdbcCache extends HttpServlet {
    static {
        try {
            Class.forName("COM.ibm.db2.jdbc.app.DB2Driver");
            Class.forName("COM.ibm.jdbc.cache.CacheDriver");
        }
    ...
}
```

Next we have to change the URL from

```
private static final String url = "jdbc:db2:sample";
```

to

```
private static final String url = "jdbc:cache:db2:sample";
```

That's it. Very simple. With `PingJdbcCache`, throughput climbed back to 205 requests per second. That's 5× performance boost over the plain `PingJdbc` servlet. See Figure 10.9.

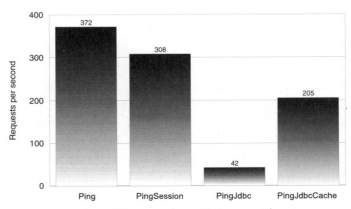

Figure 10.9. Caching JDBC connections

JSP—Java Server Pages

The next step towards real-life use is by incorporating Java Server Pages (JSP). The trend these days is towards making application development so easy that even nonprogrammers could synthesize nontrivial applications. JSP is an important step in this direction. A `PingJsp.jsp` script is as easy as

```
<html>
<head>
<title>PingJsp</title>
</head>

<H3> <% out.print("Ping JSP Script"); %> </H3>

</body>
</html>
```

When you invoke the JSP page for the very first time, the application server invokes the page compiler that transforms the JSP script into a servlet and compiles it. Future invocations of the JSP script will skip the compilation step and invoke that special servlet. The servlet and its compilation is all done automatically. You can write JSP scripts without having a clue about servlet programming. The performance, however, is another story. JSP performance, at this time, lags behind servlet performance. See Figure 10.10.

The first issue I have with JSP is that it forces the servlet to use a `Print-Writer`. As we learned earlier, servlets using `PrintWriter` are about 15 percent

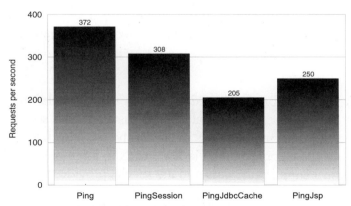

Figure 10.10. `PingJsp`—Java Server Pages

slower than those that use `ServletOutputStream`. The advantage is that all JSP-generated servlets automatically support internationalization. What if, on the other hand, we don't really need such internationalization support. In that case, you are stuck with the overhead of `PrintWriter`, like it or not. This is the classic trade-off between speeding application development and speeding the application execution. These two do not go hand in hand. It would be nice, from a performance perspective, if the JSP specification allowed developers to flag the fact that internationalization support is not necessary and to allow the page compiler to generate a servlet using `ServletOutputStream`.

So 15 percent of efficiency is due to the usage of `PrintWriter`, but `PingJsp` trails `Ping` by more than 15 percent. The rest depends on another factor. The page compilers do not generate servlet code that is as efficient as you and I could handcraft. I expect this efficiency will improve over time as application-server vendors tighten the implementations of the page compiler.

So the question is, Should you use a servlet or JSP for your application? I would use a servlet if and only if the two conditions below are satisfied:

- Performance of this application is critical. This application is going to get hit very often by a large crowd of concurrent users.

- The size of the response data is fairly small.

If either of these conditions is not met, I would use JSP for simplicity. If performance is not critical, then the answer is obvious. Otherwise, if the size of the generated response is fairly large, say, larger than 500 bytes, the performance will be dominated by the movement of data, as we have seen earlier in this chapter. That will narrow the gap between servlet and JSP performance.

RMI

There are various forms of outside sources that a servlet may go to in order to generate its response data. A database is just one such source. Another popular technique I've seen in practice is to isolate the business logic on a separate server and retrieve the response data via RMI calls to a remote object. In that case, the remote object supplies the data and the servlet provides the HTML formatting.

To measure the impact of RMI on servlet performance, we created a very simple RMI server object that returns a simple `String` object:

```
public interface RemoteServer extends Remote {
    public abstract String hiThere() throws RemoteException;
}

public class Server extends Thread implements RemoteServer {
    static public void main(String[] args) {
        try {
            Server server = new Server();
            Naming.rebind("Server", server);
            System.out.println("Server is ready...");
        }
        catch( Exception e ) {
            e.printStackTrace();
        }
    }

    public Server() throws RemoteException {
        super();
        UnicastRemoteObject.exportObject(this);
    }

    public String hiThere() {
        return "Hi There";
    }
}
```

The `hiThere()` method of the `Server` object is invoked by the `PingRmi` servlet via RMI:

```
public class PingRmi extends HttpServlet {

    private static final String prefix =
            "<html>" +
            "<head><title>Hello RMI World</title></head>" +
            "<body><h1>RMI server says ";
    private static final String suffix =
            " </h1></body></html>";
    private static final byte[] prefixBytes = prefix.getBytes();
    private static final byte[] suffixBytes = suffix.getBytes();

    private RemoteServer server;

    public void init(ServletConfig sc) {
        String url = "rmi://localhost/Server";

        try {
            server = (RemoteServer) Naming.lookup(url);
```

```
        } catch ( Exception e ) {
                e.printStackTrace();
        }
    }

    public void service (HttpServletRequest req,
                         HttpServletResponse res)
            throws ServletException, IOException {
        try {
            res.setContentType("text/html");
            ServletOutputStream out = res.getOutputStream();

            out.write(prefixBytes);
            out.print(server.hiThere()); // Make the RMI call
            out.write(suffixBytes);
        } catch ( Exception e ) {
                e.printStackTrace();
        }
    }
}
```

In our test, the RMI server and the servlet executed on the same physical box (four-way PC server) but on separate JVMs. The throughput numbers were surprisingly good considering that RMI calls necessitate socket I/O. Figure 10.11 adds PingRmi to the servlet performance mix.

RMI performance is very sensitive to the number and type of objects bounced back and forth as call-and-return arguments to the remote method. In our case,

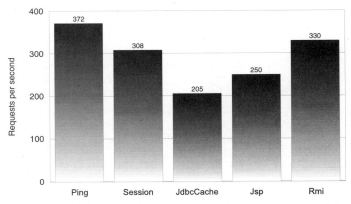

Figure 10.11. PingRmi performance relative to other servlets

we had no input parameters, and the return object was a simple `String`. In part this explains why `PingRmi` performed so well in comparison to the simple `Ping` upper bound. There were two other performance forces in this test case:

- The RMI server executed of the same physical machine. If it executed on a remote machine, we would have had to travel the whole TCP, IP, and device driver code paths. When the RMI object executes on the same machine, the underlying socket code is much cheaper because of significant shortcuts in the code path.

- On the other hand, running the RMI JVM on the same physical box steals CPU cycles from the Web application server.

Those are two competing forces that probably offset one another. If we ran the RMI server on a separate box, the results would not be much different. The deciding factor in RMI performance is serializing and deserializing call parameters and return value objects.

Key Points

- Using `print()` to send HTML data is more efficient than using `println()`. The `println()` method is more expensive, and the new line sequence is ignored by HTML parsers anyway. In practice, however, the performance difference may be negligible.

- Application servers use buffered output streams under your servlets. There is no point in using `StringBuffer append()` calls to try home-grown buffering. This practice could actually hurt performance because of excessive data movements.

- `PrintWriter` objects process output slower than does `ServletOutput-Stream`. Use a `PrintWriter` only if you need to convert from one character encoding scheme to another. If you are working only with ASCII text, use `ServletOutputStream`. It is more efficient.

- Converting Unicode characters to bytes is expensive. If you send characters down the stream, this conversion will take place under the covers. If significant portions of your data are static (they don't change between servlet invocations), then you should convert those characters to bytes in the servlet's `init()` method.

- Servlet performance is sensitive, among other things, to the amount of data generated. Larger amounts of data will equate to slower execution.

- Maintaining session state will exact a small price on performance.

- Servlets that use JDBC to get their data from a database must use some kind of connection pooling. Otherwise, performance is going to plummet as the cost of building and tearing down JDBC connections will dominate performance.

- Java Server Pages (JSP) is a convenience feature for those who don't want to bother with servlets. At this point in time, JSP implementations seem to lag behind in efficiency. A JSP script is slower than an equivalent servlet.

11

A Java Web Server

We have already touched upon the 80–20 principle in the context of software design and implementation (Optimization 15). The 80–20 principle has also played a role in the selection of optimizations covered earlier in this book. Our discussion is by no means a comprehensive account of all Java performance issues. It is simply an attempt to capture the dominant optimization opportunities that you are likely to encounter in a random Java application. To substantiate this claim, I thought it would be a good exercise to download a random Java application from the Internet and try to construct a mapping from our optimizations to their manifestations in this Java code. I also wanted to apply our optimizations to semi-real code and evaluate their true impact. I claim that the optimizations covered in this book could provide drastic improvements that could double or triple the performance and scalability of real-life Java applications.

The application we will work with in this chapter is a simple, minimal prototypical Web server written in Java [DB99]. It was written as a demonstration of a multithreaded Java server. You can view the full source code and a discussion of it at `http://developer.java.sun.com/developer/technicalArticles/Networking/Webserver/Webserver.java`. We start by introducing the original code. (We made some small modifications to get the code to compile and run, but it is faithful to the original.) We will then go through an iterative process of making incremental performance improvements.

All performance measurements in this chapter are given in terms of requests per second, where higher is better.

Version 1: The Original Server

This minimal HTTP server is capable of handling simple HTTP requests for HTML documents. It does not support CGI, servlets, or any other advanced features found in commercial servers. The Server object accepts new connections and hands them over to a worker thread for processing. Those worker threads are not created on demand. They are initialized in advance when the Server class is loaded.

The main() method of the Server starts by determining the port to listen on and then proceeds to load the server properties file. That file includes parameters such as the name of the server log file, socket read time-out, and size of the thread pool:

```
log=server.log
timeout=5000
workers=8
```

The Server then creates the thread pool and initializes the threads:

```
for (int i = 0; i < workers; ++i) {
   Worker w = new Worker();
   (new Thread(w, "worker #"+i)).start();
   threads.addElement(w);  // The thread pool
}
```

The Worker thread object doesn't do much at this point. It waits on a notify() to get started with some real work. The Server then proceeds to create the ServerSocket where new connections will be accepted

```
ServerSocket ss = new ServerSocket(port);
```

Now we are ready to go to work. The Server object goes on a never-ending while loop, accepting new connections and handing them over to a Worker thread. The Worker thread is selected from the pool of free threads:

```
while (true) {
   Socket s = ss.accept();
   Worker w = null;
   synchronized (threads) {
      if (threads.isEmpty()) {
         Worker ws = new Worker();
         ws.setSocket(s);
         (new Thread(ws, "additional worker")).start();
      } else {
          w = (Worker) threads.elementAt(0);
```

```
                    threads.removeElementAt(0);
                    w.setSocket(s); // Notify the worker thread that work is
                                    // available
            }
        }
}
```

That's it for Server main(). The rest of the action is in the Worker thread. The run() method contains an infinite loop that starts by waiting on a notify(). When the notification arrives (via setSocket()), the Worker handles a single HTTP request and then puts itself back on the pool of available threads and goes back to the wait state:

```
class Worker extends Server implements HttpConstants, Runnable {
    ...
    private Socket s;
    ...

    // The Server object calls setSocket() to notify...
    // ... the Worker of incoming work
    synchronized void setSocket(Socket s) {
        this.s = s;
        notify();
    }

    public synchronized void run() {
        while(true) {
            if (s == null) { // Nothing to do
                try {
                    wait();
                } catch (InterruptedException e) {
                    continue; // Should not happen
                }
            }
            try {
                handleClient();
            } catch (Exception e) {
                e.printStackTrace();
            }
            // Cleanup
            s = null;
            Vector pool = Server.threads;
            synchronized (pool) {
                if (pool.size() > Server.workers) {
                    return; // Too many threads, exit this one
                }
```

```
            else {
               pool.addElement(this); // Back to the pool
            }
         }
      }
   }
```

The `handleClient()` method called from within `run()` does most of the work. It reads the request from the socket, parses it, determines the target document, and sends it back. It also prepends the response HTTP headers and logs an entry in the server log. The log is a static member of the `Server` class:

```
class Server implements HttpConstants {

   ...
   // Print to the log file
   protected static void log(String s) {
      synchronized (log) {
         log.println(s);
         log.flush();
      }
   }

   static PrintStream log = System.out;
   ...
}
```

Although this is our starting point, we are not starting from ground zero. This initial version already contains two powerful optimizations. First, threads are being pooled in order to avoid a large performance penalty that results from creating and destroying threads on demand. This is an application of Optimization 37. The second major optimization relates to the fact that the `Worker` threads log the client's IP address (e.g., 9.37.123.456) in the log file as opposed to the client's host name (`dxb.raleigh.ibm.com`). Converting the IP address to a host name would require a very expensive reverse-DNS search on the performance-critical path. If host names are needed, you could easily write a utility to extract the IP addresses from the log file and replace them with fully qualified host names. That utility could run periodically in the background or even on a separate server machine. This strategy is related to Optimization 27. That optimization pushed an expensive computation out of the critical path and onto the initialization stage. We named it Precompute. In the Web server logging example we are looking at a Postcompute, but the idea is the same—move an expensive computation out of the critical path. Some computations must be performed prior to the critical path (Precompute), and some may be deferred for later (Postcompute.)

The following sections will discuss the optimizations we applied to the given code. Every version will be tested to quantify its performance gain. The test environment consisted of a client and server connected via a high-speed LAN (100 Mbps Fast-Ethernet.) The Java Web server was deployed on a four-way Netfinity server.[1] The client was a powerful 12-way AIX machine.[2] We chose a client that is more powerful than the server so that we could swamp the server and drive it to 100 percent CPU utilization. The Web server was configured to use a thread pool of eight threads, which is twice the number of processors on that machine. The client used 32 concurrent threads to repeatedly request an `index.html` file residing on the server machine.

Version 2

Caching is the performance engineer's best friend. We start by caching a few semistatic computations.

Cache the Date Response Header

The HTTP response headers contain two date headers. The `Date` header is a timestamp indicating the time the response was generated. The other header, `Last Modified`, specifies the age of the file—the last time it was modified. This is important for the browser to facilitate caching. The next time this document is requested by the user, the browser may use a locally cached value if the document has not been modified since the last timestamp. That makes two `Date` constructors per HTTP request. The `printHeaders()` method generates and writes the headers to the `PrintStream ps` object that is wrapped around the output socket. The document we are sending back is represented by a `File` object named `targ`:

```
boolean printHeaders(File targ, PrintStream ps)
    throws IOException {

   ...
```

---

[1] Pentium-II, 4X200 MHz running NT 4.0 and the IBM Win32 1.1.7 JVM.
[2] PowerPC, 12X166 MHz running AIX 4.3.2 and the IBM 1.1.6 JVM for AIX.

```
        ps.print("Date: " + (new Date()));
        ...
        ps.print("Last Modified: " +
                (new Date(targ.lastModified())));
        ...
}
```

`Date` constructors are expensive. We have already alluded to this fact in various places, including Optimization 28. Optimization 28 also suggests a solution in the form of relaxed granularity. As far as the instantaneous timestamp is concerned (`Date` header), the browser would not care if we were off by a second every once in a while. The `LazyDate` class introduced in Optimization 28 fits perfectly here. It will cache the value of the current date and refresh it once per second, spreading the cost of `Date` construction over hundreds or even thousands of requests. We add a `LazyDate` object as a private member of the `Worker` object. We will use that `LazyDate` object to generate timestamps:

```
private LazyDate today = new LazyDate(1000);
...
boolean printHeaders(File targ, PrintStream ps)
    throws IOException {
    ...
    // ** This is too accurate for our needs **
    // ps.print("Date: " + (new Date()));

    ps.print("Date: " + today.todaysDate()); // Use cached value
    ...
    ps.print("Last Modified: " +
            (new Date(targ.lastModified())));
    ...
}
```

That takes care of the first `Date` constructor. We now shift our focus to the second one, which specifies the document's Last Modified attribute.

Cache the File's *Last-Modified* Attribute

Instead of probing the system for the file's `Last-Modified` attribute on every request, we will perform this check only once per second. There's absolutely no harm in it in this scenario. Even if the file has been modified, the worst that could happen is that we would serve a one-second stale document that would have been the correct one a second ago. If you stop to think about it, this could have happened even if we never cached the Last-Modified value. Imagine an HTTP request arriving on a very busy server while the document is being modified. The document that will be served will depend on system timing issues with regard to thread scheduling. The server is indeterminate in this sense, and we exploit it. This approach is acceptable for this particular domain. It is essentially another application of Optimization 28. The FileCache class caches the last modified attribute of target files:

```
class FileCache {
    private Hashtable ht = new Hashtable();
    private long cacheRefresh; // Milliseconds

    public FileCache(long refresh) {
        cacheRefresh = refresh;
    }

    public String lastModified(File file) {
        LazyLastModified z = (LazyLastModified) ht.get(file.getName());
        if (z == null) {
            z = new LazyLastModified(file, cacheRefresh);
            ht.put(file.getName(), z);
        }

        return z.lastModified();
    }
}

class LazyLastModified {
    private File file;
    private long lastCheck;
    private String lastModified;
    private long cacheRefresh; // Milliseconds

    public LazyLastModified(File file, long refresh) {
        this.file = file;
        cacheRefresh = refresh;
        update();
    }

    public String lastModified() {
        long now = System.currentTimeMillis();
        if ((now-lastCheck) > cacheRefresh ) {
            update();
        }
```

```
        return lastModified;
    }

    // This is the expensive compuatation we are trying to avoid.
    // By design, it will seldom be called.
    private void update() {
        lastCheck = System.currentTimeMillis();
        lastModified = (new Date(file.lastModified())).toString();
    }
}
```

We incorporate this optimization into the printHeaders() method. Again, we add a private member to the Worker object to handle the caching of the Last-Modified attribute of requested files:

```
private LazyDate today = new LazyDate(1000);        // One-second
                                                    // refresh
private FileCache fileCache = new FileCache(1000);  // One-second
                                                    // refresh
...
boolean printHeaders(File targ, PrintStream ps)
    throws IOException {
    ...
    ps.print("Date: " + today.todaysDate());   // Use cached value
    ...
    // ps.print("Last Modified: " +                 // Too...
    //          (new Date(targ.lastModified()))));  // ...slow

    String lm = fileCache.lastModified(targ);  // This is...
    ps.print("Last Modified: " + lm);          // ... much better
    ...
}
```

There are about fifteen optimizations we are going to apply to this server in the course of this exercise. Figure 11.1 shows the performance improvement resulting from the elimination of the repeated Date computations.

The first two optimizations we have just performed have made a dent in the performance of the server. This improvement serves as an indicator of the substantial overhead hidden in the Date constructors.

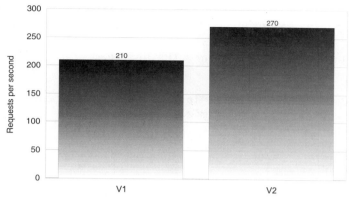

Figure 11.1. Comparing the original (version 1) to version 2

Version 3

Next on our agenda is the issue of char-to-byte conversion. A proper conversion of Unicode characters to a byte stream is expensive. We discussed this issue at length in Optimization 32 as well as in Optimization 4. Those optimizations would apply to our server code in two distinct areas: HTTP response headers and HTTP logging.

Exploit ASCII-to-Byte Conversion for HTTP Headers

We'll take on the HTTP response first. The response must be ASCII even if the document body is not. Treating the headers to a general-purpose Unicode conversion is unnecessary and inefficient. The fact that the headers are guaranteed to be ASCII opens up a substantial optimization opportunity that we can exploit (see Optimization 4). So far we have built the response incrementally via multiple print() calls:

```
static final byte[] EOL = {(byte)'\r', (byte)'\n' };
...
boolean printHeaders(File targ, PrintStream ps)
   throws IOException {
   ...
   ps.print("Server: Simple java");
   ps.write(EOL);
   ps.print("Date: " + today.todaysDate());
   ps.write(EOL);
   ...
}
```

Instead, we will build the response headers in a StringBuffer and then convert it to a byte array at once using a utility that exploits the fact that the input is ASCII:

```
boolean printHeaders(File targ, PrintStream ps)
   throws IOException {
   ...
   // Make the StringBuffer large enough to contain
   // all headers. See Optimization 8
   StringBuffer headers = new StringBuffer(512);

   // ps.print("Server: Simple java");
   // ps.write(EOL);
   headers.append("Server: Simple java\r\n");

   // ps.print("Date: " + today.todaysDate());
   // ps.write(EOL);
   headers.append("Date: " + today.todaysDate() + "\r\n");

   ...   // More headers

   // Optimization 4
   byte[] b = MyGetBytes.asciiGetBytes(headers.toString());
   ps.write(b, 0, b.length);
   ...
}
```

Along the way we made use of Optimization 8, which calls for the StringBuffer constructor to create a StringBuffer large enough to contain the expected string. We also used Optimization 4 to convert ASCII characters efficiently to bytes.

Use ASCII for Logging

A similar opportunity exists with respect to the log file. This log contains an entry describing each request handled by the server. Since I'd like my log data in ASCII format, there's no need for the generic char-to-byte conversion. I'm going to employ an ASCII shortcut. The following is the original code:

```
// Print HTTP log entries to the log file
protected static void log(String s) {
   synchronized (log) {
      log.println(s);
      log.flush();
   }
}
```

We are going to rearrange the code in two steps. First, we use Optimization 4 to perform a fast ASCII-to-byte conversion:

```
protected static void log(String s) {
    synchronized (log) {
        byte [] b = MyGetBytes.asciiGetBytes(s);
        log.write(b, 0, b.length);
        log.flush();
    }
}
```

But this is only half the story. The String object passed to this method is not a shared object. Consequently, it should not be protected by the synchronized block. It should be moved outside to reduce the synchronization scope (see Optimization 42). The following is preferred:

```
protected static void log(String s) {
    byte [] b = MyGetBytes.asciiGetBytes(s);

    synchronized (log) {
        log.write(b, 0, b.length);
        log.flush();
    }
}
```

Notice that the method signature has not changed and this modification is encapsulated in the log() method. Callers of this method are oblivious to this significant change.

Eliminate Needless Reset

The next optimization is very simple. We are just going to comment-out an unnecessary piece of code. The loop

```
// Zero out the buffer from last time
for (int i = 0; i < buf.length; i++) {
    buf[i] = 0;
}
```

is used by the handleClient() to zero out the buffer used for reading an incoming HTTP request. This computation is unnecessary (see Optimization 14), and we simply comment it out.

Reuse Threads in LIFO Order

The last optimization before we measure this version has to do with the order in which threads are selected from the pool. When a Worker thread is finished with a request, it puts itself back at the end of the Vector representing the pool:

```
Vector pool = Server.threads;
synchronized (pool) {
    ...
    pool.addElement(this); // Back to the pool
    ...
}
```

When the Server object has accepted a new connection, it selects a Worker thread from the pool. The problem is that it selects and removes the first one:

```
w = (Worker) threads.elementAt(0);
threads.removeElementAt(0);
```

There are two performance issues here. First, removing an element from the front of the Vector is inefficient because all the elements must be shifted by 1 (Optimization 17). The second issue is that the first thread in the pool has been there the longest. Therefore, it is the least likely of all the threads to find its instructions and data in the processor cache and memory. It is the most likely to encounter cache misses and page faults. It is likely to get a cold start. A better choice would be to impose a last in, first out policy on the thread pool by the use of a Stack (Optimization 38). We'll mimic a Stack behavior with our existing Vector since it is a one-line change:

```
int last = threads.size() - 1;
w = (Worker) threads.elementAt(last);
threads.removeElementAt(last);
```

The various optimizations applied to this version have resulted in another performance boost. See Figure 11.2.

Version 4

Cache the Response Headers

Every time the Worker thread handles an HTTP request, it is faced with a substantial amount of work involved in computing the response headers. Currently,

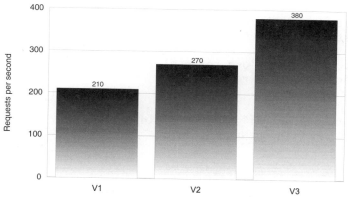

Figure 11.2.   Adding version 3 to the mix

this information is not preserved and is tossed away when the `printHeaders()` method returns. The nature of the Web is such that some documents are requested repeatedly. Some documents could be served hundreds of times per second. If we computed the response headers for the same document over and over, it would be a failure to take advantage of, and reuse, what we already know (Optimization 25). In this case, we want to cache and reuse the response headers for documents that are in "hot" demand. The only issue with caching response headers is that the `Date` header must be periodically refreshed to reflect the current timestamp. We solve this problem by expiring the cached values after one second.

We have used the `FileCache` object previously in this chapter to cache the document's `Last Modified` attribute, which is one of the response headers. It would be natural to expand the reach of the `FileCache` implementation to keep track of all the response headers, not just one. While we are at it, instead of storing the response headers in a Unicode `String` format, we can go ahead and compute the char-to-byte conversion and store the response headers in a byte array. Not only do we skip the need to compute the response headers once per request, but we also eliminate the need to perform a costly char-to-byte conversion over and over.

The new and improved `FileCache` implementation enables the storage of response headers for various documents in a byte array format. A creation timestamp is attached to each entry, and the entry will expire some time later (one second in our domain). When an entry is expired, it is removed from the `FileCache` and must be recomputed by the `printHeaders()` method.

```
class FileCache {
    private Hashtable ht = new Hashtable();
    private long cacheRefresh; // Milliseconds

    public FileCache(long refresh) {
        cacheRefresh = refresh;
    }

    public void put(File file, FileInfo fi) {
        ht.put(file.getName(), fi);
    }

    public FileInfo get(File file) {
        FileInfo fi = (FileInfo) ht.get(file.getName());
        if (fi == null) {
            return null;
        }
        long now = System.currentTimeMillis();
        if ((now-fi.getLastUpdate()) > cacheRefresh ) {
            ht.remove(file.getName());
            return null;
        }

        return fi;
    }
}
```

The FileCache is a wrapper around a Hashtable keyed by File objects and whose values are FileInfo objects. The FileInfo object holds the response headers for a particular document (file).

```
class FileInfo {
    private byte[] headers;
    private long lastUpdate;

    public FileInfo (byte[] h, long lu) {
        headers = h;
        content = null;
        lastUpdate = lu;
    }

    public void setHeaders(byte[] h) {
        headers = h;
    }

    public void setLastUpdate(long lu) {
        lastUpdate = lu;
    }
```

```java
    public byte[] getHeaders() {
        return headers;
    }

    public long getLastUpdate() {
        return lastUpdate;
    }
}
```

The first time a document is requested, the FileCache does not have a value for it, so we must go through the printHeaders() method to compute it:

```java
void handleClient() throws IOException {
    ...
    FileInfo fi = fileCache.get(targ);
    boolean OK = false;

    if (fi != null) {                    // Fast lane
        byte[] b = fi.getHeaders();
        ps.write(b, 0, b.length);
        OK = true;
    }
    else {                               // Slow, but this path is not
                                         // traveled very often
        OK = printHeaders(targ, ps);
    }
    ...
}
```

On subsequent requests within a one-second window, we are going to find the corresponding FileInfo object in the FileCache; then we take the execution "fast lane" and send the bytes straight down the stream. Otherwise, if the FileInfo is expired, we have to take the slow ride again through the print-Headers() method. However, by design, this traffic is not going to happen more than once per second. It is the responsibility of the printHeaders() method to generate the FileInfo object and add it to the FileCache:

```java
boolean printHeaders(File targ, PrintStream ps)
    throws IOException {

    ... // As before

    // Convert the headers into a byte array...
    // ...and send it down the stream
    byte[] b = MyGetBytes.asciiGetBytes(headers.toString());
    ps.write(b, 0, b.length);
```

```
    // Create a new FileInfo object and add it to the cache
    FileInfo fi = new FileInfo(b, System.currentTimeMillis());
    fileCache.put(targ, fi);
    ...
}
```

This takes care of caching the response headers from one request to the next in a one-second interval. Next we quickly dispose of a file I/O issue.

Eliminate Explicit Flushing

The log output stream is a `PrintStream` object wrapped around a `Buffered-OutputStream`:

```
log = new PrintStream(
        new BufferedOutputStream(
            new FileOutputStream(r)));
```

I like buffering I/O, but not if you are going to flush as often as the `log()` method does. It flushes every time, effectively undermining the buffering machinery:

```
protected static void log(String s) {
    byte [] b = MyGetBytes.asciiGetBytes(s);

    synchronized (log) {
        log.write(b, 0, b.length);
        log.flush();
    }
}
```

As pointed out by Optimization 31, the combination of buffering and frequent flushes could be worse than no buffering at all. To fix that problem, all we need to do is comment out the `flush()` call in `log()` and let the `BufferedOutput-Stream` implementation decide when to flush:

```
protected static void log(String s) {
        byte [] b = MyGetBytes.asciiGetBytes(s);

        synchronized (log) {
            log.write(b, 0, b.length);
/****           log.flush();    ****/        // Unnecessary
        }
}
```

Now, the implementation will collect a number of log records before flushing them to the file system. It should be pointed out that if the server crashes, we may lose a few log records that reside in the buffer and don't get a chance to be flushed. However, this is not expected to happen very often and could be considered a miniscule trade off. Besides, when the server crashes, losing a few log records is the least of our problems.

Increase Parallelism

Last, but not least, we modify the multithreading design of this server. This is a fundamental design change meant to enhance the scalability of the server. The original design had a main thread executing an infinite loop in the Server main() method. We'll call this one the Accept thread since it was in charge of accepting new connections. Once a connection was accepted by the Accept thread, it was handed over to one of the available Worker threads in the pool. This creates a scalability bottleneck in the form of sequential execution. The throughput of the server is bounded above by the speed of the Accept thread. We cannot serve more requests per second than the Accept thread can handle, regardless of the number of Worker threads in the pool (See Amdahl's Law in Chapter 7). The Accept thread presents a sequential execution stage that is built into the existing design. We need to take that design apart and eliminate the sequential stage. What we do is take away the responsibilities of the Accept thread and expand the job description of the Worker threads to include the accepting of new connections. The Worker threads from now on will listen on the port concurrently, waiting to establish new connections. Somewhere down the line, those Worker threads will collide inside the TCP/IP implementation of the Accept call, but this is a much smaller region of synchronization compared to the one we had with the Accept thread. This new design is a winner in three categories:

- It shortens the scope of sequential execution from the whole Accept thread to a few instructions in the core of the native implementation of the TCP/IP accept operation. This is a close relative of Optimization 42 that suggests the reduction of synchronized blocks.

- We eliminate the need for a thread pool and its management.

- An individual request is now handled by a single thread from start to finish. Previously, every request passed through both the Accept and Worker threads, thereby paying the penalty of a thread context-switch.

The downside of this design is that if the pool has a large number of Worker threads, all of them will get to execute and therefore increase the cache miss ratio and memory page-faults (See Optimization 38). In the previous design, we could have gotten away with a small number of active threads even if the pool was large. Most of the threads in the pool would rarely get activated. However, if this were a commercial product, we would implement a mechanism to dynamically control the number of Worker threads in the new model. It is just that we will not do it here. The new role of the Server main() method is reduced to creating the Worker threads and the ServerSocket to listen on:

```
ServerSocket ss = new ServerSocket(port);
for (int i = 0; i < workers; ++i) {
   Worker w = new Worker(ss);
   (new Thread(w, "worker #"+i)).start();
}
```

Notice that the Server object must create the ServerSocket before the Worker threads since the ServerSocket object is passed as a constructor argument to the Worker constructor.

There are corresponding changes on the Worker thread side. The whole wait() and notify() scheme is gone. The Worker takes a reference to the Server-Socket as a constructor argument and immediately goes to work:

```
class Worker extends Server implements HttpConstants, Runnable {
   ...
   private Socket s;
   private ServerSocket ss; // Listen socket for accepting new
                            // connections

   public Worker(ServerSocket ss) {
      buf = new byte[2048];  // Input buffer
      this.ss = ss;
      s = null;
   }

   public void run() {
      while(true) {
         try {
            s = ss.accept();  // Accept a new connection and ...
            handleClient();      // ...handle it.
         } catch (Exception e) {
            e.printStackTrace();
```

```
            }
        }
    }

    ...  // More implementation details
}
```

With these optimizations, we have received another performance boost, as shown in Figure 11.3.

Version 5

In this version we will aggressively expand the caching notion to any computation whose results have a likelihood of being useful on subsequent requests. We start with caching the file contents.

Cache HTML Documents

If some document is in high demand, there's no point in reading it from the file system every time. We ought to cache the document's contents in memory. We could expand the FileInfo object we used before to store the file contents as well as the response headers. That would be fine. However, if we are going to cache the document's content, we can incorporate another computing shortcut that eliminates the creation of a File object and the String manipulations leading up to it. Up to this point the mapping from URL to content was a two-step computation. First, we mapped the URL to a corresponding File object. With

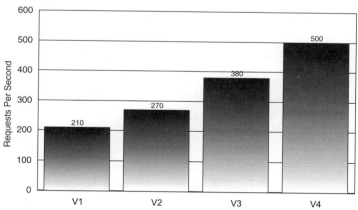

Figure 11.3.   Comparing version 4 to earlier versions

that File object at hand, we proceeded to the second step of retrieving its contents from the file system. The File object was the glue between URL and content:

```java
// Extract the filename from the HTTP request
String fname =
    (new String(buf, 0, index,i-index)).replace('/',
File.separatorChar);
if (fname.startsWith(File.separator)) {
    fname = fname.substring(1);
}
File targ = new File(Server.root, fname);
```

Why bother with the intermediate File object? If we are going to cache content, we can use the URL as a key to map directly into the corresponding content. The UrlCache helps us with this task. It is similar to the FileCache introduced earlier with the exception of using a URL String as a key:

```java
class UrlCache {
    private Hashtable ht = new Hashtable();
    private long cacheRefresh;

    public UrlCache(long refresh) {
        cacheRefresh = refresh;
    }

    public void put(String url, FileInfo fi) {
        ht.put(url, fi);
    }

    public FileInfo get(String url) {
        FileInfo fi = (FileInfo) ht.get(url);
        if (fi == null) {
            return null;
        }
        long now = System.currentTimeMillis();
        if ((now-fi.getLastUpdate()) > cacheRefresh ) {
            ht.remove(url);
            return null;
        }

        return fi;
    }
}
```

Like the FileCache, the UrlCache maintains an association between a key (URL) and a FileInfo object. While we are on the subject of document caching, we prefer to store the document in byte array rather than a String. A String of Unicode characters is slower to transmit than a byte array (Optimization 32) so we will cache the document's content in a byte array instead. The conversion of the content from Unicode to bytes will happen infrequently, when we get a document cache miss and we have to read the contents from the file system. Once the content is converted and cached, subsequent requests for the same document will take the execution fast lane. This is another subtle manifestation of pushing expensive computations out of the performance-critical path (Optimization 27). Since a document cache miss is expected to be a rare occurrence, the execution path of a cache miss is considered noncritical. This also means that we don't waste time or intellectual capital on trying to speed up the slow, noncritical execution path. For example, it would be okay to use the String.getBytes() to convert the file content into a byte array.

Again we are constructing a two-lane software highway—a fast lane that's taken most of the time and a slow one that's taken once per second (remember the 80–20 principle). The handleClient() method reads in the request, extracts the URL, and then looks in the UrlCache. If the information is cached, we get it and quickly send it down the stream. Otherwise, we take the slow route through printHeaders() and sendFile(). Those two methods will update the UrlCache for future requests:

```java
void handleClient() throws IOException {

    ... // Read the request and parse it

    FileInfo fi = urlCache.get(url);

    if (fi != null) {                               // Fast lane
        byte[] b = fi.getHeaders();
        ps.write(b, 0, b.length);
        byte[] c = fi.getContent();
        ps.write(c, 0, c.length);
    } else {                                        // Slow lane
        targ = urlToFile(url);
        if (printHeaders(targ, ps, url)) {
            sendFile(targ, ps, url);
        } else {
```

```
            send404(targ, ps);
        }
    }

    ... // Log and cleanup
}
```

Cache Client IP Addresses

The next caching optimization revolves around the creation of the log record for a particular request. A log record corresponding to an HTTP request for a URL named /index.html will typically look like

```
From 9.37.73.226: GET e:\server_root\6.0\index.html-->200
```

The log record is composed of the following tokens:

```
From <client IP address>: <HTTP Method> <file name>--><HTTP status code>
```

Composing this log record is expensive for two main reasons. First, and most important, computing the client's IP address dominates the cost as it uses

```
String ipAddr = s.getInetAddress().getHostAddress();
```

to convert a four-byte binary sequence to a dotted decimal String (such as "9.37.73.259", for example). Even though the number of clients surfing the Internet is very large, it is often the case that large number of physical HTTP clients are hidden behind an HTTP proxy that appears to the HTTP server as a single logical client. For example, there are 250,000 employees at IBM who may surf the Web but all of their HTTP requests appear to be originating from a single client, which happens to be the IBM HTTP proxy server. Consequently, caching the client's IP address may not be as crazy as it sounds at first.

The IP address cache will be a simple Hashtable. The values could be IP addresses in a dotted decimal form such as "9.37.73.226", but we can take it a step further and cache the first portion of the log record, as in "From 9.37.73.226". That eliminates the need to perform the String concatenation

```
String firstPortion = "From " + ipAddr;
```

when the IP address is present in the cache.

The secondary cost factor of the log record is found in all the String concatenations that must take place to combine various String objects into a single String. For that reason we try to cache as much as we can to avoid costly String manipulations. Consequently, we are also trying to cache the second portion of the log record that comes after the IP address:

```
: GET e:\server_root\6.0\index.html-->200
```

We simply add this field to the FileInfo object that's associated with a URL in the UrlCache object. Now the logging stage of our server works roughly like this:

- We try to retrieve the first portion of the log from the IP address cache. If it's there, fine. Otherwise, we compute it and add it to the cache for future reference.

- The same applies for the second portion of the log. We look for it in the UrlCache.

The code is given by

```
private void loggingStage(File targ, String url) {
   InetAddress ia = s.getInetAddress();   // s is the socket
   String firstHalf = (String) addressCache.get(ia);
   if (firstHalf == null) {
      firstHalf = "From " + ia.getHostAddress();
      addressCache.put(ia,firstHalf);
   }

   FileInfo fi = urlCache.get(url);
   String secondHalf = (fi == null) ?
                       null : fi.getLogSecondHalf();

   if (secondHalf == null) {
      int rCode = 0;
      if ( !targ.exists()) {
         rCode = HTTP_NOT_FOUND;
      } else {
           rCode = HTTP_OK;
      }

      secondHalf =  ": GET " +
                    targ.getAbsolutePath() +
                    "-->" +
                    rCode +
```

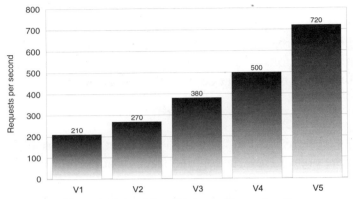

Figure 11.4.   Marching on with version 5

```
            "\r\n";
    if (fi != null) {
        fi.setLogSecondHalf(secondHalf);
    }
}

    log(firstHalf+secondHalf);
}
```

That's it for version 5. Our caching efforts have paid off with an additional boost in throughput. See Figure 11.4.

Version 6

Reuse What You Already Know

The failure to take advantage of previous results is one of the most common mistakes I have seen in commercial Java code. I have committed the same sin during the development of this server, and I will fix it now. The method responsible for putting together the log String needs to access the FileInfo object associated with the given URL. It tries to fetch the FileInfo object from the UrlCache:

```
private void loggingStage(File targ, String url) {
    ...
    FileInfo fi = urlCache.get(url);
    ...
}
```

However, the `FileInfo` object associated with this URL was already available to the caller of `loggingStage()`. The optimization is as simple as passing a reference to the `FileInfo` object as an argument to the method that needs it:

```
private void loggingStage(String url, FileInfo fi) {
  ...
/****   FileInfo fi = urlCache.get(url);  ****/  // Unnecessary
  ...
}
```

We have thus eliminated a costly `Hashtable` search.

Prefer Byte Arrays to String Objects

When we cache data that is meant for an output stream, we prefer to cache it as byte array instead of a `String` object. We apply this idea to the two portions of the log record. The first half is kept in the IP address cache and the other in the `FileInfo` object. We change their representations from a `String` object to a byte array. Instead of calling the log method once with a `String` argument, we will call it twice with a byte-array argument. The small overhead of calling the method twice is more than compensated for by eliminating the need to glue the two portions into a single `String` and having to convert it into a byte array on the fly:

```
private void loggingStage(String url, FileInfo fi)
     throws IOException {

    InetAddress ia = s.getInetAddress();

    byte[] firstHalf = (byte[]) addressCache.get(ia);
    if (firstHalf == null) {
       firstHalf = ("From " + ia.getHostAddress()).getBytes();
       addressCache.put(ia,firstHalf);
    }

    ... // Fix the second half as a byte array

    log(firstHalf);
    log(secondHalf);
  }
```

The `log()` method must also be modified to accept a byte array argument instead of a `String`:

```
protected static void log(byte[] b) throws IOException {
    synchronized (log) {
        log.write(b, 0, b.length);
    }
}
}
```

Replace a *PrintStream* with an *OutputStream*

This is a minor optimization but it illustrates the point that you don't want to deploy complex solutions that were meant for bigger problems, because performance trades off with complexity. Generally, simpler solutions for smaller problems will run faster. The log file is a case in point. We don't need and don't use the advanced functionality of a `PrintStream` or a `PrintWriter`. All we need is an output stream. Therefore, we modify the log stream from a `PrintStream` to an `OutputStream`:

```
log = /**** new PrintStream ****/   // Don't really need that
      (new BufferedOutputStream(
          new FileOutputStream(r)));
```

Buffer Output Data

The last optimization we perform is a significant one. Right now the output stream that is wrapped around the socket is unbuffered, and that may cost us multiple physical network I/O operations. This is a simple change from

```
PrintStream ps = new PrintStream(s.getOutputStream());
```

to

```
OutputStream ps = new BufferedOutputStream(s.getOutputStream());
```

Let's run another measurement. The results are given by Figure 11.5.

We got another significant boost in throughput. Profiling this version indicated that the bulk of CPU cycles are now consumed in the TCP/IP system calls such as `accept()`, `read()`, `write()`, and `close()`. There's not much that we can do about that from the application layer. Although some Java optimization issues are probably still lurking around version 6, they would demand substantial effort for diminishing returns. We have taken this server implementation from 210 requests-per-second to 925. That's more than 4× improvement.

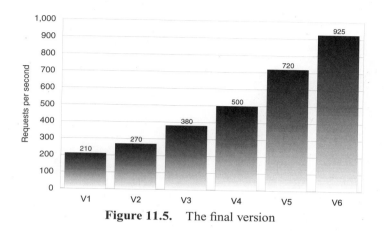

Figure 11.5.   The final version

Keep in mind that the initial implementation was already in pretty good shape from a performance perspective. It had two elements going in its favor:

- It was written by an expert Java programmer.

- It was a very simple application. Complex commercial applications would present us with many more opportunities to commit software performance mistakes.

Even so, we have managed to squeeze a 4× performance speedup by using some of the optimizations we developed in earlier chapters.

Key Point

- The performance optimizations presented in this book are capable of making a significant difference in the performance and scalability of Java code.

Caching JDBC Connections

CacheDriver.java

```
package COM.ibm.jdbc.cache;

import java.lang.*;
import java.sql.*;
import java.util.*;
import java.io.*;

public class CacheDriver implements java.sql.Driver {
  private static CacheDriver ourDriver;

  private Properties p;

  static {
    ourDriver = new CacheDriver();
    /*BEGIN REMOVE THIS CODE AND INITIALIZE CONFIG VARIABLES IF YOU WANT*/
    try {
        ourDriver.init();
    } catch (IOException e) {
        if (null!=DriverManager.getLogStream()) {
            DriverManager.println("Error Reading CacheDriver +
                                  "properties: "+e);
            e.printStackTrace(DriverManager.getLogStream());
        }
        System.err.println("Error Reading CacheDriver properties: "+e);
        e.printStackTrace(System.err);
    }
    /*END REMOVE*/

    try {
       java.sql.DriverManager.registerDriver(ourDriver);
    } catch (SQLException e) {
        DriverManager.println("Error registering driver" +
                    " COM.ibm.jdbc.cache.CacheDriver");
        DriverManager.println("Message:   "+e.getMessage());
        DriverManager.println("SQL State: "+e.getSQLState());
```

```
                        DriverManager.println("Code:        "+e.getErrorCode());
        }
}

static final String RSRC = "CacheDriver.properties";

/*BEGIN IF YOU REMOVED THE INIT STANZA,
  THEN YOU MUST CONFIGURE THESE*/
static int maxDBs = 0;
static int initConnsPerDB = 0;
static int maxPooledConnsPerDB = 0;
static int maxConnsPerDB = 0;
/*END IF*/

public void init() throws IOException {
   p = null;

   InputStream is = getClass().getResourceAsStream(RSRC);
   if (is == null) {
      throw new IOException("Cannot read resources file" +
                            "<<"+RSRC+>>");
   } else {
       p = new Properties();
       p.load(is);
       for (Enumeration e = p.propertyNames();
            e.hasMoreElements();
            System.err.println("CacheDriver Property : " +
                               (String)e.nextElement()));
   }

  {
   String nowIniting = null;
   try {
      nowIniting = "CacheDriver.maxDBs";
      if (null!=p.get(nowIniting))
         maxDBs = Integer.parseInt((String)p.get(nowIniting));
      nowIniting = "CacheDriver.initConnsPerDB";
      if (null!=p.get(nowIniting))
         initConnsPerDB =
             Integer.parseInt((String)p.get(nowIniting));
      nowIniting = "CacheDriver.maxPooledConnsPerDB";
      if (null!=p.get(nowIniting))
         maxPooledConnsPerDB =
             Integer.parseInt((String)p.get(nowIniting));
      nowIniting = "CacheDriver.maxConnsPerDB";
      if (null!=p.get(nowIniting))
         maxConnsPerDB =
             Integer.parseInt((String)p.get(nowIniting));
```

```
      } catch (Exception e) {
          System.err.println("[CACHE: Exception initializing"
                             +nowIniting+"]");
      }
   }
}

static public void abandonConnection(String key, Connection con)
            throws SQLException {
   if (con==null) {
      System.err.println("[ACK! trying to abandon NULL connection"
                     + " with key <<"+key+">>");
      (new Throwable()).printStackTrace(System.err);
      return;
   }
   ourDriver.doAbandonConnection(key,con);
}

static public void returnConnection(String key, Connection con)
            throws SQLException {
   ourDriver.doReturnConnection(key, con);
}

static final String CACHE_PREFIX = "jdbc:cache:";

static private String decomposeURL(String url) {
   if (url.startsWith(CACHE_PREFIX)) {
      return "jdbc:"+(url.substring(CACHE_PREFIX.length()));
   } else {
      return null;
      }
}

private CacheDriver () {
}

//private sun.misc.Cache conns = new sun.misc.Cache();
private java.util.Hashtable conns = new java.util.Hashtable();

private void doAbandonConnection(String key, Connection con)
        throws SQLException {
   System.err.println("[CACHE: abandoning connection <<"
                      +con+">>]");
   ConnectionPool pool = null;
   synchronized(conns) {
      pool = (ConnectionPool)conns.get(key);
```

```java
        if (pool == null) {
            System.err.println("[ACK! no stack for <<"+key+">>]");
            con.close();
            return;
        }
    }

    pool.abandonConnection(con);
}

private void doReturnConnection(String key, Connection con)
        throws SQLException {
    //System.err.println("[CACHE: releasing connection <<"
                            +con+">>]");
    ConnectionPool pool = null;

    synchronized(conns) {
      pool = (ConnectionPool)conns.get(key);
      if (pool == null) {
          System.err.println("[ACK! no stack for <<"+key+">>]");
          con.close();
          return;
      }
    }

    pool.putConnection(con);
}

private static Connection createConnection(String newurl,
                                    java.util.Properties info)
        throws SQLException {
    return DriverManager.getConnection(newurl,info);
}

public Connection connect(String url, java.util.Properties info)
        throws SQLException {
    if (this != ourDriver) return ourDriver.connect(url,info);

    String newurl = decomposeURL(url);
    if (newurl == null) return null;
    ConnectionPool pool = null;
    String key = newurl+info.toString();

    synchronized (conns) {
        if (conns.size() >= CacheDriver.maxDBs) {
            System.err.println("[CACHE: punting on connection to <<"
                            +url+">>]");
            return createConnection(newurl,info);
        }
```

```
        pool = (ConnectionPool)conns.get(key);

        if (pool == null) {
            System.err.println("[CACHE: new stack for <<"+key+">>]");
            pool = new ConnectionPool(maxPooledConnsPerDB,
                                      key,
                                      newurl,
                                      info);
            conns.put(key,pool);
        }
    }

    return pool.getConnection(newurl,info);
}

public boolean acceptsURL(String url)
        throws SQLException {
    if (this != ourDriver) return ourDriver.acceptsURL(url);
    String newurl;

    return (null != (newurl = decomposeURL(url))) &&
           (null != DriverManager.getDriver(newurl));
}

public DriverPropertyInfo[] getPropertyInfo(String url,
                            java.util.Properties info)
        throws SQLException {
  if (this != ourDriver)
     return ourDriver.getPropertyInfo(url,info);

  String newurl;
  Driver d;

  return ((null != (newurl = decomposeURL(url))) &&
          (null != (d = DriverManager.getDriver(newurl)))) ?
          d.getPropertyInfo(newurl,info) : null;
}

public int getMajorVersion() {
    return 0;
}
public int getMinorVersion() {
    return 1;
}
```

```java
    public boolean jdbcCompliant() {
        return true;
    }
}

class ConnectionPool extends java.util.Stack {
    int waiters;
    int numconns;

    public ConnectionPool (int capacity,
                           String key,
                           String url,
                           java.util.Properties info)
            throws SQLException {
        super();
        ensureCapacity(capacity);
        waiters = 0;
        numconns = 0;

        try {
            System.err.println("[CACHE: creating "+
                                CacheDriver.initConnsPerDB+
                                " initial connections for url=<<"+
                                url+
                                ">>]");
            while (numconns < CacheDriver.initConnsPerDB) {
                System.err.println("[CACHE: create initial url=<<"+url+">>]");
                Connection c = DriverManager.getConnection(url,info);
                System.err.println("[CACHE: created initial url=<<"+
                                url+
                                ">> <<"+
                                c+
                                ">>, "+
                                numconns+
                                " conns extant]");
                push(c);
                numconns++;
            }
        } catch (Error e) {
            System.err.println("[CACHE: error in creating initial connections <<"+
                            e+
                            ">>]");
            e.printStackTrace(System.err);
            throw e;
        }
    }
```

```java
    public void abandonConnection(Connection c)
            throws SQLException {

        System.err.println("[CACHE: abandoning connection <<"+c+">>]");
        synchronized(this) {
            numconns--;
        }
        c.close();
    }

    public synchronized void putConnection(Connection c) {
        //System.err.println("[CACHE: put <<"+c+">>]");
        push(c);
        if (size() > CacheDriver.maxConnsPerDB) {
            System.err.println("[ACK!: size was "+
                            size()+
                            ", max was "+
                            CacheDriver.maxConnsPerDB+
                            "]");
        }
        if (waiters > 0) {
            notify();
        }
    }

    public synchronized Connection getConnection(String url,
                                java.util.Properties info)
            throws SQLException {
        try {
            String key = url+info.toString();
            if (!empty()) {
                Connection c = (Connection) pop();
                //System.err.println("[CACHE: reuse <<"+c+">>]");
                return new CacheConnection(key,c);
            }

            if (numconns < CacheDriver.maxConnsPerDB) {
                System.err.println("[CACHE: create url=<<"+url+">>]");
                Connection c = DriverManager.getConnection(url,info);
                System.err.println("[CACHE: created url=<<"+
                            url+
                            ">> <<"+
                            c+
                            ">>, "+
                            numconns+
                            " conns extant]");
                CacheConnection cc = new CacheConnection(key,c);
                numconns++;
```

```
            return cc;
        }

        System.err.println("[CACHE: WAIT]");
        waiters++;
        do {
            try { wait(1000); } catch (InterruptedException e) {}
        } while (empty());
        waiters--;
        Connection c = (Connection)pop();
        //System.err.println("[CACHE: reuse <<"+c+">>]");
        return new CacheConnection(key,c);
    } catch (Error e) {
        System.err.println("[CACHE: error in getConnection <<"
                            +e+">>]");
        e.printStackTrace(System.err);
        throw e;
    }
  }
}
```

CacheConnection.java

```
package COM.ibm.jdbc.cache;

import java.lang.*;
import java.sql.*;
import java.util.*;

public class CacheConnection implements java.sql.Connection {

  private String key;
  private Connection con;
  private boolean abandon;

  CacheConnection(String key, Connection con) {
     this.key = key;
     this.con = con;
     this.abandon = false;
  }

  public void setAbandon() {
     System.err.println("[CACHE: abandoning connection <<"+
                         this+
                         ">>/<<"+
                         this.con+
                         ">>]");
     this.abandon = true;
  }
```

```java
public boolean getAbandon() { return this.abandon; }

public Statement createStatement() throws SQLException {
    try {
        return new CacheStatement(this,this.con.createStatement());
    } catch (SQLException e) {
        this.setAbandon();
        throw e;
    }
}

public PreparedStatement prepareStatement(String sql)
        throws SQLException {
    try {
        return new
          CachePreparedStatement(this,
                this.con.prepareStatement(sql));
    } catch (SQLException e) {
        this.setAbandon();
        throw e;
    }
}

public CallableStatement prepareCall(String sql)
          throws SQLException {
    try {
        return new
          CacheCallableStatement(this,
                this.con.prepareCall(sql));
    } catch (SQLException e) {
        this.setAbandon();
        throw e;
    }
}

public String nativeSQL(String sql) throws SQLException {
    try {
        return this.con.nativeSQL(sql);
    } catch (SQLException e) {
        this.setAbandon();
        throw e;
    }
}

public void setAutoCommit(boolean autoCommit)
        throws SQLException {
```

```java
        try {
            this.con.setAutoCommit(autoCommit);
        } catch (SQLException e) {
            this.setAbandon();
            throw e;
        }
    }

    public boolean getAutoCommit() throws SQLException {
        try {
            return this.con.getAutoCommit();
        } catch (SQLException e) {
            this.setAbandon();
            throw e;
        }
    }

    public void commit() throws SQLException {
        try {
            this.con.commit();
        } catch (SQLException e) {
            this.setAbandon();
            throw e;
        }
    }

    public void rollback() throws SQLException {
        try {
            this.con.rollback();
        } catch (SQLException e) {
            this.setAbandon();
            throw e;
        }
    }

    public void close() throws SQLException {
        Connection c = con;
        con = null;
        boolean already_closed = true;
        try {
            already_closed = c.isClosed();
        } catch (SQLException e) {
            System.err.println("[CACHE: EXN in close(): "+e+"]");
            e.printStackTrace(System.err);
            setAbandon();
        }
        if (getAbandon() || already_closed) {
```

```java
            CacheDriver.abandonConnection(key,c);
        } else {
            CacheDriver.returnConnection(key,c);
        }
    }

    public boolean isClosed() throws SQLException {
        try {
            return this.con.isClosed();
        } catch (SQLException e) {
            this.setAbandon();
            throw e;
        }
    }

//=========== Advanced features: =================

    public DatabaseMetaData getMetaData() throws SQLException {
        try {
            return this.con.getMetaData();
        } catch (SQLException e) {
            this.setAbandon();
            throw e;
        }
    }

    public void setReadOnly(boolean readOnly) throws SQLException {
        try {
            this.con.setReadOnly(readOnly);
        } catch (SQLException e) {
            this.setAbandon();
            throw e;
        }
    }

    public boolean isReadOnly() throws SQLException {
        try {
            return this.con.isReadOnly();
        } catch (SQLException e) {
            this.setAbandon();
            throw e;
        }
    }

    public void setCatalog(String catalog) throws SQLException {
        try {
            this.con.setCatalog(catalog);
```

```java
        } catch (SQLException e) {
            this.setAbandon();
            throw e;
        }
    }

    public String getCatalog() throws SQLException {
        try {
            return this.con.getCatalog();
        } catch (SQLException e) {
            this.setAbandon();
            throw e;
        }
    }

    public void setTransactionIsolation(int level)
            throws SQLException {
        try {
            this.con.setTransactionIsolation(level);
        } catch (SQLException e) {
            this.setAbandon();
            throw e;
        }
    }

    public int getTransactionIsolation() throws SQLException {
        try {
            return this.con.getTransactionIsolation();
        } catch (SQLException e) {
            this.setAbandon();
            throw e;
        }
    }

    public SQLWarning getWarnings() throws SQLException {
        try {
            return this.con.getWarnings();
        } catch (SQLException e) {
            this.setAbandon();
            throw e;
        }
    }

    public void clearWarnings() throws SQLException {
        try {
            this.con.clearWarnings();
        } catch (SQLException e) {
```

```
                   this.setAbandon();
                   throw e;
                }
           }
      }
}
```

CacheStatement.java

```java
package COM.ibm.jdbc.cache;

import java.lang.*;
import java.sql.*;
import java.util.*;

public class CacheStatement implements java.sql.Statement {

   protected CacheConnection c;
   protected Statement stmt;

   public CacheStatement(CacheConnection c,Statement stmt) {
      this.c = c;
      this.stmt = stmt;
   }

   public ResultSet executeQuery(String sql) throws SQLException {
      try {
         return this.stmt.executeQuery(sql);
      } catch (SQLException e) {
         c.setAbandon();
         throw e;
      }
   }
   public int executeUpdate(String sql) throws SQLException {
      try {
         return this.stmt.executeUpdate(sql);
      } catch (SQLException e) {
         c.setAbandon();
         throw e;
      }
   }

   public void close() throws SQLException {
      try {
         this.stmt.close();
      } catch (SQLException e) {
         c.setAbandon();
         throw e;
      }
   }
```

```
public int getMaxFieldSize() throws SQLException {
    try {
        return this.stmt.getMaxFieldSize();
    } catch (SQLException e) {
        c.setAbandon();
        throw e;
    }
}

public void setMaxFieldSize(int max) throws SQLException {
    try {
        this.stmt.setMaxFieldSize(max);
    } catch (SQLException e) {
        c.setAbandon();
        throw e;
    }
}

public int getMaxRows() throws SQLException {
    try {
        return this.stmt.getMaxRows();
    } catch (SQLException e) {
        c.setAbandon();
        throw e;
    }
}

public void setMaxRows(int max) throws SQLException {
    try {
        this.stmt.setMaxRows(max);
    } catch (SQLException e) {
        c.setAbandon();
        throw e;
    }
}

public void setEscapeProcessing(boolean enable) throws SQLException
{
    try {
        this.stmt.setEscapeProcessing(enable);
    } catch (SQLException e) {
        c.setAbandon();
        throw e;
    }
}
```

```java
public int getQueryTimeout() throws SQLException {
    try {
        return this.stmt.getQueryTimeout();
    } catch (SQLException e) {
        c.setAbandon();
        throw e;
    }
}

public void setQueryTimeout(int seconds) throws SQLException {
    try {
        this.stmt.setQueryTimeout(seconds);
    } catch (SQLException e) {
        c.setAbandon();
        throw e;
    }
}

public void cancel() throws SQLException {
    try {
        this.stmt.cancel();
    } catch (SQLException e) {
        c.setAbandon();
        throw e;
    }
}

public SQLWarning getWarnings() throws SQLException {
    try {
        return this.stmt.getWarnings();
    } catch (SQLException e) {
        c.setAbandon();
        throw e;
    }
}

public void clearWarnings() throws SQLException {
    try {
        this.stmt.clearWarnings();
    } catch (SQLException e) {
        c.setAbandon();
        throw e;
    }
}
```

```java
public void setCursorName(String name) throws SQLException {
    try {
        this.stmt.setCursorName(name);
    } catch (SQLException e) {
        c.setAbandon();
        throw e;
    }
}

public boolean execute(String sql) throws SQLException {
    try {
        return this.stmt.execute(sql);
    } catch (SQLException e) {
        c.setAbandon();
        throw e;
    }
}

public ResultSet getResultSet() throws SQLException {
    try {
        return this.stmt.getResultSet();
    } catch (SQLException e) {
        c.setAbandon();
        throw e;
    }
}

public int getUpdateCount() throws SQLException {
    try {
        return this.stmt.getUpdateCount();
    } catch (SQLException e) {
        c.setAbandon();
        throw e;
    }
}

public boolean getMoreResults() throws SQLException {
    try {
        return this.stmt.getMoreResults();
    } catch (SQLException e) {
        c.setAbandon();
        throw e;
    }
}
}
```

CacheCallableStatement.java

```java
package COM.ibm.jdbc.cache;

import java.lang.*;
import java.sql.*;
import java.util.*;

import java.math.BigDecimal;

public class CacheCallableStatement
        extends CachePreparedStatement
        implements java.sql.CallableStatement {

  protected CallableStatement cstmt;

  public CacheCallableStatement(CacheConnection c,
                                CallableStatement cstmt) {
    super(c,cstmt);
    this.cstmt = cstmt;
  }

  public void registerOutParameter(int parameterIndex, int sqlType)
        throws SQLException {
    try {
      this.cstmt.registerOutParameter(parameterIndex, sqlType);
    } catch (SQLException e) {
        c.setAbandon();
        throw e;
      }
  }

  public void registerOutParameter(int parameterIndex,
                                   int sqlType,
                                   int scale)
        throws SQLException {
    try {
      this.cstmt.registerOutParameter(parameterIndex, sqlType,
                                      scale);
    } catch (SQLException e) {
        c.setAbandon();
        throw e;
      }
  }
```

```java
public boolean wasNull() throws SQLException {
   try {
      return this.cstmt.wasNull();
   } catch (SQLException e) {
      c.setAbandon();
      throw e;
   }
}

public String getString(int parameterIndex) throws SQLException {
   try {
      return this.cstmt.getString(parameterIndex);
   } catch (SQLException e) {
      c.setAbandon();
      throw e;
   }
}

public boolean getBoolean(int parameterIndex) throws SQLException {
   try {
      return this.cstmt.getBoolean(parameterIndex);
   } catch (SQLException e) {
      c.setAbandon();
      throw e;
   }
}

public byte getByte(int parameterIndex) throws SQLException {
   try {
      return this.cstmt.getByte(parameterIndex);
   } catch (SQLException e) {
      c.setAbandon();
      throw e;
   }
}

public short getShort(int parameterIndex) throws SQLException {
   try {
      return this.cstmt.getShort(parameterIndex);
   } catch (SQLException e) {
      c.setAbandon();
      throw e;
   }
}
```

```java
    public int getInt(int parameterIndex) throws SQLException {
       try {
          return this.cstmt.getInt(parameterIndex);
       } catch (SQLException e) {
            c.setAbandon();
            throw e;
         }
    }

    public long getLong(int parameterIndex) throws SQLException {
       try {
          return this.cstmt.getLong(parameterIndex);
       } catch (SQLException e) {
            c.setAbandon();
            throw e;
         }
    }

    public float getFloat(int parameterIndex) throws SQLException {
       try {
          return this.cstmt.getFloat(parameterIndex);
       } catch (SQLException e) {
            c.setAbandon();
            throw e;
         }
    }

    public double getDouble(int parameterIndex) throws SQLException {
       try {
          return this.cstmt.getDouble(parameterIndex);
       } catch (SQLException e) {
            c.setAbandon();
            throw e;
         }
    }

      public BigDecimal getBigDecimal(int parameterIndex, int scale)
              throws SQLException {
         try {
            return this.cstmt.getBigDecimal(parameterIndex, scale);
         } catch (SQLException e) {
              c.setAbandon();
              throw e;
           }
      }
```

```java
public byte[] getBytes(int parameterIndex) throws SQLException {
   try {
      return this.cstmt.getBytes(parameterIndex);
   } catch (SQLException e) {
       c.setAbandon();
       throw e;
   }
}

public java.sql.Date getDate(int parameterIndex)
      throws SQLException {
   try {
      return this.cstmt.getDate(parameterIndex);
   } catch (SQLException e) {
       c.setAbandon();
       throw e;
   }
}

public java.sql.Time getTime(int parameterIndex)
      throws SQLException {
   try {
      return this.cstmt.getTime(parameterIndex);
   } catch (SQLException e) {
       c.setAbandon();
       throw e;
   }
}
public java.sql.Timestamp getTimestamp(int parameterIndex)
         throws SQLException {
   try {
      return this.cstmt.getTimestamp(parameterIndex);
   } catch (SQLException e) {
       c.setAbandon();
       throw e;
   }
}

   //========= Advanced features: ===============

public Object getObject(int parameterIndex) throws SQLException {
   try {
      return this.cstmt.getObject(parameterIndex);
   } catch (SQLException e) {
       c.setAbandon();
       throw e;
   }
}
}
```

CachePreparedStatement.java

```java
package COM.ibm.jdbc.cache;

import java.lang.*;
import java.sql.*;
import java.util.*;
import java.math.BigDecimal;

public class CachePreparedStatement
        extends CacheStatement
        implements java.sql.PreparedStatement  {

  protected PreparedStatement pstmt;

  public CachePreparedStatement(CacheConnection c,
                                PreparedStatement pstmt) {
      super(c,pstmt);
      this.pstmt = pstmt;
  }

  public ResultSet executeQuery() throws SQLException {
      try {
         return this.pstmt.executeQuery();
      } catch (SQLException e) {
          c.setAbandon();
          throw e;
      }
  }

  public int executeUpdate() throws SQLException {
      try {
         return this.pstmt.executeUpdate();
      } catch (SQLException e) {
          c.setAbandon();
          throw e;
      }
  }

  public void setNull(int parameterIndex, int sqlType)
        throws SQLException {
      try {
         this.pstmt.setNull(parameterIndex, sqlType);
      } catch (SQLException e) {
          c.setAbandon();
          throw e;
      }
  }
```

```java
public void setBoolean(int parameterIndex, boolean x)
      throws SQLException {
   try {
      this.pstmt.setBoolean(parameterIndex, x);
   } catch (SQLException e) {
      c.setAbandon();
      throw e;
   }
}

public void setByte(int parameterIndex, byte x)
      throws SQLException {
   try {
      this.pstmt.setByte(parameterIndex, x);
   } catch (SQLException e) {
      c.setAbandon();
      throw e;
   }
}

public void setShort(int parameterIndex, short x)
      throws SQLException {
   try {
      this.pstmt.setShort(parameterIndex, x);
   } catch (SQLException e) {
      c.setAbandon();
      throw e;
   }
}

public void setInt(int parameterIndex, int x) throws SQLException {
   try {
      this.pstmt.setInt(parameterIndex, x);
   } catch (SQLException e) {
      c.setAbandon();
      throw e;
   }
}

public void setLong(int parameterIndex, long x) throws SQLException
{
   try {
      this.pstmt.setLong(parameterIndex, x);
   } catch (SQLException e) {
      c.setAbandon();
      throw e;
   }
}
```

```
public void setFloat(int parameterIndex, float x)
      throws SQLException {
   try {
      this.pstmt.setFloat(parameterIndex, x);
   } catch (SQLException e) {
      c.setAbandon();
      throw e;
   }
}

public void setDouble(int parameterIndex, double x)
      throws SQLException {
   try {
      this.pstmt.setDouble(parameterIndex, x);
   } catch (SQLException e) {
      c.setAbandon();
      throw e;
   }
}
public void setBigDecimal(int parameterIndex, BigDecimal x)
      throws SQLException {
   try {
      this.pstmt.setBigDecimal(parameterIndex, x);
   } catch (SQLException e) {
      c.setAbandon();
      throw e;
   }
}

public void setString(int parameterIndex, String x)
      throws SQLException {
   try {
      this.pstmt.setString(parameterIndex, x);
   } catch (SQLException e) {
      c.setAbandon();
      throw e;
   }
}

public void setBytes(int parameterIndex, byte x[])
      throws SQLException {
   try {
      this.pstmt.setBytes(parameterIndex, x);
   } catch (SQLException e) {
      c.setAbandon();
      throw e;
   }
}
```

```
public void setDate(int parameterIndex, java.sql.Date x)
      throws SQLException {
  try {
    this.pstmt.setDate(parameterIndex, x);
  } catch (SQLException e) {
     c.setAbandon();
     throw e;
   }
}

public void setTime(int parameterIndex, java.sql.Time x)
      throws SQLException {
  try {
    this.pstmt.setTime(parameterIndex, x);
  } catch (SQLException e) {
     c.setAbandon();
     throw e;
   }
}

public void setTimestamp(int parameterIndex,
                         java.sql.Timestamp x)
      throws SQLException {
  try {
    this.pstmt.setTimestamp(parameterIndex, x);
  } catch (SQLException e) {
     c.setAbandon();
     throw e;
   }
}

public void setAsciiStream(int parameterIndex,
                           java.io.InputStream x, int length)
      throws SQLException {
  try {
    this.pstmt.setAsciiStream(parameterIndex, x, length);
  } catch (SQLException e) {
     c.setAbandon();
     throw e;
   }
}

public void setUnicodeStream(int parameterIndex,
                             java.io.InputStream x,
                             int length)
      throws SQLException {
  try {
```

```java
        this.pstmt.setUnicodeStream(parameterIndex, x, length);
    } catch (SQLException e) {
        c.setAbandon();
        throw e;
    }
}

public void setBinaryStream(int parameterIndex,
                            java.io.InputStream x,
                            int length)
        throws SQLException {
    try {
        this.pstmt.setBinaryStream(parameterIndex, x, length);
    } catch (SQLException e) {
        c.setAbandon();
        throw e;
    }
}

public void clearParameters() throws SQLException {
    try {
        this.pstmt.clearParameters();
    } catch (SQLException e) {
        c.setAbandon();
        throw e;
    }
}

public void setObject(int parameterIndex,
                      Object x,
                      int targetSqlType,
                      int scale)
        throws SQLException {
    try {
        this.pstmt.setObject(parameterIndex, x, targetSqlType,
                             scale);
    } catch (SQLException e) {
        c.setAbandon();
        throw e;
    }
}

public void setObject(int parameterIndex,
                      Object x,
                      int targetSqlType)
        throws SQLException {
    try {
```

```
                    this.pstmt.setObject(parameterIndex, x, targetSqlType);
            } catch (SQLException e) {
                c.setAbandon();
                throw e;
            }
    }

    public void setObject(int parameterIndex, Object x)
            throws SQLException {
        try {
            this.pstmt.setObject(parameterIndex, x);
        } catch (SQLException e) {
            c.setAbandon();
            throw e;
        }
    }

    public boolean execute() throws SQLException {
        try {
            return this.pstmt.execute();
        } catch (SQLException e) {
            c.setAbandon();
            throw e;
        }
    }
}
}
```

CacheDriver.properties

```
CacheDriver.maxDBs=2
CacheDriver.initConnsPerDB=2
CacheDriver.maxPooledConnsPerDB=8
CacheDriver.maxConnsPerDB=8
```

B

Simple Java Web Server

Server.java

```java
import java.io.*;
import java.net.*;
import java.util.*;

import UrlCache;
import MyGetBytes;
import LazyDate;
import FileInfo;

class Server implements HttpConstants {

    // Print to stdout
    protected static void p(String s) {
        System.out.println(s);
    }

    // Print to the log file
    protected static void log(byte[] b) throws IOException {
        synchronized (log) {
            log.write(b, 0, b.length);
        }
    }

    static OutputStream log = null;

    /* our server's configuration information is stored
     * in these properties
     */
    protected static Properties props = new Properties();

    // Where worker threads stand idle
    static Vector threads = new Vector();

    // The web server's virtual root
    static File root;
```

```
// Timeout on client connections
static int timeout = 5000;

// Max # worker threads
static int workers = 5;

static String serverRoot = null;

// Load www-server.properties from java.home
static void loadProps() throws IOException {
    File f = new File(serverRoot +
                      File.separator +
                      "server.properties");
    if (f.exists()) {
        InputStream is =
            new BufferedInputStream(
                new FileInputStream(f));
        props.load(is);
        is.close();
        String r = null;

        if (root == null) {
            root = new File(serverRoot);
        }
        r = props.getProperty("timeout");
        if (r != null) {
            timeout = Integer.parseInt(r);
        }
        r = props.getProperty("workers");
        if (r != null) {
            workers = Integer.parseInt(r);
        }
        r = props.getProperty("log");
        if (r != null) {
            p("opening log file: " + r);
            log = new BufferedOutputStream(
                    new FileOutputStream(r));
        } else {
            p("logging to stdout");
        }
    } else {
        p("Config file " +
        f.getAbsolutePath() + " does not exist ");
    }

}
```

```java
    static void printProps() {
        p("root="+root);
        p("timeout="+timeout);
        p("workers="+workers);
    }

    public static void main(String[] args) throws Exception {
        if(args.length != 2) {
            System.out.println("Usage: java Server <port> " +
                                    "<serverRoot>");
            return;
        }

        int port = Integer.parseInt(args[0]);
        serverRoot = args[1];
        p("Port is " + port + " serverRoot is " + serverRoot);
        loadProps();
        printProps();

        ServerSocket ss = new ServerSocket(port);

        // Start worker threads
        for (int i = 0; i < workers; ++i) {
            Worker w = new Worker(ss);
            (new Thread(w, "worker #"+i)).start();
            threads.addElement(w);
        }
    }
}

class Worker extends Server implements HttpConstants, Runnable {
    final static int BUF_SIZE = 2048;
    static final byte[] EOL = {(byte)'\r', (byte)'\n' };
    UrlCache urlCache = new UrlCache(1000);
    LazyDate today = new LazyDate(1000);
    Hashtable addressCache = new Hashtable();

    // Buffer to use for requests
    byte[] buf;
    // Socket to client we're handling */
    private Socket s;
    private ServerSocket ss;

    public Worker(ServerSocket ss) {
        buf = new byte[2048];
        this.ss = ss;
        s = null;
    }
```

```
public synchronized void run() {
   while(true) {
      try {
         s = ss.accept();
         handleClient();
      } catch (Exception e) {
          e.printStackTrace();
         }
      }
}

void handleClient() throws IOException {
   File targ = null;
   InputStream is = new BufferedInputStream(s.getInputStream());
   OutputStream ps =
      new BufferedOutputStream(s.getOutputStream());
   /* Abandon the connection unless data
    * arrives before the timeout expires
    */
   s.setSoTimeout(Server.timeout);

   try {
   /* We only support HTTP GET, and don't
    * support any fancy HTTP options,
    * so we're only interested really in
    * the first line.
    */
      int nread = 0, r = 0;

outerloop:
      while (nread < BUF_SIZE) {
         r = is.read(buf, nread, BUF_SIZE - nread);
         if (r == -1) {
            /* EOF */
            return;
         }
         int i = nread;
         nread += r;
         for (; i < nread; i++) {
            if (buf[i] == (byte)'\n' ||
                buf[i] == (byte)'\r') {
               break outerloop;
            }
         }
      }
```

```java
        boolean doingGet;
        int index; // Beginning of file name
        if (buf[0] == (byte)'G' &&
            buf[1] == (byte)'E' &&
            buf[2] == (byte)'T' &&
            buf[3] == (byte)' ') {
          doingGet = true;
          index = 4;
        } else {
            // We don't support this method */
            String str = "HTTP/1.0 " +
                            HTTP_BAD_METHOD +
                            " unsupported method type: ";
            byte [] b = str.getBytes();
            ps.write(b, 0, str.length());
            ps.write(buf, 0, 5);
            ps.write(EOL);
            ps.flush();
            s.close();
            return;
        }

        int i = 0;
        for (i = index; i < nread; i++) {
          if (buf[i] == (byte)' ') {
              break;
          }
        }

        String url = new String(buf, 0, index,i-index);
        FileInfo fi = urlCache.get(url);
        if (fi != null) {
          byte[] b = fi.getHeaders();
          ps.write(b, 0, b.length);
          byte[] c = fi.getContent();
          ps.write(c, 0, c.length);
        } else {
            targ = urlToFile(url);
            if (printHeaders(targ, ps, url)) {
              sendFile(targ, ps, url);
            } else {
                send404(targ, ps);
            }
        }
    }

    loggingStage(url,fi);
```

```
        } finally {
            ps.flush();
            s.close();
        }
}

private void loggingStage(String url, FileInfo fi)
    throws IOException {

    InetAddress ia = s.getInetAddress();

    byte[] firstHalf = (byte[]) addressCache.get(ia);
    if (firstHalf == null) {
        firstHalf = ("From " + ia.getHostAddress()).getBytes();
        addressCache.put(ia,firstHalf);
    }

    byte[] secondHalf = (fi == null) ?
        null : fi.getLogSecondHalf();
    if (secondHalf == null) {
        File targ = urlToFile(url); //dxb
        int rCode = 0; //dxb moved up from printHeaders()
        if ( !targ.exists()) { //dxb
            rCode = HTTP_NOT_FOUND;
        } else {
            rCode = HTTP_OK;
        }

        secondHalf = (": GET " +
                    targ.getAbsolutePath() +
                    "-->"+
                    rCode+
                    "\r\n").getBytes();
        if (fi != null) {
            fi.setLogSecondHalf(secondHalf);
        }
    }

    log(firstHalf);
    log(secondHalf);
}

private File urlToFile(String url) {
    String fname = url.replace('/', File.separatorChar);
    if (fname.startsWith(File.separator)) {
        fname = fname.substring(1);
    }
```

```java
    File targ = new File(Server.root, fname);
    if (targ.isDirectory()) {
        File ind = new File(targ, "index.html");
        if (ind.exists()) {
            targ = ind;
        }
    }

    return targ;
}

boolean printHeaders(File targ,
                     OutputStream ps,
                     String url)
    throws IOException {

    boolean ret = false;
    StringBuffer headers = new StringBuffer(512);

    if (!targ.exists()) {
        headers.append("HTTP/1.0 " +
                       HTTP_NOT_FOUND +
                       " not found\r\n");
        ret = false;
    } else {
        headers.append("HTTP/1.0 " + HTTP_OK+ " OK\r\n");
        ret = true;
    }

    headers.append("Server: Simple java\r\n");
    headers.append("Date: " + today.todaysDate() + "\r\n");

    if (ret) {
        if (!targ.isDirectory()) {
            headers.append("Content-length: "+
                           targ.length() +
                           "\r\n");

            headers.append("Last Modified: " +
                           (new Date(targ.lastModified())) +
                           "\r\n");

            String name = targ.getName();
            int ind = name.lastIndexOf('.');
            String ct = null;
            if (ind > 0) {
```

```
                    ct = (String) map.get(name.substring(ind));
                }
                if (ct == null) {
                    ct = "unknown/unknown";
                }
                headers.append("Content-type: " + ct + "\r\n");

            } else {
                headers.append("Content-type: text/html\r\n");
            }
        }

        // Fast ASCII-to-byte conversion
        byte[] b = MyGetBytes.asciiGetBytes(headers.toString());

        ps.write(b, 0, b.length);
        FileInfo fi =
            new FileInfo(b, System.currentTimeMillis());
        urlCache.put(url, fi);

        return ret;
    }

void send404(File targ, OutputStream ps) throws IOException {
    ps.write(EOL);
    ps.write(EOL);
    String str = "Not Found\n\n"+
                 "The requested resource was not found.\n";
    byte [] b = str.getBytes();
    ps.write(b,0,str.length());
}

void sendFile(File targ,
              OutputStream ps,
              String url) throws IOException {
    InputStream is = new FileInputStream(targ.getAbsolutePath());

    try {
        int n;
        byte [] b = new byte[8192];
        ps.write(EOL);
        b[0] = (byte) '\r';
        b[1] = (byte) '\n';
        int blen = 2;

        while ((n = is.read(buf)) > 0) {
            ps.write(buf, 0, n);
```

```java
                // Assuming everything fits in a single buffer...
                System.arraycopy(buf,0,b,blen,n);
                blen += n;
            }

            FileInfo fi = urlCache.get(url);
            if (fi != null) {
                byte [] c = new byte[blen];
                System.arraycopy(b,0,c,0,blen);
                fi.setContent(c);
            }
        } finally {
            is.close();
        }
    }

    // Mapping of file extensions to content types
    static Hashtable map = new Hashtable();

    static {
        fillMap();
    }

    static void setSuffix(String k, String v) {
        map.put(k, v);
    }

    // Partial list of HTTP content types...
    static void fillMap() {
        setSuffix(".htm", "text/html");
        setSuffix(".html", "text/html");
        setSuffix("", "content/unknown");
        setSuffix(".zip", "application/zip");
        setSuffix(".tar", "application/x-tar");
        setSuffix(".gif", "image/gif");
        setSuffix(".jpg", "image/jpeg");
        setSuffix(".jpeg", "image/jpeg");
        setSuffix(".text", "text/plain");
        setSuffix(".txt", "text/plain");
    }

}

// Partial list of HTTP status codes...
interface HttpConstants {
    public static final int HTTP_OK = 200;
    public static final int HTTP_BAD_REQUEST = 400;
```

```
            public static final int HTTP_UNAUTHORIZED = 401;
            public static final int HTTP_NOT_FOUND = 404;
            public static final int HTTP_BAD_METHOD = 405;
        }
```

FileInfo.java

```java
    import java.util.*;
    import java.io.*;

    class FileInfo {
        private byte[] headers;
        private byte[] content;
        private long lastUpdate;
        private byte[] logSecondHalf;

        FileInfo (byte[] h, long lu) {
            headers = h;
            content = null;
            lastUpdate = lu;
            logSecondHalf = null;
        }

        public void setHeaders(byte[] h) {
            headers = h;
        }

        public void setContent(byte[] c) {
            content = c;
        }

        public void setLastUpdate(long t) {
            lastUpdate = t;
        }

        public void setLogSecondHalf(byte[] s) {
            logSecondHalf = s;
        }

        public byte[] getHeaders() {
            return headers;
        }

        public byte[] getContent() {
            return content;
        }
```

```java
    public long getLastUpdate() {
        return lastUpdate;
    }

    public byte[] getLogSecondHalf() {
        return logSecondHalf;
    }
}
```

UrlCache.java

```java
import java.util.*;
import java.io.*;
import FileInfo;

class UrlCache {
    private Hashtable ht = new Hashtable();
    private long cacheRefresh;

    public UrlCache(long refresh) {
        cacheRefresh = refresh;
    }

    public void put(String url, FileInfo fi) {
        ht.put(url, fi);
    }

    public FileInfo get(String url) {
        FileInfo fi = (FileInfo) ht.get(url);
        if (fi == null) {
            return null;
        }
        long now = System.currentTimeMillis();
        if ((now-fi.getLastUpdate()) > cacheRefresh ) {
            ht.remove(url);
            return null;
        }

        return fi;
    }
}
```

LazyDate.java

```java
import java.util.*;

class LazyDate {
```

```
        private long lastCheck = 0; // Never checked before
        private String today;
        private long cacheRefresh;

        public LazyDate(long refresh) {
            cacheRefresh = refresh;
            update();
        }

        public String todaysDate() {
            long now = System.currentTimeMillis();
            if ((now-lastCheck) > cacheRefresh) {
                update();
            }

            return today;
        }

        private void update() {
            lastCheck = System.currentTimeMillis();
            today = (new Date()).toString();
        }
    }
```

MyGetBytes.java

```
    public class MyGetBytes {
        public static byte[] asciiGetBytes(String buf) {
            int size = buf.length();
            int i;
            byte[] bytebuf = new byte[size];

            for (i = 0; i < size; i++) {
                bytebuf[i] = (byte)buf.charAt(i);
            }

            return bytebuf;
        }
    }
```

server.properties

```
    log=server.log
    timeout=5000
    workers=8
```

Bibliography

[AHU74]   A. Aho, J. Hopcroft, and J. Ullman, *The Design and Analysis of Computer Algorithms*, Addison-Wesley, Reading, MA (1974).

[BEN82]   J. L. Bentley, *Writing Efficient Programs,* Prentice-Hall, Englewood Cliffs, NJ (1982).

[BM97]   B. Meyer, *Object-Oriented Software Construction, Second Edition*, Prentice-Hall PTR, Englewood Cliffs, NJ (1997).

[BM99]   D. Bulka and D. Mayhew, *Efficient C++*, Addison-Wesley, Reading, MA (1999).

[BR95]   A. Binstock and J. Rex, *Practical Algorithms for Programmers,* Addison-Wesley, Reading, MA (1995).

[BW97]   J. Beveridge and R. Wiener, *Multithreading Applications in Win32,* Addison-Wesley, Reading, MA (1997).

[CAM91]   M. Campbell et al., "The Parallelization of UNIX System V Release 4.0," Proceedings of the Winter 1991 USENIX Conference.

[CM98]   Chet Murthy, private communication (1988).

[DB99]   D. Brown, "A Simple, Multithreaded Web Server," http://developer.java-soft.com/developer/technicalArticles/Networking/Webserver/index.html.

[GH95]   E. Gamma, R. Helm, R. Johnson, and J. Vlissides, *Design Patterns: Elements of Reusable Object-Oriented Software*, Addison-Wesley, Reading, MA (1994).

[GJS96]   J. Gosling, B. Joy, and G. Steele, *The Java Language Specification*, Addison-Wesley, Reading, MA (1996).

[HP96]   J. Hennessy and D. Patterson, *Computer Architecture: A Quantitive Approach*, Morgan Kaufmann, San Francisco, CA (1995).

[JE99]   J. Engel, *Programming for the Java Virtual Machine*, Addison-Wesley, Reading, MA (1999).

[JH98]   J. Hunter and W. Crawford, *Java Servlet Programming*, O'Reilly & Associates, Inc., Cambridge, MA (1999).

[KNU97a] D. E. Knuth, *The Art of Computer Programming: Fundamental Algorithms, Volume I*, Third Edition, Addison-Wesley, Reading, MA (1997).

[KNU97b] D. E. Knuth, *The Art of Computer Programming: Seminumerical Algorithms, Volume II*, Third Edition, Addison-Wesley, Reading, MA (1997).

[KNU97c] D. E. Knuth, *The Art of Computer Programming: Sorting and Searching, Volume III*, Second Edition, Addison-Wesley, Reading, MA (1998).

[LEA97]   D. Lea, *Concurrent Programming in Java*, Addison-Wesley, Reading, MA (1997).

[LY97]   T. Lindholm and F. Yellin, *The Java Virtual Machine Specification*, Addison-Wesley, Reading, MA (1997).

[NBF96]   B. Nichols, D. Buttlar, and J. P. Farrell, *Pthreads Programming: A Posix Standard for Better Understanding*, O'Reilly & Associates, Inc., Cambridge, MA (1997).

[PFI98]   G. Pfister, *In Search of Clusters, Second Edition*, Prentice-Hall PTR, Upper Saddle River, NJ (1998).

[PH97]   D. Patterson and J. Hennessy, *Computer Organization and Design: The Hardware/Software Interface*, Morgan Kaufmann, San Francisco, CA (1998).

[SB99]   S. Ball, Supercharged strings, *Java Report,* Vol. 4, No. 2, Feb. 1999.

[SF99]   "SanFrancisco Performance Tips & Techniques Redbook," http://www-4
.ibm.com/software/ad/sanfrancisco/library.html.

[SS98]   Scott Snyder, private communication (1998).

[WB99]   A. Wirfs-Brock, Complex Java applications—Breaking the speed limit,
Java Report, Vol. 4, No. 1, Jan. 1999.

Index

Addison-Wesley Professional

How to Register Your Book

Register this Book

Visit: **http://www.aw.com/cseng/register**
Enter the ISBN*
Then you will receive:

- Notices and reminders about upcoming author appearances, tradeshows, and online chats with special guests
- Advanced notice of forthcoming editions of your book
- Book recommendations
- Notification about special contests and promotions throughout the year

*The ISBN can be found on the copyright page of the book

Visit our Web site

http://www.aw.com/cseng
When you think you've read enough, there's always more content for you at Addison-Wesley's web site. Our web site contains a directory of complete product information including:

- Chapters
- Exclusive author interviews
- Links to authors' pages
- Tables of contents
- Source code

You can also discover what tradeshows and conferences Addison-Wesley will be attending, read what others are saying about our titles, and find out where and when you can meet our authors and have them sign your book.

Contact Us via Email

cepubprof@awl.com
Ask general questions about our books.
Sign up for our electronic mailing lists.
Submit corrections for our web site.

cepubeditors@awl.com
Submit a book proposal.
Send errata for a book.

cepubpublicity@awl.com
Request a review copy for a member of the media interested in reviewing new titles.

registration@awl.com
Request information about book registration.

We encourage you to patronize the many fine retailers who stock Addison-Wesley titles. Visit our online directory to find stores near you.

Addison-Wesley Professional
One Jacob Way, Reading, Massachusetts 01867 USA
TEL 781-944-3700 • FAX 781-942-3076